HIGH-IMPACT
DAY TRADING

HIGH-IMPACT DAY TRADING

Powerful Techniques for Exploiting Short-Term Market Trends

Robert M. Barnes

IRWIN
Professional Publishing®
Chicago • London • Singapore

Times Mirror
Higher Education Group

Library of Congress Cataloging-in-Publication Data
Barnes, Robert M.
  High-impact day trading: powerful techniques for exploiting short-term
market trends / Robert M. Barnes
    p. cm.
  ISBN 0–7863–0798–6
  Includes index.
    1. Commodity futures—United States.   2. Primary Commodities—Prices—
United States—Charts, diagrams, etc.   3. Investment analysis—United States.
  HG6046 .B336   1996
  332.63/28—dc20   96–11268

Printed in the United States of America
1 2 3 4 5 6 7 8 9 0 B S 3 2 1 0 9 8 7 6

CONTENTS

LIST OF TABLES

LIST OF FIGURES

Table #	Title

LIST OF CHARTS

Most traders and almost all services, manuals, and even books dwell on certain aspects of trading: methodology (trend following/contrary/patterns, etc.); how to construct and use methods (graphically/computerized, etc.); occasionally, historical tests of the methods to find out best operating settings for those methods; and, perhaps, evaluate which methods(s) might suit the trader psychologically.

But there are many topics missing amongst all of these helpful sources. Foremost, except for a very small handful of books, these sources do not address a very major problem of trading: overnight price movement, with its often huge gaps that mean big losses to the trader, who cannot correct his position until the opening when all the news has been discounted and price adjustments adverse to his position have already taken place.

The message here is that serious traders who need real risk reduction in leveraged trading like futures must strongly consider day trading and have an effective plan to reap the benefits of that dynamic, high-profit potential mode of trading.

It is not enough to just grab any old method (a moving average, for example) and plop it into place for day trading. A good review of current methods, their theory and practical points, both good and bad, should be conducted. (See Chapter 1 for this review.)

But the trader must also be visionary and get to the root, the essence of the particular possibilities and pitfalls of day trading, and come up with new and truer ways to handle the price movements within the day. (See Chapter 2 for an in-depth discourse and discovery of the general way, and a brand-new, natural way to handle day price moves.)

Further, the trading approach must be simple but strong, practical rules that are usable by computer advocates and by other traders who deeply understand and appreciate the markets and the day trade approach, but who only use graphs when trading. (See Chapter 3 for easy calculations and sound trading strategies for diverse audiences.)

Above all, the method of day trading must be substantially profitable for a large number of instruments under many conditions for different trading styles. (In Chapter 4, we examine nearly 20 commodities individually over various time frames and dates and test for and find profitable method settings that produce profits ranging from under $1,000 to over $5,000, before costs, per contract for a typical month of trading—plenty of profit opportunity for the day trader, for both speculative and conservative trading stances!)

Finally, the trader should think of practical ways/tips for molding and improving the methodology for his own use. (Chapter 5 covers filtering candidates to trade, late day trading, and single versus multiple trade considerations, amongst other topics.)

The book should be used as an investigation into seriously considering day trading as a preferred medium. The reader should then carefully consider the innovative, perhaps truer, and yet also more practical method, the mountain/valley approach, for trading. He should understand, approve of, and learn how to apply the rules for trading the method, either graphically or by computer. Lastly, our trader should choose a portfolio of commodities and use the suggested parameter settings for a conservative or speculative approach to trading, or research settings on his own.

Have a satisfying journey into the exciting world of day trading!

Robert M. Barnes

CHAPTER 1

The Steaming Cauldron of Day Trading and Trading Methods

THE TRADER'S PROBLEM

Traders, whether they be individual speculators, brokers, or CTAs, have their own special goals and styles. Some want long-term, large profits. Others insist on many small profits and few losses and tend to trade quite often. Underlying these methodologies are what we call a "comfort level" approach to making money. All traders want to make fantastic profits, but they differ on risk taking. Some will take some risk, others will tolerate little, while a few will suffer any risk (as far as their bank accounts allow) to make millions.

No one wants losses (unless they're masochists). But losses not only exist, they're here.

Traders who use long-term, trend-following methods pile up big gains in times of opportune, big moves, but lose badly during choppy, little-trend times. Short-term traders, on the other hand, are able to nip losses to manageable levels during desultory times by going for small profits, but they often cannot accumulate substantial gains in their accounts in big-trend market times because they don't hold on to the big movers.

Which style does the best over the long run is dependent upon the trader's risk tolerance preference (long term big gain and loss periods versus short term small gains and losses; big return/risk versus small return/risk) and the type of markets that predominate.

If we are going through big-trend times, then everyone will benefit, but the long-term trend follower will (generally) show the larger net profit while suffering about the same risk (losses) as the short termer. Should choppy markets predominate, the short-term trader will most likely have a better profit bottom line and certainly a superior risk profile (less losses per dollar profit). However, the lack of trends and large price volatility could make both traders lose enough to seriously, or even irreparably, damage their accounts.

This is the crux of the commodity trader's major problem.

THE NATURE OF OVERNIGHT RISK/LOSSES

Both types of traders, from the extremes of long-term trend follower to short-term profit-taker, suffer from at least three major risk (loss) sources: the day-to-day price volatility; the overnight price gap; and the very nature of their trading methods.

Day-to-day price volatility is a bedrock, inescapable risk that all traders face. Basically, it is the price change magnitudes that happen within the day (daily range) or, more commonly known and felt by traders, the price variations that happen from close to close. While the former influences those traders with shorter time horizons and profit goals (within-day price tracking and hourly prices, for example), the latter affects *all* traders. Large price changes not only greatly influence what position is taken and when the trader takes it, but they also greatly determine the price levels, the entry price of the position. A sudden surge in one direction could trip a buy signal, but the trader has to get in at a high price and is "set up" for the inevitable price retracement/ loss potential somewhere along the line because of that big move. Close-to-close price variation, an unavoidable price variation that affects all traders having positions held overnight, is the biggest risk.

Even if our trader could track prices more closely during the day, thus lessening overnight, close-to-close (when many methods traders make their decisions) risk, a second type of risk occurs that cannot be avoided: the overnight price gap.

From yesterday's close to today's opening price, anything can, and often does, happen. Announcements after the close or at the open (such as the PPI, Fed Reserve interest rate changes, unemployment figures, etc.) greatly affect prices on the opening of trading, the result of which is at least 50–50, good or bad, for the hapless trader who happens to have a position before that. But much also occurs during the period from the close (late afternoon) to midmorning, a period of 16 hours or so that constitutes almost 2/3 of the entire day. Not only foreign events (during their business hours), but also domestic occurrences, can profoundly change prices at the next opening. Nothing short of stepping aside his position each night can help the trader avoid this inevitable risk. This places a floor, or minimum risk, that the trader must face.

Finally, the *nature* of quantitative trading methods make for a certain degree, or minimum, of risk. Trend-following methods require large moves in the direction of the next or contemplated trend to get into a new position. By definition, the new position is accepting a move and a dimunition of gain or increase in loss against the *current* position. Contrary methods do the opposite, looking for the new move to signal a counter move. But some of the time the new move is the beginning or extension of a trend, and the contrarian is about to lose by fighting that trend.

So the very nature of overnight position-holding, the gap in price, and the weaknesses of every method create a floor, or rock-bottom risk with which every trader must deal. Of course, our trader would like to reduce this risk considerably, and maybe even increase net profit (icing on the cake), but still preserve the money-making potential.

REDUCE THE RISK, KEEP/INCREASE THE PROFIT

What we need is a way to get around the overnight price volatility and gap curses and to come up with a strong trading method to boot. In a word, we need a way to increase the returns and lower the risk.

We'll work on reducing risk first. Figure 1–1 shows two price series, one daily close-to-close, the other for minute to minute closes in a day. Three conclusions can be drawn from this and real data (see Charts 1–1 and 1–2). First, day-to-day price variations or volatility is larger than that for 1-minute price changes within the day. Also, there are gaps between one day's closing and the next day's opening on a number of occasions (see Chart 1–1), while there are none in the 1-minute interval data (simply because the data are continuous—the open for each minute is the close of the prior minute). Third, the price change from the beginning of the period to the end, shown in both Figure 1–1(a) and Chart 1–1, is (often) larger than for the comparable 1-minute interval, shown in Figure 1–1(b) and Chart 1–2. This gives the long-term trader more profit potential on longer-term data (daily versus 1-minute). We don't know about short-term trading—in and out—but it is a good guess that the larger price variation in daily data would give the trader more opportunities for short-term goals, whether trend or contrary oriented, because of the larger price variations in daily data (which is what he is playing upon, anyway).

F I G U R E   1–1

Daily and Within-Day Prices

a. Daily prices

A

B

b. Day 1-minute prices (1 day)

a

b

CHART 1–1

June Swiss Franc 60-Minute Price Chart

USE WITHIN-DAY DATA

Whether we use 1-minute, 5-minute, or 15-minute data, it is clear that risk (measured by price change) will be reduced compared to overnight data—we have considerably reduced overnight price change variation and eliminated the gap from closing to opening by switching to within-day data.

But what about profit potential? It is still not clear whether long-term trading or short-term goals trading is more profitable with daily data. One consideration is where prices will end up, or even range, during one period versus the other. In Figure 1–1 (a) daily prices end up and have larger range than the single day's

C H A R T   1–2

June Swiss Franc 1-Minute Price Chart May 25, 1995

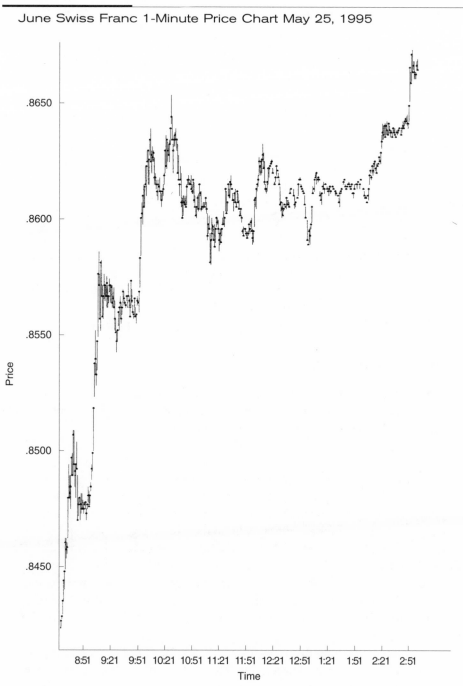

beginning to end shown in (b), but that could have been reversed, and the within-day trend could have actually gone further.

Likewise, there is only one day represented in Figure 1–1 (b). If every day in Figure 1–1 (a) had similar profit opportunity to that in (b), the trader could have many profitable trades, all somewhat near the one depicted in (a), but adding up to much more than the one trade in (a). Even if there were only moderate gain possibilities in each day, it is quite possible that the sum total of those opportunities would still be greater than the one profit trade in (a). We could still use strong, reliable, trend-following methods, or whatever could most reliably capture the moderate profit potential in (b) many times over many days, even if only trading once or twice each day.

Taking the small profits shown in Figure 1–1 (b) multiple times in the day might sound good, but if costs (slippage and commissions) and the generally smaller daily range is considered, it becomes unclear whether net profits can be made at all. Even though there are "mini-trends" during the day (see Chart 1–2), they are not as extensive (large) as those trends that develop over many days. But like their counterparts that appear over many days, day trends do proliferate. They don't pop up every day, but neither is there only one per year, or some other infrequent occurrence.

So here we have the problem: to get real reduction in risk, we must go to day trading. To get real profits (i.e., overcome commissions, slippage, and small moves), we must aim our firepower to increase the odds of a successful trade and maximize the size of the profit for each trade.

We'll review some current methods that could possibly be used for day trading.

CURRENT METHODS

The half dozen or so approaches described here by no means cover all day trade or general methods that could conceivably be used, but they are representative and pretty well cover the broad spectrum. We will evaluate them and see if any could actually be used to reduce risk and significantly increase profit size in the difficult day environment.

1. *Moving Averages.* Probably the most well-known and popular of all methods, moving averages are used to separate significant trend beginnings from meaningless swiggles and sideways movements—distinguish the signal from the noise. It is easy to compute—simply add up the last N days' prices and divide by N. The moving averages method has been used successfully in many business and scientific endeavors.

The assumption is that the moving average best represents the current growth of the trend, and that the most recent prices could mean a significant departure from the current trend, which could now be turning in the direction of those recent prices.

The rules for trading the averages are relatively straightforward.

If actual, recent prices diverge significantly from this growth trend (the moving average), such as falling below the line in a bull trend or moving above the line in a bear trend, the current trend itself is then suspect, and a change in trend direction may very well be taking place.

Figure 1–2 depicts this method. The trader calculates and constructs the moving average on the chart and looks for prices to rise above or below it to trade.

F I G U R E   1–2

Moving Average Method

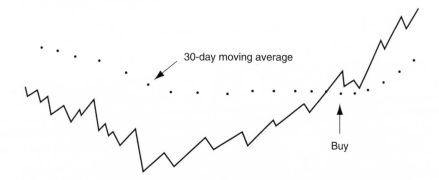

In Figure 1–2 a 30-day average is plotted over prices, and the trader goes long when prices rise above the average and enters short positions when prices fall below the average. Some traders also specify a minimum penetration of the averages by current prices. For example, prices must rise five cents for soybeans above the current average for the trader to go long.

When there are big, lengthy trends present this method is probably one of the very best at catching them. In day trading there are sometimes large trends slowly building from the beginning of the day to the end. The great majority of the time, however, the price movements do not last the whole day, nor do they go far. Moving averages are notoriously known for getting caught in many whipsaws, going long and then having prices sink and trip a short position and then going long again after prices rebound to trip another signal, and so on. Even though it will pick up the occasional big price move, moving averages simply is not suited for the many short-lasting, small price movements that predominate in day trading.

2. *Breakout Methods.* Perhaps even more popular than moving averages, the breakout method is also directed at finding and climbing aboard major trends.

In its simplest form, the breakout method is easy to compute and can be easily seen on a graph. Figure 1–3(a) shows the basic formula. If prices are in a downtrend or sideways range, then a rise of so many points or a certain percentage of price above the high of the range or lowest point in a downtrend signifies a break of the current trend or range. This is somewhat like finding one or a few malfunctioning, newly produced parts on an assembly line in a factory and suspecting a significant flaw in the manufacturing process. Thus a new situation, a new trend, is declared. The trader then goes long when a price rise of X points or more happens above the trading range or downtrend bottom point.

The other two situations are similar but a little more sophisticated. Figure 1–3(b) shows the same situation, a trading range, but here the trader hypothecates a *length of time* that prices are outside the current trend or condition as crucial in determining whether a major trend change has occurred. The assumption here is that the size of the price change away from the trend is not the issue. Rather, it is the *number* of prices that are (suspected to be) not part of the current trend that is important,

FIGURE 1-3

The Breakout Methods (3)

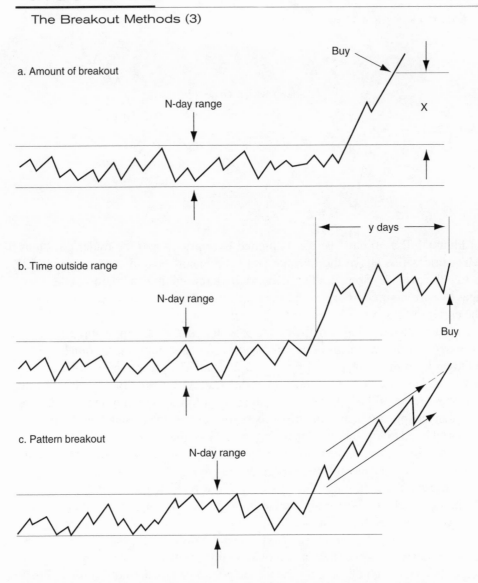

a. Amount of breakout

b. Time outside range

c. Pattern breakout

and hence a critical number of them signals a new trend. In this situation the trader buys when prices remain outside the current sideways trend for at least Y days.

Another form of the breakout method evaluates the *way* in which prices diverge outside the current trend. Figure 1–3(c) depicts this situation. A number of divergent patterns could be postulated: ever increasing prices; flag, head and shoulder, and other chart formations; and a channel projection (shown here). Once an unusual pattern has formed outside the current trading range or trend, the trader takes a position in the direction of the chart formation.

Like the moving average method, the breakout method is very good (and is probably the quickest) at catching big trends. This is particularly true for the most popular version, the single breakout, shown in Figure 1–3 (a). However, like moving averages, the breakout method is vulnerable to whipsaws—if the trader chooses too small a breakout amount, he could continually alternate between longs and shorts, while too large a choice could mean very few, but very profitable, trades. Even in the latter case one or two losses could kill the total profit picture because there are so few trades.

The major problem with this and the moving average approach is that one single event—a move of a certain size—defines a transition from one trend to another, when in truth the marketplace is far more sophisticated. For example, one or a group of traders could go on a buying spree and then retire from buying without having stimulated a follow-through by other buyers. It is the *persistence* of a statistically verifiable and reliable buying action that confirms that we do have a trend change, as prices continue to develop and progress in the new direction.

The second and third variations do attempt to bring in the elements of persistence and reliability, in the form of days persisting in a possible new trend situation or an unusual pattern. As we will see later in the chapter on theory, this is indeed a launching pad to coming up with a plausible, viable way to not only improve the batting average or successful percentage of total trades, but also to enlarge the average profit per trade.

3. *The Oscillator Method.* An offshoot of moving averages, the oscillator method attempts to sense when a top or bottom is forming and to predict the end of that top or bottom. This propels the trader, who is expecting a new trend to start soon, to jump in prematurely.

Essentially, the trader looks for a point at which the rate of price changes is turning towards the new trend direction. Formally, when differences of successive moving averages bottom (become most negative) and then become less so (come up from the bottom) by so many points, then a long position is taken. Likewise, a short position is taken when these differences top out at some positive number and drop by so many points.

Figure 1–4 depicts a situation of taking a long position. Prices are initially falling, in a downtrend, bottom, and then begin to rise and start a new uptrend. The oscillator, in the bottom graph, reaches its bottom before prices do and starts moving up from there before prices do. If we use a breakout-type criteria on the oscillator, not on prices, we can in effect time the new uptrend in the oscillator. More importantly, we can predict the subsequent start of an uptrend in prices themselves.

Oscillators can catch many big trends just as, or even before, they start to get underway, and this will help to improve the size of the profitable trade in the day environment.

However, there are many negatives. At least three variables are needed to optimize, or best fit, the oscillator method to a particular market: the number in the moving average; the span of time or number of days between moving averages to detect rounding tops and bottoms; and the best size for a signal trigger (amount of oscillator rise from the bottom or drop from the top).

FIGURE 1–4

Oscillator Method

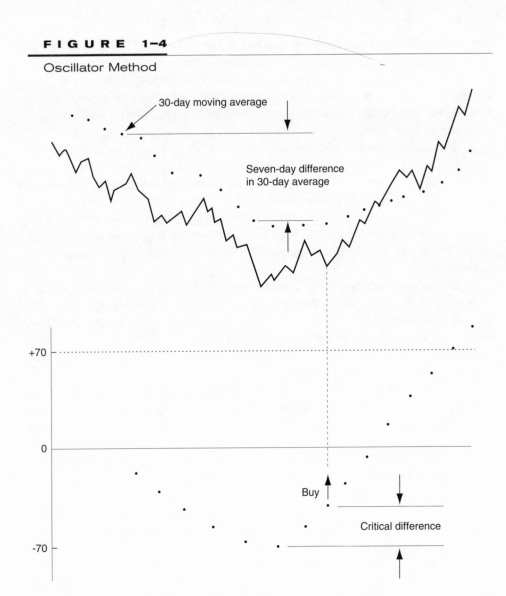

But the main problem is the sensitivity of the oscillator method. Like a moving average, it can be tricked into long or short positions by small or large false upturns and downturns of the oscillator. It is especially sensitive because the index trigger is a second difference and can be set off by small variations in prices. If the trader were to counter or deaden this sensitivity by enlarging the index position trigger size, he unfortunately would then be making the buy/sell actions take place later, at about the same time as the moving averages themselves.

4. *The RSI Method.* The Relative Strength Index (RSI) is an indicator generally used to seek out overbought and oversold conditions, although it could also be used in the traditional trend-following mode.

The RSI measures the strength of upside movement versus the total of upside and downside price changes over an interval of time. Formally, it is the average of positive price change *magnitudes* divided by the average of positive and negative price change *magnitudes,* times 100. When the RSI is near 100, the condition is considered overbought (too many positive changes in a row, so it is vulnerable to a move downwards, or negative price changes) and should be sold. When the RSI is near zero (all negative price changes), the condition is thought to be oversold and should be bought.

Figure 1–5 details this method. A downwards slanting price movement bottoms and turns sharply upwards, where (at the end) the RSI turns high positive (near 100) and indicates an overbought condition, so the trader goes short at that high RSI point.

The advantage of this method is that it is good in choppy and cyclic markets, but it fares poorly in highly trended markets. Unfortunately, day trading has lots of choppy conditions, good for this method, but the profit per trade in that environment is small and next to nothing after costs are considered. The success rate has to be so high that any losses hurt, and one or two big trends could kill the net profit situation, when the RSI trade is against the trend. Stops could help lessen

F I G U R E   1–5

RSI Method

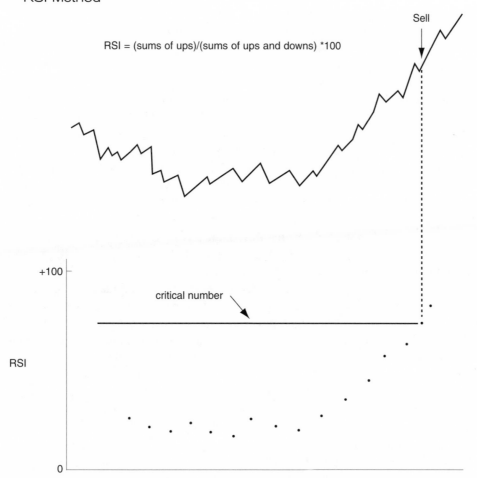

RSI = (sums of ups)/(sums of ups and downs) *100

Sell

+100

critical number

RSI

0

the loss, but the trader would still need a very high batting average to get the average profit per trade after costs to significantly above zero.

5. *%R Method.* Another popular method for initiating counter trend positions or entering trades/taking profits advantageously in a current trend is the "%R" method. It is emblematic of another class of methods, stochastics. Similar to the RSI method, the %R method also looks for overbought and oversold conditions, but it uses raw prices and ranges rather than net price changes.

Today's %R is equal to the period's high minus today's close, divided by the difference between the period's high and low, times 100, to give it a scale between 0 and 100. When the index gets near zero (say 10), the trader should sell, basically because prices are closing and bumping up against the period's top range, and the assumption is that prices will not break through the range. Likewise, longs are taken when the index climbs to near 100 (say 90), as, again, prices are not expected to fall below the interval's low range number, but instead bounce upwards.

Figure 1–6 displays the concept well. Prices have bounced around in a range up until the last day on the chart, when prices close at the high of the range. This produces a %R of next to zero and tells the trader to sell (either sell short to start a new position or sell out his long to cover the current position).

Again, like the RSI, the %R method should be expected to do well in tight or bouncing markets, where prices bounce back and forth. While there are many times in the day trading environment when prices fluctuate in tight or moderate ranges (and they predominate price movements), this and all other contrary methods have to be "right on" in choosing those range peaks and valleys in order to get a high batting average and at least a moderate profit per trade. Unfortunately, this kind of accuracy is too much to expect, since there are enough moderate and large trends around to significantly decrease the trade success rate and average profit per trade (mostly because the ranges are so small and lead to small contrary profits).

6. *The Congestion Phase Method.* The congestion phase method and the next method, the Taylor overnight method, are really built for price phenomena occurring over several days. They point to price events which are likely to occur in a day's time, and they could indicate a side of the market to take for one day or a price rise/fall potential for that day. Transferring directly the phenomena to within-day time intervals would make extremely tight goals or price patterns and would not make profit sense for the day trader.

The congestion phase method refers to an unlikely continuance of a pattern, setting up the real chance for an opposite event. In particular, strings of like price changes from close to close beget moves of good size the other way. Price changes of good size two days in a row have a high probability of making prices go strongly in the opposite direction by the next close, so the trader could benefit by taking a position opposite to the two-day string of same direction price closings.

Figure 1–7 depicts this approach. On days two and three the prices have closed higher. Note that this is by a certain minimum amount each day, otherwise all sorts of two-day moves would qualify and the chance of an opposite phenomena would realistically be only 50 percent—pure luck! This produces counter moves the fourth day and a sharply lower closing. The trader should have shorted on the close of the third day, expecting the drop the next day.

% R Method

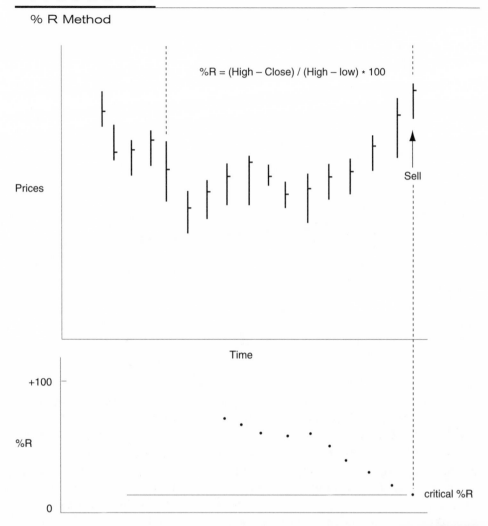

$$\%R = (High - Close) / (High - low) * 100$$

From a day trade perspective, it might be advantageous to short on the opening of the fourth day, expecting a further drop from then to the close. Much of the time, however, prices will have dropped considerably on the opening, leaving little chance and profit opportunity for our erstwhile short trader. At best, half the time he will have had an opportunity to short at the opening at the same or higher prices than the prior close.

In truth, while there probably are some special occasions when day trade from one side and preplanned profits are available, there are only a small number of these rare, pure opportunities. And, of course, provision must be made for losses, which could either be numerous, or large, or both.

7. *Taylor Overnight Method.* Similar in some way to the congestion phase approach, the Taylor overnight method also looks for two- and three-day phenomena, opening the door to certain one-day (day trading) possibilities, where certain price scenarios are most likely to occur.

Congestion Phase Timing

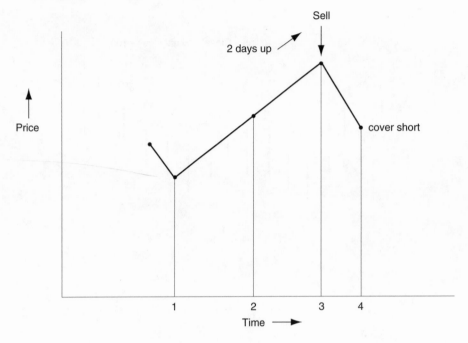

Basically, this approach forecasts a cycle or wave of price action that allows the trader to first establish a position at a good price, to later cover at a nice profit, and, finally, to initiate an opposite counter-trend position to complete the cycle.

In Figure 1–8 an uptrend is in effect. Upon an opening (see day 2) that is lower than the previous close (day 1), the trader will buy if prices continue to drop, making (ultimately) low prices on the day and thereafter going to higher prices. Prices then will continue higher over the next two days, getting into new higher ground (for the trend) in one of the two days, whereupon the trader will take profits. Finally, during the next day or two prices will open higher but fail to make new highs, at which point the trader should go short.

Day trading opportunities present themselves on the day of the initial buy (day 2 in our example), as the trader can simply liquidate the long at the end of the day, with high odds that the trade will have produced an upside positive change from the open to the close. Otherwise, the trader might consider the same strategy on the following day (day 3 in our example), where odds still favor an overall increase in prices, continuing the recovery and continuance of the uptrend.

However, there are some tricky points here. We don't know that prices will not continue to drop on day 2 after we initiated the long position. What guarantees that further reaction to the uptrend isn't in store? Prices could close lower than the open just as well as partially recovering. Three days of lower closings in uptrends are not unheard of, so day trade longs on either of the second two days could be disastrous.

F I G U R E   1–8

Taylor Overnight Method

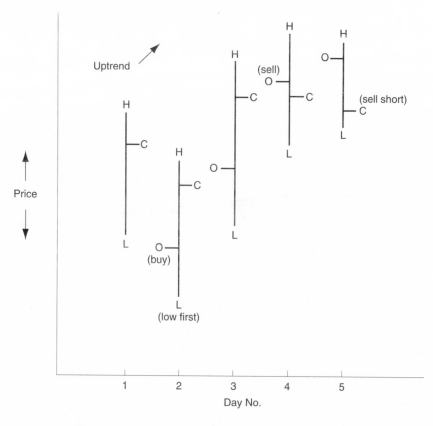

Unfortunately, while markets have a tendency to move in partial cycles, neither the length or depth of these "reactions" to the trend (the mini-cycle) is set in stone. This leaves the profitability and success rate of these "sure" trades very much up in the air and certainly does not induce feelings of reliability or big profits in our minds.

DAY TRADE NEEDS

We do need to feel, once we have decided upon day trading as the way of securing substantial profits with reduced risk, that we can count on a timing method that will give us a high success rate, large gains, and small losses.

Unfortunately, few if any of the methods we reviewed fill that bill.

Moving averages will get whipsawed with too many losses even while they capture a few good trends. The net effect is little net profit, if any, and a horrible success rate (30 percent, as with overnight trading).

Oscillators come closer, in that they grab trends early and get most of the profit, but they often go for spurious trends, thus diluting the success rate and bringing average profit to zero or below.

Breakout methods have results similar to moving averages, as the single size breakout goes for the big move, gets aboard late when it's right, loses badly when it's wrong, and otherwise gets average success rates and low per trade profit results. The other two versions, waiting for time to confirm the existence of a major trend and a pattern tester, are more subtle and may produce profits, but they must be elaborated upon and tested.

Contrary methods such as RSI and %R do well in many choppy and moderate markets that do indeed abound, but they do poorly in the few trended days, and, along with the small profit per trade in choppy markets due to small range and high costs (slippage and commissions), they are doubtful in producing net profits and/or high trade success rates.

Finally, special situation methods like the congestion phase and the Taylor overnight methods open the door to some high probability day trade situations, but they are few and far between, and their sizable losses and low success rates (50–50 chance of the special event occurring) make them questionable for use in regular, reliable day trading.

We need a reliable method for accurately choosing large profit opportunities for day trading. We need a method that has a high trade success rate and high profit per trade. This means finding a technique that aims for large profit opportunities and has a high reliability rate (meaning one that picks out the few and leaves the many small and moderate moves on the table).

To get this kind of accuracy, we need to rethink what makes large trends and put together a most accurate definition of trend itself. .

CHAPTER 2

The Mountain/Valley Trend Theory

In the prior chapter we saw that the best trading strategy to use for day trading was to find big trends and then select and time them well. That is, we must be quite sure that we have selected a trend (to get high success rate) and that we have chosen relatively big trends and timed the trade for the earliest possible entry (to maximize profit per trade). This is necessary because day ranges are small, meaning small-sized trends as compared to long-term, overnight trends; and costs (slippage and commissions) are large relative to profit opportunity.

This impels us to obtain as accurate and useful a definition of trend as possible.

Most trading strategies make some assumption about trends. Moving averages assume that the trend can be represented by the averages themselves. The major problem here is that the averages always lag behind current price and trend developments, and, hence, any analysis will always be after the fact.

Breakout approaches do better in that they (the simple type) are current and react at the same time as trend movements develop: a simple large move may perhaps signals a change in the current trend to another major one, right then and there. However, the trader is dependent upon just one price change, a simple move in one day. But perhaps this was a fluke and prices will soon react strongly the other way. One day, unfortunately, does not a trend make.

Oscillators use the same trend definition as moving averages, but they also look at hill tops and valley bottoms as possibly ending the current trend and starting another. Often those tops do turn out to be the final top of an uptrend, but just as often the tops are just temporary plateaus, following which the uptrend resumes. And so this approach is prone to identifying false-trend tops and bottoms, leading to lower success rates and profit per trade numbers.

At the other end of the spectrum are contrary methods, which assume a completely different trend definition. Basically, RSI, %R, and others think that price bulges and strong price movements presage the end of the current trend and not the start of a new, oppositely directed one. These methods are really attempting to jump ahead of the actual trend development, and this leads to some (even many) false trend calls, with subsequent large losses, unless tight stops are placed. Tight stops, however, can lead to many false starts on trends, as each false-trend signal is cut off and then reinstituted shortly thereafter as the current trend resumes.

WHAT IS A TREND?

Before we try and settle upon a good trend definition, we should describe some qualities it should have.

Consistency

The definition should work the same in all different time periods (yearly, weekly, daily, hourly), time frames (1984 trends can be chosen as easily and will look similar to those in 1994), and across commodities (that is, trends should appear the same, so that you could remove the name label and price axis and not know if it was gold or corn trends being measured on the chart).

Reliability

We would like to know if a definition were used once and implied a minimal extension of the current trend beyond the initial identification, that in the future the trader could count on at least this minimal extension. Also, the identification should enjoy a high success, meaning a low rate of false identification of new or changed trends.

Flexibility

Trends are not exactly the same each time. Some are straight up, some moderately vacillate, and some wildly thrash back and forth, often creating false counter-trend signals. We would want our trend definition to have the intelligence to realize that a trend was still in progress, whether it monotonously droned on upwards/downwards or visciously slashed back and forth.

SOME REAL TREND EXAMPLES

Before we pin down a definition, let's look at some real examples to see if there are any other qualities and insights we can derive from pictorial representation.

Chart 2–1 shows S&P on a daily basis, and a mild, straightforward uptrend is in progress much of the time. Note that there are periods of almost continual new trend highs, but there is a predominance of back and forth, up and down periods, where the trend would make good upwards progress, lose some ground, and then regain it plus some.

C H A R T   2–1

S&P Daily Continuous Prices: Uptrend, Moderate Volatility

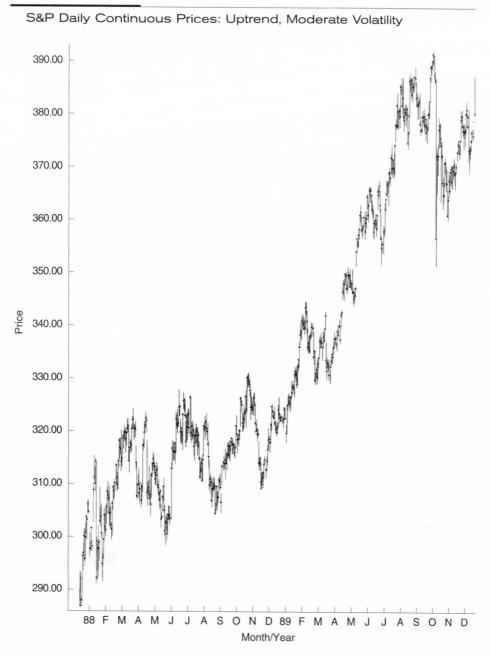

Chart 2–2 also depicts an uptrend, but with wild, not mild, trend features. Here the trend eventually goes far, but the reactions along the way and the violent counter-trend movements are both large and unpredictable. Note the common tie between mild and wild times in Chart 2–1 and Chart 2–2: higher closes eventually build the two (different) trends.

CHART 2-2

S&P Daily Continuous Prices: Uptrend, Great Volatility

Chart 2–3 shows a mild downtrend for silver. This example is almost the duplicate of Chart 2–1 except that prices step down instead of step up, with all other attributes being the same—some straight (down) trend periods intermingled with many small wiggles and squiggles (reactions) against the (down) trend.

Chart 2–4 displays the wild side of silver. Prices eventually career down to a real low point at the end, but, meanwhile, all hell breaks loose in between, with

C H A R T   2–3

Comex Silver Daily Continuous Prices

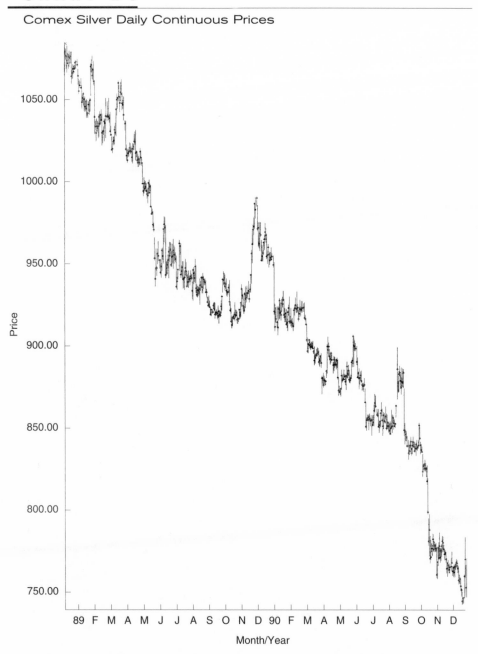

some periods of sharp down runs, other times of zig zag, huge price recoveries, and seeming new uptrends. But again, new lows make the difference and keep the trend headed downwards.

What about trends and price movements within the day? First of all, trends look a little different on different time scales within the day, even though the same basic trend is represented on all time frames. Charts 2–5, 2–6, and 2–7 represent

C H A R T   2–4

Comex Silver Daily Continuous Prices

the same commodity (sugar) for the same day but on 1-, 5-, and 15-minute charting bases respectively. What you notice is a *granularity* difference. The three time
frames show the same trend, but the 1-minute graph shows the pimples, warts, and
every up and down wiggle prices can and do make within the trend, whereas the
15-minute graph gives a cursory overview (only 24 prices plotted) of the trend,
showing where it started, a few milestones in between, and where it ended. On one

CHART 2-5

1-Minute Prices for Sugar #11 on April 17, 1995

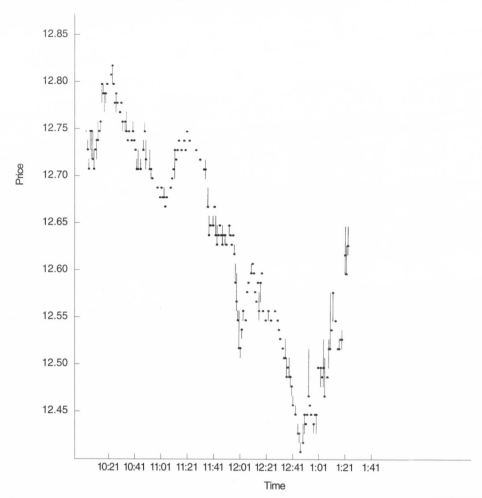

hand the 1-minute graph shows too much detail, which can throw off even a good trend definition with too much randomness, while the 15-minute representation jumps too quickly to allow a reliable call about trends to be made. But again, trade success will depend upon how good the trend definition is, and how much and what type of data it needs.

So we have to consider which time frame—1 minute, 5 minute, 15 minute, or whatever—to use to best apply the trend definition and enjoy trade success.

Finally, let's look at types of trends within the day. We'll use a 5-minute basis chart, the middle ground between the 1- and 15-minute extremes. Chart 2–8 shows S&P futures mildly oscillating and ending up at the high point of the day. Note that the same things can be said about mild day trends as were said about mild daily-basis uptrends (Chart 2–1)—there are periods of straight up price movement, but also many mildly vacillating back and forth periods, for and

CHART 2-6

5-Minute Prices for Sugar #11 on April 17, 1995

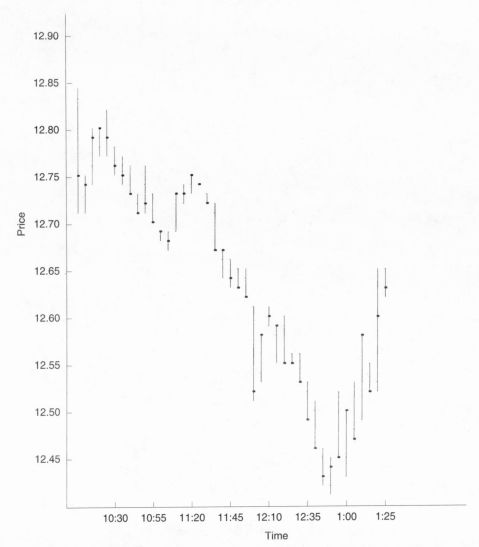

against the trend. The major difference: the size of the trend itself (smaller in intra-day movements) from beginning to end and within price movements (again, smaller than with daily-basis price volatility).

Chart 2–9 shows 5-minute S&P prices in a relatively strong uptrend within the day, but with also relatively violent reactions to the uptrend. Again, this situation is analogous to daily-basis prices in Chart 2–2, but with intraday prices far less violent.

Chart 2–10 depicts 15-minute silver prices with a relatively strong down-trend but mild price volatility, especially as compared to Chart 2–3, its daily-basis counterpart. Again, note the lessened price variation in the intraday chart. Also,

C H A R T   2–7

15-Minute Prices for Sugar #11 on April 17, 1995

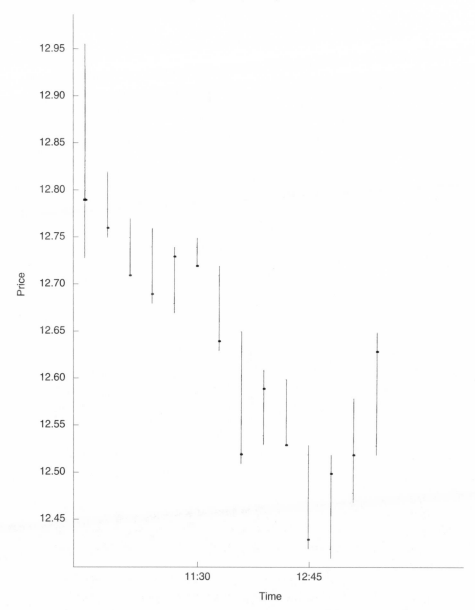

the most noticeable feature, as in the daily-basis data (Chart 2–3) about the continued trendedness, is the sequence of lower lows along the way.

Chart 2–11 displays the wild side of silver and is the within-day counterpart of Chart 2–4. Everything is smaller in Chart 2–11—the trend size from beginning to end and the price variation from 15-minute interval to the next 15-minute interval. Even though it wildly vacillates, the trend makes newer and newer lows until the end of the day.

CHART 2-8

5-Minute Prices for S&P on June 19, 1995

TRENDS ARE DIFFERENT

We've looked at different time frames of the same trend for a commodity and noticed a lot of similarities (extent of trend, type of price variation the same on different time scales), but also some differences (more detail and reactions in smaller time frames).

We should expect some trend differences between commodities. For example, T-bills will exhibit long, drawn-out trends, while orange juice uptrends will skyrocket in an unbroken line and then churn around on daily bases. But there can also be different acting trends in the same commodity, due to different circumstances. For example, in wheat a drought(supply) uptrend will tend to be more drawn out and have greater price variation than a similar demand uptrend, such as when the Russians first bought wheat and prices steadily trickled higher and with less price variation. For comparisons, look at Chart 2-1 versus 2-2, Chart 2-3 versus 2-4, and even within the day, Chart 2-8 versus 2-9, and Chart 2-10 versus 2-11.

C H A R T   2–9

5-Minute Prices for S&P on June 5, 1995

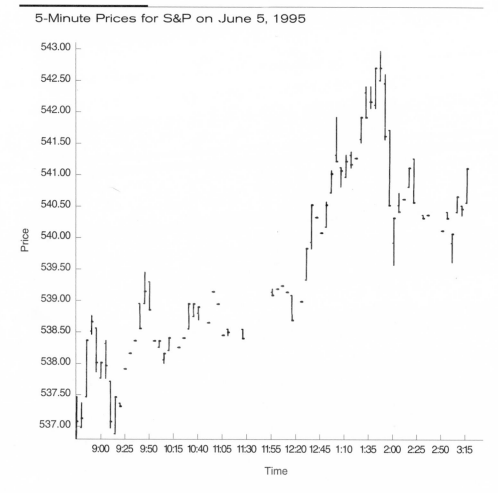

Figure 2–1 presents the two extremes and middle ground, where most trends abide. Situation (a) depicts an unbalanced, pure demand chart picture, such as an orange crop freeze or oil crisis, where prices essentially go up almost every day from start A to end B (after which they stabilize and go sideways).

Situation (c) is the other extreme. There is still a great amount of price increase from start E to finish F, but prices react and vary all over the place in between. In this situation many measures of trend-moving averages and breakout, for example—would give opposite trend signals and get badly burned in the middle. Even contrary definitions would not necessarily work well, since small and large reactions would be mixed in, triggering opposite trend signals too soon and not at all and necessitating the trader to institute many stops to get out of positions going against the major trend.

Situation (b) is the middle ground between the two extremes, with a long-lasting and good-sized length of trend and with moderate reactions to it along the way.

This is also the most prevalent for both daily and within-day price trends.

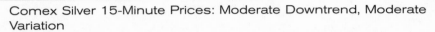

C H A R T   2–10

Comex Silver 15-Minute Prices: Moderate Downtrend, Moderate
Variation

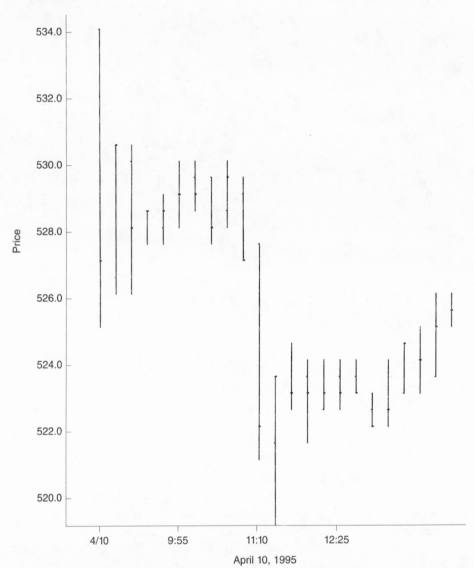

April 10, 1995

THE TREND DEFINITION

What is a trend? Perhaps we should back off and take another perspective, a "natural" view. What do we think about when we think "trend"? We obviously think
"higher" for an uptrend, not only from beginning to end, but at many check points
along the way.

Consider a mountain. If you were hiking up it, you would follow a path or
go over rocks that would lead to clearings and temporary plateaus, or local tops,
each one higher than the next. If you knew how many there were, you could gauge

C H A R T   2–11

Comex Silver 15-Minute Prices: Large Downtrend,
Large Variation

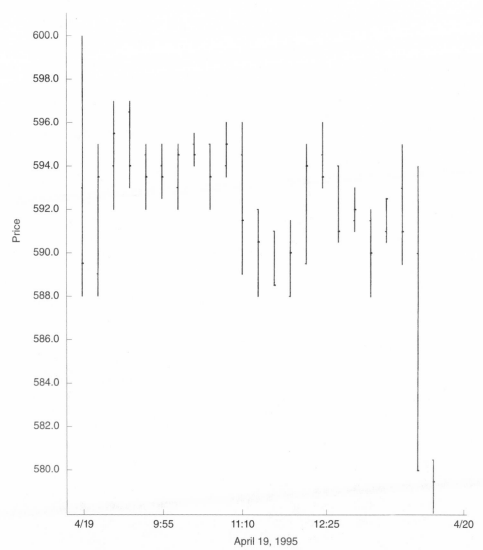

April 19, 1995

how much of the mountain you had already climbed. Even at the beginning, you know you're climbing a mountain after you've gone a sizable distance upwards and reached the first, second, or third intermediate top.

Of course, some judgment or foreknowledge must tell you you're climbing a mountain and not a hill. Similarly, with major uptrends and downtrends in the stock and commodity markets some sort of minimal size of intermediate tops and/or numbers of intermediate tops must convince you that it is a major, not minor, trend about to get underway. You obviously cannot (or are unlikely to) go for the first intermediate top, for it might just be a large hill (false trend), nor can you wait for 50 successively higher tops, since the trend will probably be finished by then.

FIGURE 2–1

Different Trend Styles

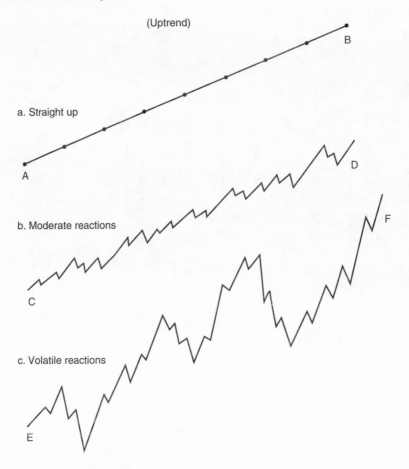

(Uptrend)

a. Straight up

b. Moderate reactions

c. Volatile reactions

There is a happy and crucial medium. We can use far fewer than 50, but we need more than one higher intermediate top.

We can, of course, experiment and test real situations to find out where that happy medium is for each commodity and type of situation (here we are talking about day trading). And we will do that in Chapter 4.

But there is another viewpoint which can help us. From a statistician's stance we can calculate gross, pure probabilities of events. Here we will postulate that prices randomly (with no real drift or cause to go up or down significantly) fluctuate up and down with equal probability. So, if we calculate the probability of one high or low next appearing on the scene, each has only a 50 percent probability. But if we stipulate two successive tops without new corresponding bottoms, the chances are only 50 percent times 50 percent (because they're independent events, supposedly), or 25 percent ($\frac{1}{2} \times \frac{1}{2} = \frac{1}{4}$, or 25 percent chance of two tops in a row).

Going further out, four tops in a row (with no bottoms in between) have only a $\frac{1}{2} \times \frac{1}{2} \times \frac{1}{2} \times \frac{1}{2} = \frac{1}{16}$, or 6¼ percent chance. Now we can start to postulate that such a rare event (and further on out, 5 in a row, or 6, etc.) is not random and must mean that these successive tops are the start of something big—a major (continuing) drift upwards.

Figure 2–2 depicts the trend definition, as a mountain (uptrend) or a valley (downtrend).

F I G U R E   2–2

The Trend Definition: Mountain/Valley

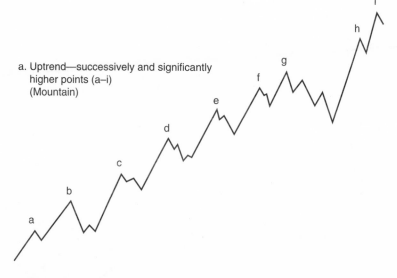

a. Uptrend—successively and significantly
   higher points (a–i)
   (Mountain)

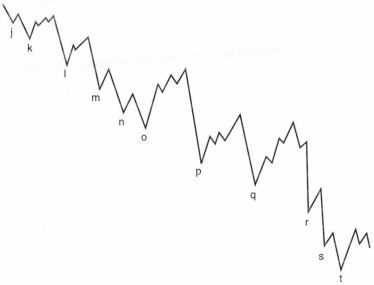

b. Downtrend—successively and significantly
   lower points (j–t)
   (Valley)

The definition makes sense from a natural and a mathematical viewpoint. It is also practical, getting around some of the obstacles met by other definitions, moving averages and breakouts, which essentially emphasize the occurrence and magnitude of the first hill, and contrary methods, which assume that first hill is *only* a hill and is not part of a mountain.

This definition is a natural one to sift out meaningless local hills and go for the real mountains (trends) only (to increase the success rate), and at the same time choose the big trends (to increase the profit per trade).

The next chapter will address practical strategies for using the mountain/valley trend definition for day trading.

CHAPTER 3

Good Strategies and Easy Calculations

Now that we have a good definition for trend, we have to apply it to the day trading environment and come up with sound strategies.

BASIC CALCULATIONS

But first we must sharpen our pencils to do the basic calculations.

As you recall, the real, true calculation is simply looking for higher high points to define an uptrend, and lower lows to delineate a downtrend. (When we refer to a high or low point, or in any reference to points, we mean the *closing* price of a period in the day.) It's that simple. But we must find out where to start, what constitutes a significant new high or low, and determine how many new highs constitute a real, big uptrend (that will take some research—see Chapter 4). Finally, all together, we must determine what trading rules we should use. (See the summary at the end of this chapter for a complete set of trading rules.)

Figure 3–1 shows the basic calculation. If we are in situation (a), a downtrend, we are looking for prices to start swinging up to start a new uptrend. Therefore, we are looking for the first or next high point, so many of which will finally constitute an uptrend signal. (Note that we're always in either an uptrend or downtrend. Refer to Figure 3–5 and discussion to arrive at the very first trend— some explanation is needed before we jump to that.)

We test the price differences between a suspected new high point and the last high point (or last low, if the downtrend is still plunging and we are at the lowest price, but more on that later, in Figure 3–2). Basically, the new potential high point must equal or exceed the last high point by a fixed number of points, M, chosen by the trader, to qualify as the new high point. The first test will be a suspected first high less the lowest low (see Figure 3–2).

If prices were in an uptrend, then we are continually testing to find the next (significant) downtrend, so we are looking for new low points. If we already have

FIGURE 3–1

The Basic Calculation

a. Currently in downtrend

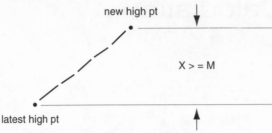

new high pt

latest high pt

$X >= M$

b. Currently in uptrend

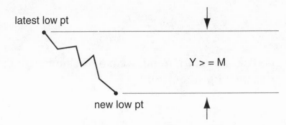

latest low pt

$Y >= M$

new low pt

c. Currently in uptrend: new highs, reset lows

new high

(start over the lows!)

current high

low 1

low 2

low 3

low points following the most recent high point in the uptrend, then we are look-ing for the next low point. We compare a suspected new low point (see situation (b) in Figure 3–1) and take the difference between the latest low and suspected new low. If the difference equals or exceeds M, then we label that recent point as the new or latest low point.

If we are at a new high point in the uptrend and are looking for a possible first low point, then we apply the above test to this latest high point minus the sus-pected new low point. If the difference equals or exceeds M, then the price is deemed to be the first low point in a possible new downtrend.

A note of caution: Every time the current trend makes a new milestone (new high in an uptrend or new low in a downtrend), we must reset the low point in uptrends and high points in downtrends and start over with finding new low points,

FIGURE 3-2

The Basic Test

(Currently in a trend)

M = minimum distance required between new highs or new lows

a. Currently in Uptrend: test for new lows

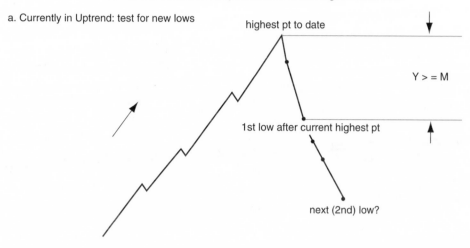

b. Currently in Downtrend: test for new highs

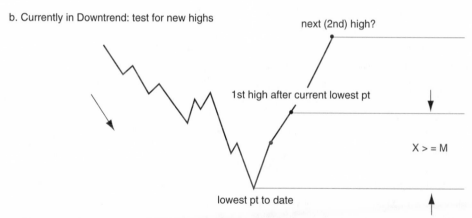

simply because the trend is still climbing upwards, and by definition there is no downtrend yet, as they only start from the highest peak of uptrends. Likewise uptrends start only from the lowest low in downtrends, by definition. See Figure 3–1, situation (c), for new highs in an uptrend and restarting the low points all over again.

Figure 3–2 extends this basic testing to show that we are looking for many (successive) low points in current uptrends to find the next downtrend and many high points in downtrends to find the next uptrend.

In situation (a) we are in an uptrend, and we are testing for many new lows to find a new downtrend. At the highest point to date we again (as we did before at lower high points) look for lower points to possibly start a downtrend. The first lower price is tried. If it passes the difference test from above, we label it the first low. If not, we wait for either a lower price to test (high point minus the lower price greater than or equal to M) or a new high point in the uptrend, which auto-matically cancels and resets all of the previous low points.

If we do get a first low, we start looking for the new low, which we will label and define when the first/latest low minus the new suspected low is greater than or equal to M. If this happens, it is labeled the next low, and in our situation (a), it is now the second low.

The opposite type of calculation and reasoning, but same philosophy, is applied to looking for uptrends in current downtrend markets.

In situation (b) in Figure 3–2, we start from the lowest point in the down-trend to date (to date could mean from the start, right away, or at some later point in the downtrend) and look for significant higher points in a possible uptrend. We keep testing the first high point and later ones to see if they are at least M points higher than the lowest point to date, allowing us to label that higher point as the first real, significant high point. Likewise, once a first high point is chosen, the next possible higher point is compared to that high point (here the first); then the new one is labeled the next high point (here the second one).

Charts 3–1 and 3–2 give examples of these basic calculations. An example of only one price difference needed to establish a new low point in an uptrend is depicted in the first situation: After closing price (A), a drop of more than 10 points (.0010) establishes a new low close after the most recent high close (A). (We chose 10 points as the critical number of points beforehand.)

The second situation shows the same uptrend (same day), but two price changes are required to establish a new low point in the uptrend: After making new high close (C) just before 10:00 A.M. prices slip a bit at the next 5-minute mark and then finally drop by the end of the following period, closing by a total of more than 10 points from (C) to (D).

Chart 3–2 shows similar situations, but in a current downtrend. The first tells us that only one difference is needed to establish the next new high point (B) after a new low closing (A) is made at around 11:20. (We arbitrarily set 5 points, .0005, as the critical difference M in Figure 3–1 to determine a new starting high.)

The next situation, however, requires two major price changes in order to identify a new high point in the downtrend: Prices close at new low (C) around 10:30 A.M. the same day, then take two 5-minute periods to make up the necessary 5 points to record a new high.

BASIC STRATEGIES: REVERSING POSITIONS

Figure 3–3 carries the calculations further, applying strategies for finding new uptrends and taking longs, and new downtrends and going short.

In situation (a) prices are in a downtrend and hit new lows (latest low point). From there prices recover and make a significant new (first) high at point 1, where the price difference between that point and the latest low point (X) is greater than or equal to M, our minimum/critical distance between successive highs or from low to first high. Continuing, new highs are posted at points 2, 3, 4, 5, and 6. Notice that sometimes it takes only one new price to establish new highs (points

C H A R T   3–1

Basic New Low Calculation in Uptrend:
(B) One Price Drop Needed
(D) Two Price Drops Needed

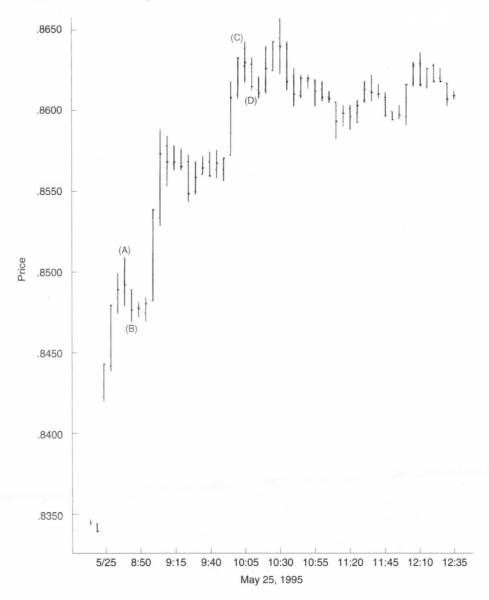

May 25, 1995

2, 3, and 6), while for others it takes several price changes to make new highs (points 4 and 5).

In any case, we have six new significant highs in the downtrend. Does this signify a new uptrend? This is the second variable with which the trader must deal—how many new tops determine a good probability that a new uptrend is underway?

C H A R T   3–2

Basic New High Calculation in Downtrend:
(B) One Price Drop Needed
(D) Two Price Drops Needed

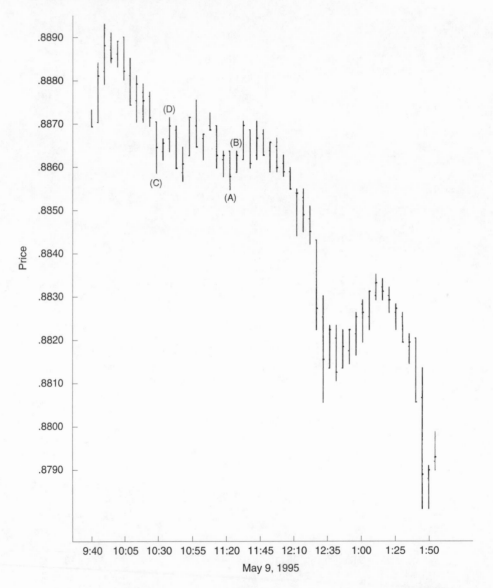

May 9, 1995

There are two variables to predetermine: minimum price *difference* between new highs/lows and *number* of new highs/lows required before a new trend is declared.

Situation (b) shows just the opposite situation—we are currently in an uptrend, looking for a new downtrend. From each latest high point reached we go through the same routine of looking for significant new lows and waiting until a large enough, critical number of them have been found, identifying a new downtrend. In this situation, point 1 is the first significant low, having dropped at least

FIGURE 3-3

The Basic Strategies: Reversing Positions

M = minimum distance between new highs or new lows

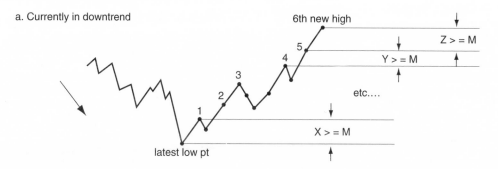

a. Currently in downtrend

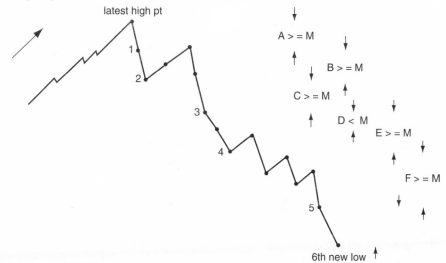

b. Currently in uptrend

M points. Point 2 drops B points, equal to or more than M points, and hence is our second low (only one day was required). Point 3 was arrived at after four more price changes. And so on. All told, we find six significant lower points by the end of the chart. If six new lows were the critical number, we would have declared the falling price series a new downtrend at point 6.

Charts 3–3 through 3–5 show three examples of taking longs from scratch or from being a pronounced downtrend.

Chart 3–3 shows a monster move in sugar at the end of the day (April 28, 1995). The bottom, reached at about 12:00 P.M. is followed by six successive higher 5-minute closings at points (A), (B), (C), (D), (E), and (F). The trader thus enters at (F) at 12.87 and exits on the close at 13–30, at a 43 point profit. (We assume a minimum price difference at 1 point.)

CHART 3-3

Six Higher Closings to Enter Long
(5-Minute Chart for Sugar #11)

April 28, 1995

Chart 3–4 details T-bonds for February 28, 1995. The lowest point is reached around 12:30 P.M. and is followed by six successive higher closings at points (A), (B), (C), (D), (E), and (F), where a long is taken and held until the closing, for a profit of approximately 22 tics, or $688 before commissions and slippage. (This assumes a minimum price difference between successive higher closings of 1 tick.)

In Chart 3–5, wheat is displayed for May 12, 1995. It reaches a bottom just before 11:00 A.M., then makes successive higher 5-minute closings at point (A), (B), (C), (D), (E), and (F), where a long position is taken at about 361 and is held until the closing of the day at 367-1/2, for a profit of about five cents, assuming minimum closing differences of 1/8 cent.

On the other side, Charts 3–6 to 3–8 show the trader taking shorts in uptrends or from a high point in the day.

A mirror image of Chart 3–3, Chart 3–6 shows sugar slowly cascading downwards until heavy selling enters around 12:30 P.M. Using a minimal 1 tick

CHART 3-4

Six Higher Closings to Enter Long
(1-Minute Chart for T-Bonds)

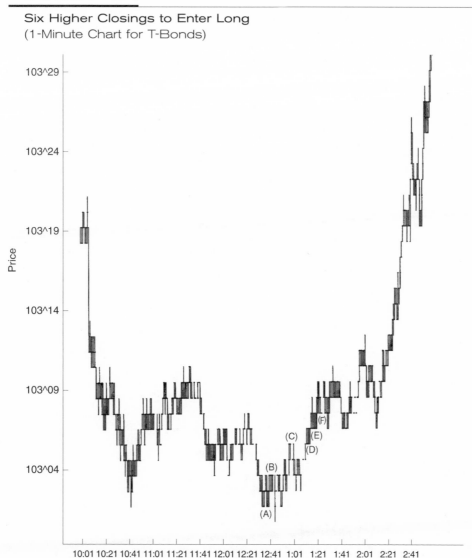

February 28, 1995

between successive lower closings on a 5-minute basis, our intrepid trader would enter a short position at the sixth point (F), at around 11:20 A.M. at 13–90, and hold to the close for a 20 tick profit.

Chart 3–7 shows an active T-bond futures for February 23, 1995, which starts out rising to almost 104 before falling just before noon. Six successive lower 1-minute closings, with 1 point the minimum successive close difference, tells the trader to go short at (F), around 103–16. Prices close that day at 102–26.

Finally, Chart 3–8 shows an active soybean moving at first sideways on June 2, 1995, and then moving sharply downwards after 12:40 P.M. Successive lower

CHART 3-5

Six Higher Closings to Enter Long
(5-Minute Chart for Wheat)

May 12, 1995

closing counts, with a minimum successive closing difference of 1/8 cent, give the trader an opportunity to go short at point (F) at around 1 P.M. at 588, and hold until the closing bell at 584.

BASIC STRATEGIES: REENTERING POSITIONS

What should the trader do when he is stopped out of his position? A stop is a money management artifice used to keep his losses small, not necessarily to signal a new

CHART   3—6

Six Lower Closings to Enter Short
(5-Minute Chart for Sugar #11)

April 10, 1995

position or even the end of a trend (although some regard it as that; otherwise they might stay in their position and wait out the storm until their trend resumed). The trader has a mechanism for reversing to the other trend (see the previous section on reversing positions), but no natural one for reentering the current trend when the trader has quit his position. Has the trend quit when he has been stopped out? No, but it is equally true that there is no evidence that the trend is continuing, unless you take the *absence* of new trend points as meaning the trend has at least temporarily stopped.

CHART 3-7

Six Lower Closings to Enter Short
(1-Minute Chart for T-Bonds)

February 23, 1995

    That is the clue we will use to reinstitute new positions with the old trend
after stop outs of previous positions. A continuing signal, or reconfirmation, will
tell us the old trend has resumed and we can reinstitute positions with that trend.
Specifically, this means at least one new high for an uptrend and one new low for
a downtrend. This is similar to requiring one more high than previously required
to get a long signal in the first place—sort of like extra assurance that the original
signal was right in the first place!

C H A R T   3—8

Six Lower Closings to Enter Short
(5-Minute Chart for Soybeans)

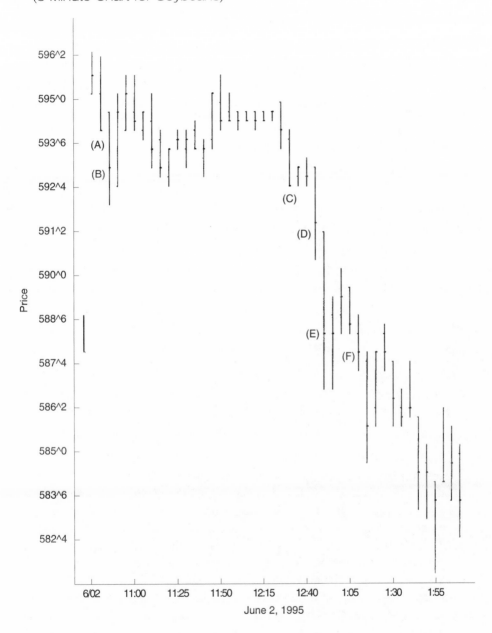

Figure 3–4 depicts reentry of longs and shorts and stop outs.

In situation (a), an uptrend and long position before stop out, a new high occurs (above the last high in the trend and after the stop out), signaling the trader to reinstitute the long at that time. Situation (B) shows the opposite, a stop out of a short followed by a new low in the downtrend, at which point the trader reinstitutes his short.

FIGURE 3–4

The Basic Strategies: Reentering Positions

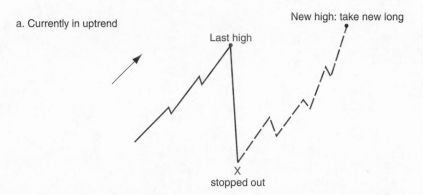

a. Currently in uptrend

New high: take new long

Last high

X
stopped out

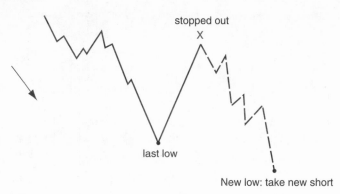

b. Currently in downtrend

stopped out
X

last low

New low: take new short

Charts 3–9 and 3–10 show examples of reentering longs after being stopped out.

Coffee prices immediately head upwards in Chart 3–9, signaling a long position (a minimum difference of .01 points, say), after a predetermined signal of four successive new high closings on a 5-minute basis, at close (D). If a stop were set at .50 points, our trader would have been stopped out just before 10:00 A.M. at point (E). But a fifth successive higher closing (new high territory for the uptrend) at close (F) told him to reenter the long, for the long ride up and huge profit over 5 points—nearly $2,000 for the day!

In Chart 3–10, sedate Eurodollar futures might have signaled a long for our intrepid trader at close (C) if he had chosen a .01 point minimum difference and three successive upticks to signal a long. A tight stop of .02 points would have prematurely closed his long at close (D). But a new high closing at (E) would have propelled him back into a long, to then enjoy a .13 points eventual profit by the closing.

Charts 3–11 and 3–12 likewise present cases where shorts have been stopped out and then reentered after new lows have been made.

C H A R T   3–9

Stopped Out of a Long: Reentered for Profit
(5-Minute Chart for Coffee)

June 15, 1995

In Chart 3–11 coffee prices break sharply right after the opening bell and perhaps signal a short after three successive lower closings at (C) (minimum difference of .01 points) on a 5-minute closing basis, but even a 1 point stop would be tripped at least by close (D). A wise trader could have reentered the short at a new (fourth) successive closing at point (E) and eventually enjoyed over 3 points profit by the day's close.

C H A R T   3-10

Stopped Out of a Long: Reentered for Profit
(5-Minute Chart for Eurodollar)

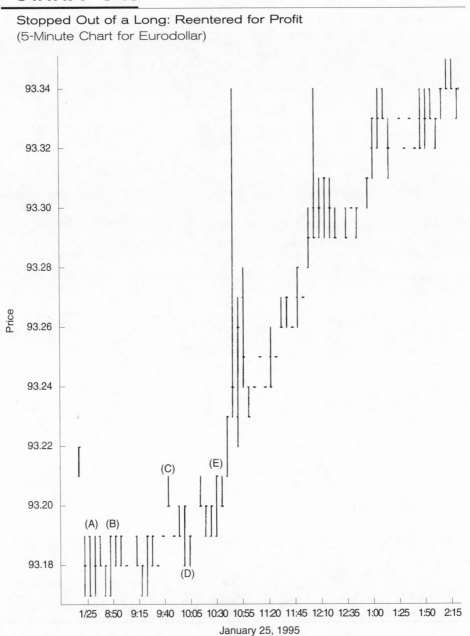

Finally, in Chart 3–12 Japanese yen prices spurt up initially but don't signal a long (if the trader had chosen four successive new high or low closings to enter a long or short, respectively, and a minimum of .0001 points price difference on a 5-minute closing basis). Instead, a short is signaled at close (D). But prices rise sharply and would stop him out at close (E) if a .0025 stop size had been used. However, a new low closing at (F) sparks him to reenter the short, for an eventual profit of .0015 by the day's closing.

C H A R T   3–11

Stopped Out of a Short: Reentered for Profit
(5-Minute Chart for Coffee)

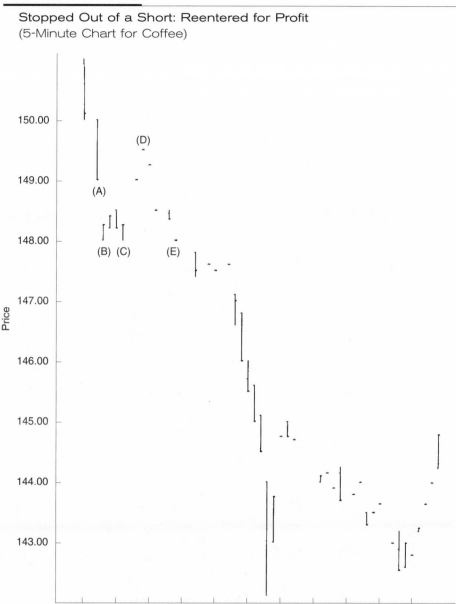

June 23, 1995

BASIC STRATEGIES: INITIAL POSITIONS

Usually, discussions of initial positions come first, in order to get the trader started. We looked at reversing positions first, however, because the basic concept of successive higher or lower closings was easiest and straightforward to explain when only one new trend was being considered, and the reference points and calculations were clear.

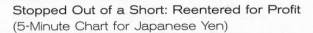

C H A R T   3–12

Stopped Out of a Short: Reentered for Profit
(5-Minute Chart for Japanese Yen)

April 28, 1995

At the beginning of the day the trader not only must apply the successive higher and lower closing finding procedures, he must be *simultaneously* looking for long or short positions, not just one, as he does when he is already in a trend and is looking only for the other (opposite directed) trend. Also, as we shall see, the trader will have to readjust the starting point references for long and short trend possible starting points.

The trader will be keeping two sets of counters and reference points, one for a possible short and one for a possible long position, from the very first price.

The philosophy, and practical good that results, of having adjustable starting points for longs and shorts emanates from looking for trend beginnings from the lowest point reached before an uptrend and the highest point reached before a downtrend begins, simply because the trader is looking for the *longest extent* of the major trend in the day. An uptrend may start later than the opening, at a point considerably lower than the start, and the extend to the close quite a distance (but perhaps not far if measured from the opening of the day).

Figure 3–5 reviews the four possible ways the first long and short positions will be initiated in the day.

Situation (a) shows one of two possible ways to start up trading with a long position. An uptrend starts right away from the start (opening) price, and prices never retreat. The trader counts succeeding significantly higher closings (as in the "reversing positions" section presented prior), then takes the long when the number of new high closings equals M, the (M)agic, critical number to trigger a position.

F I G U R E   3–5

The Basic Strategies: Initial Positions

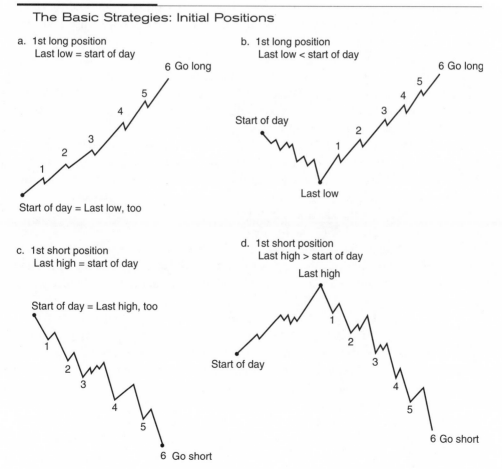

Along the way, however, he is also keeping track of possible shorts by looking for lower closings and a (M)agic number of successive closings. These lower closings have to be figured from the highest point to date (as in the "reversing positions" section described earlier), which is continually readjusted upwards as prices also go to new, higher ground. The number of lower closings is consequently readjusted back to zero as this happens. In reality, we are looking both for longs and for shorts at the same time, but the successive long or short counter is building up for one while readjusting back to zero for the other at the same time.

This situation becomes both murkier and yet more clear in situation (b). From the start of the day prices fall, making lower closings and perhaps building the lower close counter up, but we are also still looking for higher closings and readjusting the lowest point for the day still lower as prices make new lows. Finally, at the point called "last low," the (final) bottom is reached, and the higher closings counter resets to zero for the final time. After that point, first and successive significant new high closings are made until the critical (M)agic number of higher closing count is reached (six in this example) and a long is declared. (All the while we are also resetting the lowest close counter to zero if new day high closings are made, or adding to the low counter if significant new lows are made.)

Situation (c) shows the mirror image of (a), but a short position is taken. Right away from the opening prices fall, making significant new low closings and thus building up a counter of successive new, significant lower closings until, at point 6, the magic number of new lows is reached and a short is taken. Again, since we don't know until point 6 whether the trader is going long or short on the first trade, not only is the lower closing counter monitored and adjusted (built upwards), but the higher closing counter is also monitored and readjusted to zero as significant new lower closings are made, because the lower closing process could stop, and successive significant higher closings and a big enough higher closing counter could still trigger a long, as it did in (b). (That's why the trader has to continue monitoring and adjusting both higher and lower closing counters at the same time; he doesn't yet really know which one will trigger a signal, until it finally does on one of the counters.)

Situation (d) is the short analog to (b). Prices are making new higher closings, maybe even building up the higher closing counter (but haven't yet triggered a long), until the last higher closing in the day has been reached. From his point prices tumble and significant lower closings (from the last high closing) are made until the lower closing counter hits the (M)agic short trigger number (here six) and a short is taken at point 6.

Chart 3–13 (Live cattle 5-minute closes for May 26, 1995) depicts examples of initiating a first long in the day. (1) We evaluate when prices take off right from the opening with the low closing of the day equal to the opening price; and (2) we allow trend testing from *lower* closes after the start. Let's stipulate three successive higher closings of any size as the signal to go long.

For the first situation, the trader would count the number of new higher closings from the opening price only, arriving at (A), right near the opening as the first one; at point (B) around 12:30 for the second one; and at point (C) around 1:00 P.M., near the end of the day, as the third and final (position trigger) price.

Testing for Long from First Close Only and
from the Lowest Low Closing
(5-Minute Chart for Live Cattle)

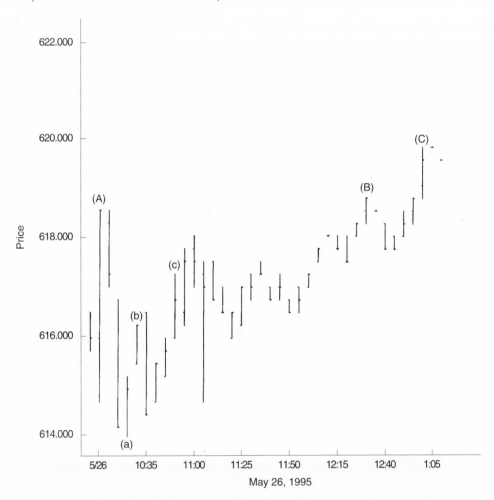

May 26, 1995

   However, if we count from new lower closings (made at the last close just before (a)), we have successive higher closings at points (a), (b), and (c) before 11:00 A.M., and an entry price of 61.75 (sorry, graph is off by a decimal place—I'll blame the commercial graphing package!), resulting in a total profit of about .20 points by day's end. Quite a difference compared to using the day's starting price only to look for new longs or shorts!

   Chart 3–14 shows a similar situation for Japanese yen—it rises a bit at first, then dips, but rises firmly to present a nice, big long position profit opportunity.

   If we started from the first close and looked for longs and shorts only from that point, using four successive higher closes of any magnitude to establish a long position, that position would be taken at point (D) after four successively higher

C H A R T   3–14

Testing for Long Position from First Close Only and
from the Lowest Low Closing
(5-Minute Chart for Japanese Yen)

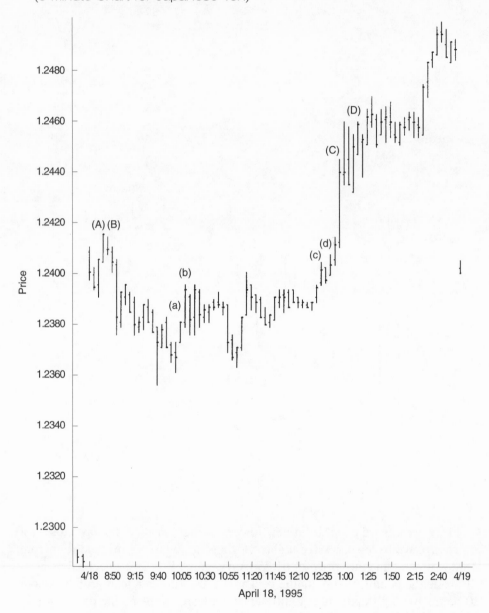

April 18, 1995

closings at (A), (B), (C), and finally (D). While the profit made at the end of the
day is respectable, about .0030 points, it is not spectacular and wastes a good part
of the move to enter the long.

However, if our hearty trader had waited for lower closings and looked for
four successive higher closings relative to that starting point, he would enter a

long position at point (d), around 1:00 P.M. at about 1.2410, a lot lower than start-ing from the first closing only. The profit at the end would have been .0080 points, more than twice (almost three times) the profit of the previous possibility, the opening-only approach.

Charts 3–15 and 3–16 give examples of initiating short positions in instances where the shorts are figured from the first close of the day and from the latest high closing.

C H A R T   3–15

Testing for Short Position from First Close Only and
from Highest Closing
(5-Minute Chart for Live Cattle)

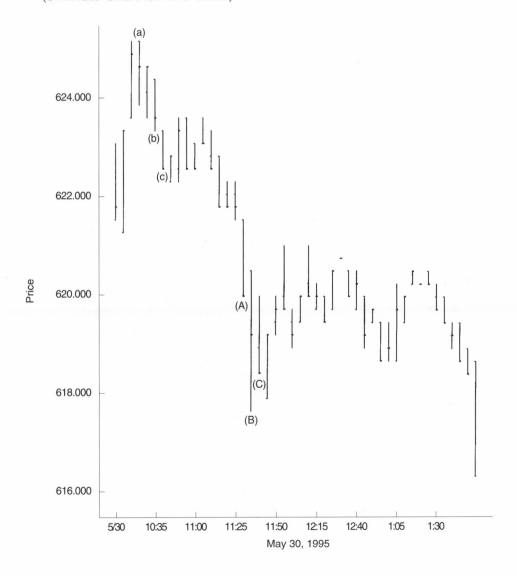

May 30, 1995

C H A R T   3–16

Testing for Short Position from First Close Only and
from Highest Closing
(5-Minute Chart for Live Cattle)

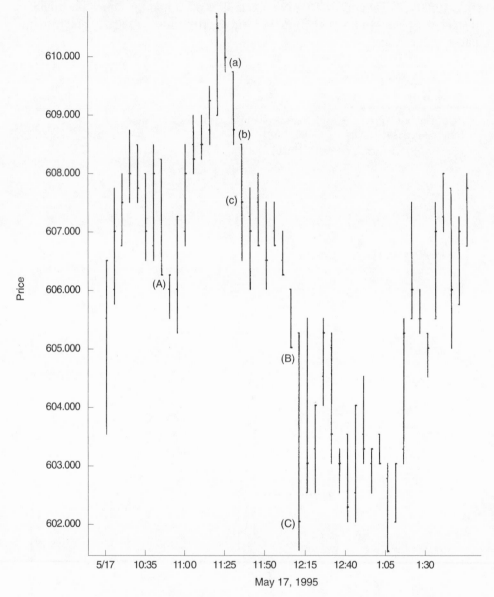

May 17, 1995

In Chart 3–15, live cattle 5-minute prices for May 30, 1995, start out at around 62.20 (sorry, decimal off again), move up, and then sharply, but erratically, fall to the final low closing of around 61.65 by day's end. If the trader uses the opening-only approach as reference for short positions, he would go short at point (C) after three successive lower closes from the first close (using three as the magic number for successive lower closings to go short). The position is entered at about 61.85 and closed out at 61.65, resulting in a moderate profit of .20 points, or $80.

If he had waited for the highest close, just prior to (a) at 10:15 A.M. or so, he would have gone short at closing (c), at about 62.25. He would have closed out at a profit of .60 points, $240, triple the profit from the opening-only approach!

A similar situation is depicted in Chart 3–16 for the same commodity, live cattle, but with even more dramatic results.

If our trader had used only the start from which to figure shorts, again using three successive lower closings relative to the first close only to enter a short, he would have entered the short after (A), (B), and then at (C), at nearly the low of the day, 60.20. The short position would have lost nearly .60 points, or $240, by the closing. However, if he had figured new low closing from the highest closing, he would have triggered a short at 60.77 at closing price (C) and closed the short out at the same price on the close, resulting in no gain (but better off by .60 points or $240!).

PLACING SIZE AND TIME STOPS FOR TRADES

In the next section we will discuss how to end the trade successfully at the end of the day. If the trade goes against the trader, he may have to close the position out in order to protect against large losses.

Figure 3–6 shows two ways to help reduce the size of loss on losing trades. In (a) a size stop is instituted for longs (a specified number of points *below* the price at which the long was originally taken) and for shorts (a designated number of points *above* the price at which the short was entered). Both stops are monitored and executed only on the *time basis* (interval closings) used—1, 5, or 15 minute, or whatever interval was used by the trader to analyze, detect, and enter the original position. (See the next chapter for testing and choosing the right time basis.)

In (b) time stops are used instead. After the trader enters a long, a specified amount of time is allowed to pass (to give the trade time to work out, especially for initial reactions and turbulence). If the trade has not worked out by the end of that time, or at all subsequent time intervals as used to enter the position (meaning that prices at the present time are *lower* than the long entry price), then he exits the trade.

The same goes for short positions—if after a specified time, and at all other time points beyond that point, prices ever go above the original entry price, then the trader closes out the position.

CLOSING OUT THE POSITION

This trading approach tries to maximize the size of the profit on each trade. The assumption is that, to get the most from a trend, the trader should time the entry as quickly as possible and then hold a position until the end of the trend (at the end of the day)—to buy or sell and then hold on. Rather than going for a fixed profit, which might sometimes, but not often, be as big as the trend eventually becomes,

FIGURE 3-6

Size and Time Stops for Each Day Trade

a. Size stop

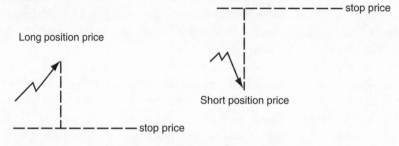

b. Time stop

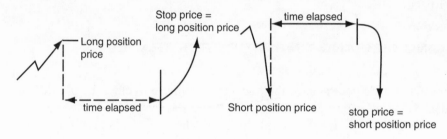

the trader goes from the profit which, on average, will be the largest, as compared to profit taking, step asides, and stop outs: the average of the trend itself.

This is why we strongly advise holding on to the trade, unless reversed or stopped out, *to the end of the day.*

SUMMARY OF TRADING RULES

The following set of rules summarizes, for graphical and computer use, the exact rules for day trading using the mountain/valley method.

We will use arithmetic operators +, −, *, / to mean add, subtract, multiply, or divide.

1. *Initially*

    a. Set the unit of trading (UNIT) = (See next chapter for individual settings for each commodity. Example: 0.5 cents for silver)

    b. Set the critical higher/lower closing counter (A3) = (See next chapter. Individual for each commodity. Example: 4 for Swiss franc)

    c. Set up new low closing (NL) = close of the first period in the day (if 1-minute basis, the end of the first minute; for a 5-minute basis, the end of the first 5-minute period)

    d. Set up new high closing (NH) = close of first interval, too

  e. Set up new low counter (NLCTR) = 0

  f. Set up new high counter (NHCTR) = 0

  g. Set up local new high (LNH) = close of first interval

  h. Set up local new low (LNL) = close of first interval

  i. Set up local new low counter (LNLCTR) = 0

  j. Set up local new high counter (LNHCTR) = 0

  k. Set up trend (TR) = 0

2. *Looking for the First Trend* (1st Trade (Trend, or TR, = 0)

   Get the close for each new interval C(I) and do all the following that apply:

   a. If C(I) – UNIT > = NH [a significant new high closing is made]
      then

      redefine   NH   = C(I) [new high closing]

                 LNL   = C(I) [new local low closing set to C(I)]

                 LNLCTR = 0 [local new low counter set to zero]

   b. If C(I) – UNIT > = LNH [a local new high closing is made]
      then

      redefine   LNH   = C(I), [new local high closing made]

      redefine   LNHCTR = LNHCTR + 1 [increase local high counter by 1]

      also, if LNHCTR > = A3 [local new high counter equals or exceeds A3]
      then initiate long position, set stops, and set trend to long (TR = 1).
      However, if LNHCTR < A3 then go back to beginning of step 2
      with new (next) time interval.

   c. If C(I) + UNIT < = NL [new low closing is made]
      then

      redefine NL   = C(I) [new low is made]

      redefine LNH   = C(I) [local new high closing set to C(I)]

      redefine LNHCTR = 0 [local new high counter set to zero]

   d. If C(I) + UNIT <= LNL [local new low is made]
      then

      redefine LNL   = C(I) [local new low closing is made]

      redefine LNLCTR = LNLCTR + 1 [increase new low counter by 1]

      also, if LNLCTR > = A3 [local new low counter equals/exceeds A3],
      then initiate a new short position, set stops, and set trend to short
      (TR = –1); otherwise, if LNLCTR < A3, then go back to beginning of
      step 2 with new (next) time interval.

3. *When in Uptrend* (TR = 1).

   Get the close for the new interval C(I) and

   a. IF C(I) – UNIT >= NH [new high closing is made]

then

redefine NH   = C(I) [new high closing set to C(I)]

redefine NHCTR = NHCTR + 1 [increase new high counter by 1]

redefine NL   = C(I) [start over with new low set to C(I)]

redefine NLCTR = 0 [reset new low counter to zero]

and test if NHCTR > = A3 [new high counter equals/exceeds A3];

if so, then go long, set stops, set trend TR = 1, unless already long;

otherwise (if NHCTR < A3), then go back to beginning of step 3 and new (next) time interval.

b. If C(I) + UNIT <= NL [new low closing in uptrend is made]

then

redefine NL   = C(I) [set new low closing to C(I)]

redefine NLCTR   = NLCTR + 1 [increase new low counter by 1]

and if   NLCTR > = A3 [new low counter equals or exceeds A3],

then go short (reverse if long), set stops, and set trend (TR = –1);

otherwise (if NLCTR < A3) go back to beginning of step 3 and new (next) time interval

c. If neither a. nor b. hold true, then check for stops if currently in a long position, and return to the beginning of step 3 with a new time interval, even if stopped out.

4. *When in Downtrend (TR = –1).*

Get the close for the next time interval, C(I), and

a. If C(I) + UNIT <= NL [new low closing is made]

then

redefine NL   = C(I) [set new low closing to C(I)]

redefine NLCTR = NLCTR + 1 [increase new low counter by 1]

redefine NH   = C(I) [start over, new high set to C(I)]

redefine NHCTR = 0 [reset new high counter to zero]

and if   NCLTR > = A3 [new low counter equals or exceeds A3]

then go short, set stops, and set trend (TR = –1) if not already short;

otherwise (if NLCTR < A3), go back to beginning of step 4 and new (next) time interval.

b. If C(I) – UNIT >= NH [new high closing in downtrend is made]

then

redefine NH   = C(I) [set new high closing to C(I)]

redefine NHCTR = NHCTR + 1 [increase new high counter by 1]

and if NHCTR > = A3 [new high counter equals/exceeds A3]

then go long (reverse if short), set stops, and set trend (TR = 1); otherwise, if NHCTR < A3 [new high counter less than A3], then go back to beginning of step 4 with next time interval.

c. If neither a. nor b. are true, then check short position (if any) for stops, and return to beginning of step 4, even if stopped out.

CHAPTER 4

Real Settings for
Serious Traders

The final step is to find some good parameter settings for major commodities. This chapter looks for good operating conditions for conservative and speculative modes of trading for many time frames (1-, 5-, 15-, 30-, and 60-minute time intervals within the day) and unusual characteristics for each particular commodity. We cover two grains, two meats, three foods, three metals, two energies, two interest rates, four currencies, and the major stock indices.

Each commodity is examined separately. A typical day's graph or more is presented and price action is discussed to set the tone and analysis for trading that commodity. Historical tests for a month's period of 1-, 5-, 15-, 30-, and 60-minute basis data are then conducted using the mountain/valley method, the findings are discussed, and good settings are chosen and discussed. Graphs depict some of the action trades, and tables present day-by-day details of better trading.

Each of these different trading modes should be looked at from your own trading perspective: Are you conservative or aggressive? What time frame can you handle? (Some can only chart prices and will gravitate towards 5-, 15-, 30- or even 60-minute time frames, while others can computerize the strategy and trade even on a 1-minute basis.)

Some caveats and words of wisdom about the results:

1. As always, the computer runs are the best for that period and do not necessarily represent what the trader would face in the future. The choice for good operating conditions for the future are based on these test periods and the author's judgment about future trading conditions.

2. Some technical minutiae:

- Prices and times on the graphs will not match exactly with those in the tables because of different data collection procedures by the graphing software (a commercial product) and the DOS program developed and used by the author. The cumulative and individual profit results over the commodities tested are not significantly affected.

- Individual and total profits exclude costs (transaction slippage and commissions), which will vary significantly from trader to trader and brokerage to brokerage. Some can get $10 for day trade commissions, while others may pay $50 or more. Some traders will jump on a signal and call the floor direct for excellent fills that are close to the signal price (maybe even better, as this is a trend-following method, and buy trigger points often come at the end of a long upsurge, and a profit taking or shorting attempts period is just around the corner, enabling our trader to actually buy lower than the signaled price). Others will have some coffee, take a nap, and casually enter the trade perhaps by the end of the day, or by lunch at best, a sure way to lose money.

- Times shown reflect oddball starting (first appearance) of trading, and so a fifteen minute period would be added to an actual start of 10:33 EDT, for a next period end at 10:48. Again, if you set your graph up on a price vendor's machine to be exactly at quarter hour, you should not see significant price pattern differences.

- Trades are closed out at the end of the last interval tested. (For example, if a 15-minute time interval is used, the end of the last interval might occur before the day's actual, official settlement. No short duration intervals are allowed.)

- $Max.Loss and $Max.Gain are the worst dollar loss against and gain for that position on that day, until the trade is closed out.

For the most part, only two parameters are tested: the trading unit size (or multiples thereof) the trader stipulates to make a closing significantly higher than the previous high closing; and how many of these successive higher closings it takes to trigger a long position. In some cases stops may improve results, as might the omission of late-in-the-day trades, or the exclusion of more than one trade per day. (See Chapter 5 for a more complete discussion of these possibilities.)

Which are the best settings for you? It depends upon your trading outlook—are you concerned about safety of capital (a conservative stance) or aggressiveness in building capital at the expense of safety (the speculative approach)? Also, if you are able to computerize this method on your spreadsheet or DOS application in Windows, then you can use any of the intervals, whichever shows the most profit (speculative stance) or most safety per dollar of profit (the conservative attitude). If not, and you only have a charting service at your disposal and will manually follow higher and lower closings on charts, then you would probably choose anything at or above 15-minute time intervals.

Currencies

BRITISH POUND

Perhaps the most opportune, and certainly the most volatile, of the currencies, the pound has over the years presented many trades with big long and short trend moves, typically moving between $1.30 and $2.50 per pound, plenty of action for the most demanding. Yet, because it moves so fast, traders can get into trouble by getting in too late or by getting in too early in anticipation of a new trend.

TYPICAL DAY MOVEMENTS

British pound prices move in the day in three distinct patterns: a good trend with low/moderate price volatility (the kind we really want!); a moderate trend with sizable volatility; and no trend, with awful turbulence (watch out!). They all appeared in March 1995, the month of our data, so we'll be in for a good test.

Chart BP–1 perfectly displays those lick-your-chops opportunities. Prices start out at $1.6000 per pound, then work steadily downwards with little price

C H A R T   BP–1

Typical Day British Pound Price Action

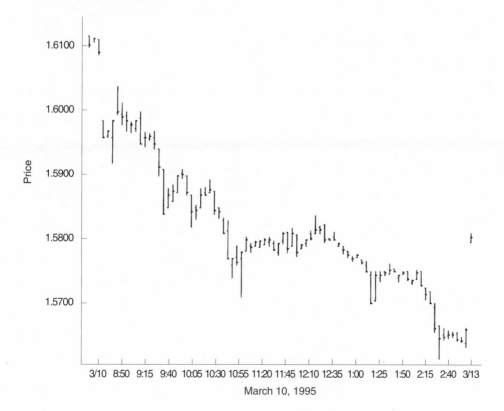

March 10, 1995

reactions (50 points or so maximum), until bottoming at day's end at 1.5700, a 300 point net move. Yummy! If we are lucky, several to half a dozen or so days in a month might be of this type.

Chart BP–2 illustrates a more typical one, however. Prices kick off at 1.6200, go nowhere until late morning, then sharply rise to over 1.6400, retreat sharply, rise again to 1.6500, then retreat even more sharply, and finally settle at about 1.6400. There is still net profit to be made (some portion of 200 points), but late entry, whipsaw reactions, and possible fake trend signals could erode, erase, and even make negative the possible profits. Be careful, trend trader!

Finally, Chart BP–3 depicts a trend methodologist's worst nightmare: prices going net nowhere and violently thrashing about between the day's start and end. On March 14, prices start at 1.5830, run up to 1.5880, race back down again to 1.5810, go back up again to 1.5880, and give the trader one big ping-pong headache.

GREAT SETTINGS FOR BRITISH POUNDS

Despite all of the above admonitions, British pound day trading can be quite lucrative. We tested our method on March 1995 price data on 1-, 5-, 15-, 30-, and 60-minute bases and found four very good settings for conservative and speculative trading modes.

Table 4.BP.C1 details 17 trades taken with 13 successive higher closings on a 1-minute basis with two minimal ticks (4 points) needed to trigger a long signal. A good success rate results (only seven losses), with a net total profit of $4,300,

C H A R T   BP–2

Typical Day British Pound Price Action

March 7, 1995

C H A R T   BP–3

Typical Day British Pound Price Action

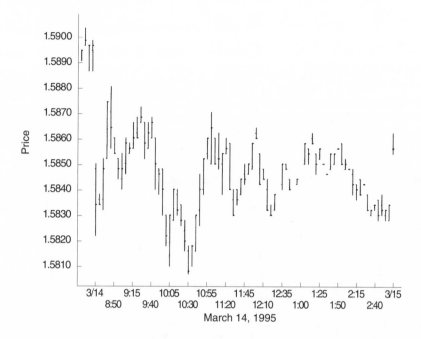

March 14, 1995

$253 per trade, outstanding numbers for 1 month. Chart BP–4 depicts one successful trade put on by a harried trader tracking 1-minute data. If you can, follow each numbered higher closing and see that the 13th higher closing, from a bottom at about 10:40 EDT, occurred at 11:35 CDT (12:35 EDT). Exhausting, but well worth it to the trader by day's end, for a profit of $625.

A slightly less conservative mode is taken in Table 4.BP.C5, where nine successive higher closings of 2 ticks are needed for a long position, using the 5-minute data intervals. Ironically, only two (small) losing trades result, giving almost as big a net profit ($3,562), and a large profit per trade ($324). A typical trade is shown in Chart BP–5, where the first lower closing (1) occurs after the big peak at 1.6460 or so, then is quickly followed by (2) through (6). After a short pause (when an upwards reaction occurs), the strong selling continues the streak until point (9) at 10:34 EDT (9:34 CDT), where the short is taken at 1.6384 and is held until the closing at 1.6226, for a profit of $988 before costs.

Speculative mode trading is best exemplified by 15-minute data intervals and a policy of taking longs when only two successive higher closings of at least 12 ticks (24 points) occur. See Table 4.BP.S15 for 15-minute results. This mode/setting results in dramatic overall performance ($6,062 net profit for the month), with the biggest loser of $333. Only five trades are losses, out of 21 total, a better than 75 percent success rate.

Chart BP–6 depicts a situation of two trades taken in the day, a short and then a long late in the day. The first, a short, is taken at point (B) after falling the required 24 points once at (A) and then at (B) for the short signal. The position is

T A B L E   4.BP.C1

Trade Results: Mountain/Valley Day Trade Method*
British Pound: Conservative Mode, 1-Minute Data

Date	Position	Time In	Price In	Time Out	Price Out	$P/L	$Max. Loss	Time	$Max. Gain	Time
3/2/95	Long	1135	1.603	1400	1.613	625	−312	1140	1188	1216
3/3/95	Long	1230	1.6248	1400	1.6274	162	−75	1234	300	1240
3/6/95	Short	911	1.638	1406	1.6234	912	−238	1013	1500	1131
3/7/95	Long	1019	1.6246	1404	1.642	1088	0	1019	1625	1249
3/8/95	Short	1121	1.6132	1350	1.6064	425	−100	1159	1200	1217
3/8/95	Long	1350	1.6064	1403	1.6062	−12	−50	1359	38	1356
3/10/95	Short	828	1.586	1404	1.5648	1325	−312	849	1562	1326
3/13/95	Long	855	1.5898	1338	1.5892	−38	−112	901	488	1046
3/13/95	Short	1338	1.5892	1403	1.5896	−25	−75	1347	38	1352
3/15/95	Long	907	1.5914	1403	1.596	288	−25	908	775	1101
3/17/95	Long	912	1.5822	1403	1.5834	75	−162	1052	162	1001
3/20/95	Short	1116	1.5766	1403	1.5732	212	−100	1157	538	1232
3/21/95	Short	935	1.5798	1405	1.5858	−375	−400	1117	138	956
3/24/95	Short	949	1.5872	1400	1.5918	−288	−425	1000	88	1059
3/28/95	Long	1018	1.6088	1403	1.6134	288	−50	1050	412	1118
3/31/95	Long	929	1.629	1030	1.6216	−462	−462	1030	162	935
3/31/95	Short	1030	1.6216	1407	1.62	100	−100	1329	538	1032
$Total						4300				
$Ave/Trade						253				

* Settings: Minimum successive high/low closing difference = .0004 dollars
        No. successive high/low closings = 13

held until 1:50 P.M. EDT (12:50 CDT), after two successive higher prices at (a) and (b) occur, starting from the bottom just before 1:30 P.M. at 1.5975 or so. Two profits, $1,000 and $125, result on the day.

Finally, the most speculative instance of trading is set up on 60-minute intervals and requires only one change of 32 points or more for a short or long. A total of 28 trades results, 16 of which are profitable. Refer to Table 4.BP.S60 for 60-minute speculative results. A net of $5,475 is recorded, with $196 profit per trade. A typical trade is shown in Chart BP–7, where a short is taken two hours into the day at point (A) at 1.5804 and is held until the close, for a profit of $425.

C H A R T   BP–4

Conservative Mode Trading: 1-Minute Prices for British Pound

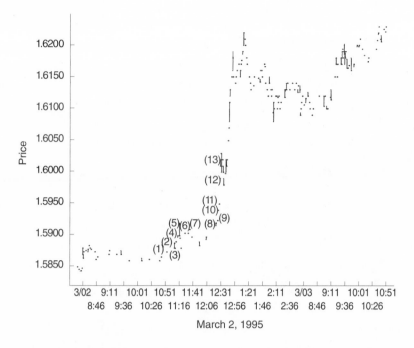

March 2, 1995

T A B L E   4.BP.C5

Trade Results: Mountain/Valley Day Trade Method*
British Pound: Conservative Mode, 5-Minute Data

Date	Position	Time In	Price In	Time Out	Price Out	$P/L	$Max. Loss	Time	$Max. Gain	Time
3/6/95	Short	934	1.6384	1359	1.6226	988	−200	1010	1400	1130
3/7/95	Long	1034	1.6348	1359	1.6424	475	−62	1124	988	1249
3/8/95	Short	1124	1.6134	1359	1.6056	488	−88	1159	1212	1219
3/10/95	Short	904	1.5834	1359	1.565	1150	−288	909	1212	1355
3/13/95	Long	929	1.5914	1352	1.5886	−175	−175	1352	362	1114
3/13/95	Short	1352	1.5886	1359	1.5894	−50	−50	1359	0	1352
3/15/95	Long	914	1.595	1358	1.596	62	−138	924	475	1045
3/17/95	Long	919	1.5834	1358	1.5836	12	−200	1054	12	1120
3/20/95	Short	1110	1.5782	1359	1.5736	288	0	1110	512	1235
3/28/95	Long	1034	1.6104	1359	1.6134	188	−138	1049	275	1119
3/31/95	Short	1020	1.6226	1359	1.6204	138	−38	1023	362	1116
$Total						3562				
$Ave/Trade						324				

* Settings: Minimum successive high/low closing difference = .0004 dollars
     No. successive high/low closings = 9

C H A R T   BP–5

Conservative Mode Trading: 5-Minute Prices for British Pound

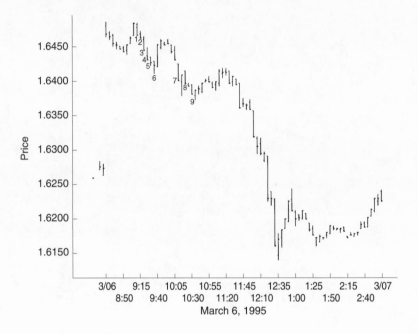

March 6, 1995

C H A R T   BP–6

Speculative Mode Trading: 15-Minute Prices for British Pound

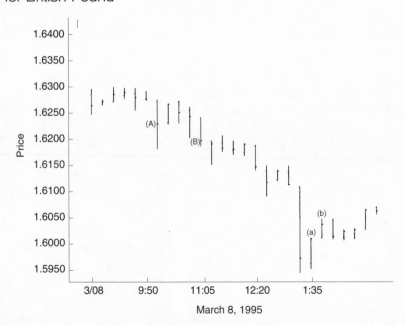

March 8, 1995

C H A R T   BP–7

Speculative Mode Trading: 60-Minute Prices
for British Pound

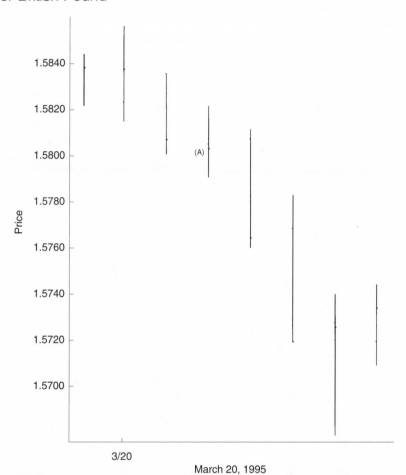

March 20, 1995

T A B L E   4.BP.S15

Trade Results: Mountain/Valley Day Trade Method*
British Pound: Speculative Mode, 15-Minute Data

Date	Position	Time In	Price In	Time Out	Price Out	$P/L	$Max. Loss	Time	$Max. Gain	Time
3/2/95	Long	1140	1.598	1357	1.6136	975	0	1140	1188	1222
3/3/95	Long	840	1.618	1359	1.6264	525	−125	855	625	1333
3/6/95	Short	834	1.643	1359	1.6226	1275	−150	849	1688	1136
3/7/95	Long	1034	1.6348	1359	1.6424	475	0	1034	988	1249
3/8/95	Short	1005	1.6196	1250	1.6036	1000	0	1005	1412	1220
3/8/95	Long	1250	1.6036	1359	1.6056	125	−150	1305	175	1350
3/9/95	Long	904	1.619	949	1.6136	−338	−338	949	12	919
3/9/95	Short	949	1.6136	1359	1.609	288	−125	1020	288	1359
3/10/95	Short	934	1.5816	1359	1.565	1038	0	934	1062	1349
3/13/95	Long	834	1.5876	1204	1.5896	125	−100	849	550	1119
3/13/95	Short	1204	1.5896	1359	1.5894	12	−250	1233	12	1359
3/15/95	Long	919	1.5934	1358	1.596	162	0	919	538	1104
3/16/95	Short	904	1.589	1359	1.5866	150	−250	919	262	1105
3/17/95	Long	903	1.58	1358	1.5836	225	0	903	275	1005
3/20/95	Short	1049	1.5776	1359	1.5756	250	−62	1104	500	1234
3/21/95	Short	919	1.5814	1359	1.5856	−262	−300	1119	188	1004
3/24/95	Short	1106	1.5864	1359	1.5912	−300	−362	1136	0	1106
3/28/95	Long	1020	1.609	1359	1.6134	275	−62	1050	362	1235
3/30/95	Long	1019	1.5992	1359	1.599	−12	−100	1044	62	1147
3/31/95	Long	904	1.6256	1019	1.6236	−125	−125	1019	312	934
3/31/95	Short	1019	1.6236	1359	1.6204	200	0	1019	438	1117
$Total						6062				
$Ave/Trade						289				

* Settings: Minimum successive high/low closing difference = .0024 dollars
    No. successive high/low closings = 2

T A B L E   4.BP.S60

Trade Results: Mountain/Valley Day Trade Method*
British Pound: Speculative Mode, 60-Minute Data

Date	Position	Time In	Price In	Time Out	Price Out	$P/L	$Max. Loss	Time	$Max. Gain	Time
3/1/95	Long	1116	1.5824	1358	1.5844	125	0	1116	125	1358
3/2/95	Long	1126	1.592	1357	1.6136	1350	0	1126	1375	1228
3/3/95	Long	920	1.6184	1112	1.618	−25	−25	1112	225	1026
3/3/95	Short	1112	1.618	1246	1.6254	−462	−462	1246	0	1112
3/3/95	Long	1246	1.6254	1359	1.6264	62	0	1246	62	1359
3/6/95	Short	920	1.6398	1359	1.6226	1075	−100	1020	1400	1321
3/7/95	Long	1020	1.6282	1320	1.635	425	0	1020	850	1220
3/7/95	Short	1320	1.635	1359	1.6424	−462	−462	1359	0	1320
3/8/95	Short	1020	1.619	1320	1.6022	1050	0	1020	1375	1220
3/8/95	Long	1320	1.6022	1359	1.6056	212	0	1320	212	1359
3/9/95	Long	920	1.6194	1020	1.6158	−225	−225	1020	0	920
3/9/95	Short	1020	1.6158	1359	1.609	425	0	1020	425	1359
3/10/95	Short	920	1.5878	1359	1.565	1425	0	920	1425	1359
3/13/95	Long	921	1.5896	1218	1.591	88	0	921	412	1122
3/13/95	Short	1218	1.591	1359	1.5894	100	0	1218	100	1359
3/15/95	Long	920	1.5932	1358	1.596	175	0	920	488	1020
3/16/95	Short	1020	1.589	1359	1.5866	150	0	1020	162	1120
3/17/95	Long	920	1.5828	1358	1.5836	50	−50	1214	75	1120
3/20/95	Short	921	1.5804	1359	1.5756	425	0	921	525	1322
3/21/95	Long	1120	1.586	1359	1.5856	−25	−100	1319	0	1120
3/22/95	Long	1325	1.5888	1359	1.587	−112	−112	1359	0	1325
3/23/95	Long	920	1.5954	1359	1.5932	−138	−175	1118	0	920
3/24/95	Short	920	1.591	1359	1.5912	−12	−38	1313	150	1120
3/28/95	Long	1021	1.6092	1359	1.6134	262	0	1021	300	1321
3/29/95	Long	1324	1.6128	1359	1.6122	−38	−38	1359	0	1324
3/31/95	Long	920	1.626	1020	1.6226	−212	−212	1020	0	920
3/31/95	Short	1020	1.6226	1329	1.6232	−38	−38	1329	312	1120
3/31/95	Long	1329	1.6232	1359	1.6204	−175	−175	1359	0	1329
$Total						5475				
$Ave/Trade						196				

* Settings: Minimum successive high/low closing difference = .0032 dollars
        No. successive high/low closings = 1

DEUTSCHE MARK

The German mark has been considered the dowdy sister of the other European currencies, the British pound and Swiss franc, perhaps because of the more conservative government in Germany. Its long-term trends are smaller than those of its cousins, but they are still adequate and have produced some large moves over the years, especially against the dollar.

TYPICAL DAY PRICE MOVEMENTS

The German mark has basically three types of day movements, all with about an equal chance of occurrence: a moderate to good trend from start to finish; a very choppy market with no real net movement from start to finish; and a mixture in which one or two trends may result, but price volatility is fairly large throughout the day.

Chart DM–1 shows a nice, typical (up)trend from .7070 to .7140, a 70 point move. But one should keep in mind that the initial dip from .7100 to .7070 may be enough to trip some trend-following methods into going short and having to reverse to long, resulting in a short loss. For the rest of the day (from the bottom) the volatility is relatively small.

A different scenario, loathesome to the trend follower, is presented in Chart DM–2. Here prices move in a scissorlike fashion between basically .7150 and .7170, a 20 point plus range—enough to do damage to the trend trader going long at the top of the range and short at the bottom—not a winning approach!

C H A R T   DM–1

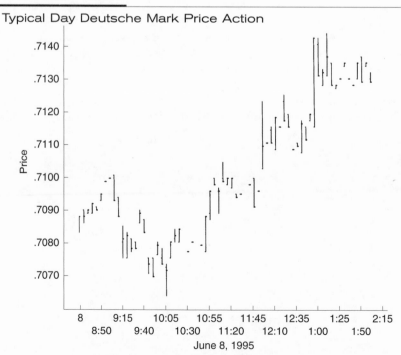

Typical Day Deutsche Mark Price Action

June 8, 1995

C H A R T   DM–2

Typical Day Deutsche Mark Price Action

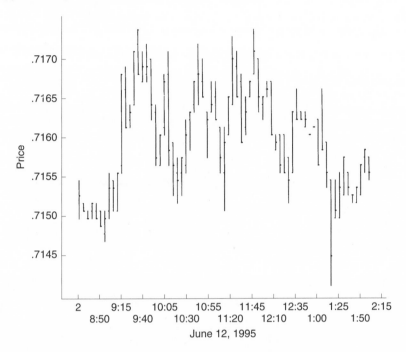

June 12, 1995

Lastly, a combination of trends and considerable volatility are depicted in Chart DM–3. Prices do make two distinct trends, one southward from .7140 to .7100 and one northbound to .7130. Meanwhile, prices fluctuate for and against these trends afterwards. Some combination of trend and contrary or limited profit taking would be best for this market.

SOME GOOD SETTINGS FOR DEUTSCHE MARK

We tested the mountain/valley method on the German mark price data for the month of June 1995. Price intervals tested consisted of 1-, 5-, 15-, 30-, and 60-minute price bases. Four modes of operating, two conservative and two speculative, are presented here.

The first one, Table 4.DM.C5–1, is one of the two conservative modes, both of which use the same price interval, 5-minute price data. They are conservative in two different ways: one requires less difference between successive higher closings, but more successive higher closings, to get long. Table 4.DM.C5–1 is the one that needs more successive higher closings. Interestingly, more trades result—about twice as many—than with the mode that requires fewer number of closings but larger differences. Table 4.DM.C5–1, the larger number of differences made, shows good total profits of $2,600 with about 30 trades, or $90 per trade. Except for one trade ($462), losses are kept at around $200 or less.

C H A R T   DM–3

Typical Day Deutsche Mark Price Action

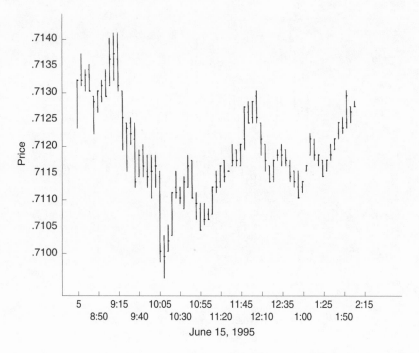

June 15, 1995

Chart DM–4 displays one successful trade. Prices start slipping ever so slightly at the start of trading on June 22, 1995, but traverse steadily south on successive lower closings from point (A) until point (F), where, at 9:04 A.M., a short is taken at .7238 and is held until the close at .7176, for a profit of $775.

A stiffer combination of successive difference size (7 ticks) and number of differences (four) to take a position is detailed in Table 4.DM.C5–2. The combination produces less trades, but it results in a healthy profit of $1,300 and per trade profit of $100. Also, the largest loss is now only $262, an improvement. Chart DM–5 gives us a nice, typical long trade for June 23,1995. After dipping a bit, prices steadily move successively higher from points (A) to (D), where a long is signaled at 9:24 A.M. at .7210. The long is held until the close at .7241, for a gain of 31 points, or $388.

A hot time is to be had by the speculative mode trader using 30-minute intervals in Table 4.DM.S30. A need for only two successive higher close differences of 5 ticks or more to go long lets the trader become quite active and successful, totaling 30 some trades, 18 of them successful, with the largest loss at only $162, a profit sum of $4,362, and a per trade average of $145. Not bad! Chart DM–6 graphs a successful long trade for June 26, 1995. Prices move pretty much consistently up and at point (B) a long is initiated at 9:49 A.M. at .7209 and is held until the end at .7270, for a profit of 61 points, or $762.

Finally, a speculative stance for hour-followers is detailed in Table 4.DM.S60. Only one higher or lower closing by 16 points allows the trader to go long or short, respectively. (This is pure breakout version, then.) A respectable

T A B L E   4.DM.C5–1

Trade Results: Mountain/Valley Day Trade Method*
Deutsche Mark: Conservative Mode, 5-Minute Data

Date	Position	Time In	Price In	Time Out	Price Out	$P/L	$Max. Loss	Time	$Max. Gain	Time
6/1/95	Long	855	0.704	1123	0.714	1250	−125	925	1250	1123
6/2/95	Short	1027	0.708	1158	0.7064	200	−75	1031	312	1038
6/5/95	Long	911	0.7124	1358	0.7122	−25	−25	1358	325	1200
6/7/95	Long	947	0.7142	1359	0.713	−150	−200	1128	0	947
6/8/95	Long	1153	0.7115	1357	0.7132	212	−62	1155	362	1258
6/9/95	Short	814	0.7139	1359	0.7156	−212	−612	959	12	834
6/12/95	Long	900	0.7153	1359	0.7158	62	−12	1327	225	930
6/13/95	Short	929	0.7153	1359	0.7131	275	−50	934	288	1214
6/14/95	Long	859	0.7166	1054	0.7169	37	0	859	225	949
6/14/95	Short	1054	0.7169	1249	0.7184	−188	−188	1249	100	1114
6/14/95	Long	1249	0.7184	1359	0.7164	−250	−250	1359	0	1249
6/15/95	Long	824	0.7132	944	0.7114	−225	−225	944	100	904
6/15/95	Short	944	0.7114	1149	0.7121	−88	−88	1149	188	1004
6/15/95	Long	1149	0.7121	1359	0.7125	50	−112	1254	88	1354
6/16/95	Short	1054	0.7159	1359	0.717	−138	−275	1134	0	1054
6/19/95	Short	819	0.7166	1009	0.7177	−138	−138	1009	100	904
6/19/95	Long	1009	0.7177	1359	0.7171	−75	−300	1104	25	1335
6/20/95	Long	1144	0.7212	1359	0.7217	62	−112	1224	100	1339
6/21/95	Long	1335	0.7226	1359	0.7239	162	0	1335	325	1345
6/22/95	Short	904	0.7238	1359	0.7176	775	−138	1004	938	1104
6/23/95	Long	824	0.7194	1300	0.7234	500	−50	844	725	1149
6/23/95	Short	1300	0.7234	1359	0.7241	−88	−112	1345	0	1300
6/26/95	Short	844	0.722	1156	0.7211	112	0	844	350	954
6/26/95	Long	1156	0.7211	1359	0.7223	150	0	1156	162	1351
6/27/95	Long	1145	0.7263	1359	0.7242	−262	−262	1359	0	1145
6/28/95	Long	854	0.723	1009	0.7193	−462	−462	1359	0	1145
6/28/95	Short	1009	0.7193	1359	0.7177	200	0	1009	538	1024
6/29/95	Long	856	0.7202	1359	0.727	850	−150	926	1038	1226
6/30/95	Long	1004	0.7255	1359	0.7255	0	−150	1019	100	1220
$Total						2600				
$Ave/Trade						90				

* Settings: Minimum successive high/low closing difference = .0001 dollars
            No. successive high/low closings = 6

profit total of $1,400 and $70 per trade result over some 20 trades. Chart DM–7 details a short taken at 9:17 A.M. at point (A) on June 2, 1995, after dropping heavily from the opening to .7148, that is held through some price recovery at the end for a good profit of 48 points, or $600.

C H A R T   DM–4

Conservative Mode Trading: 5-Minute Prices for Deutsche mark

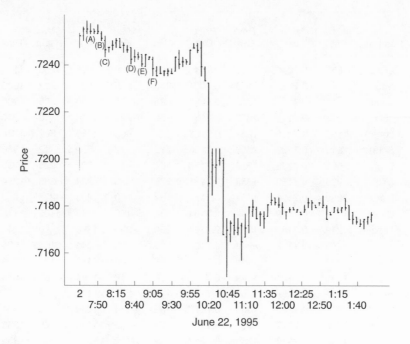

June 22, 1995

T A B L E   4.DM.C5–2

Trade Results: Mountain/Valley Day Trade Method*
Deutsche mark: Conservative Mode, 5-Minute Data

Date	Position	Time In	Price In	Time Out	Price Out	$P/L	$Max. Loss	Time	$Max. Gain	Time
6/1/95	Long	951	0.7067	1123	0.714	912	−88	956	912	1123
6/2/95	Short	1018	0.7088	1158	0.7064	300	−25	1022	412	1038
6/5/95	Long	935	0.7139	1358	0.7122	−212	−212	1358	138	1200
6/8/95	Long	1153	0.7115	1357	0.7132	212	−62	1155	362	1258
6/13/95	Short	949	0.7143	1359	0.7131	300	−112	954	162	1214
6/19/95	Short	1104	0.7153	1359	0.7171	−225	−325	1335	0	1104
6/21/95	Long	1345	0.7252	1359	0.7239	−162	−162	1359	0	1345
6/23/95	Long	924	0.721	1359	0.7241	388	−50	938	525	1149
6/26/95	Short	934	0.7204	1359	0.7233	−238	−250	1351	150	954
6/27/95	Long	1145	0.7263	1359	0.7242	−262	−262	1359	0	1145
6/28/95	Short	1019	0.7172	1359	0.7177	−62	−225	1130	275	1024
6/29/95	Long	1001	0.7222	1359	0.727	600	−50	1006	788	1226
6/30/95	Long	1220	0.7263	1359	0.7255	−100	−138	1355	0	1220
$Total						1300				
$Ave/Trade						100				

* Settings: Minimum successive high/low closing difference = .0007 dollars
    No. successive high/low closings = 4

C H A R T   DM–5

Conservative Mode Trading: 5-Minute Prices
for Deutsche mark

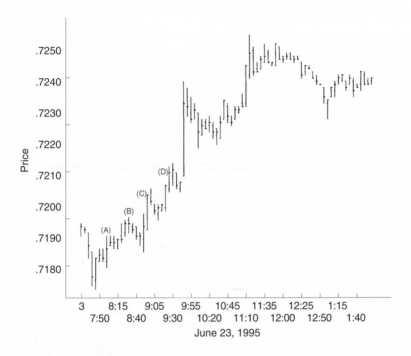

June 23, 1995

C H A R T   DM–6

Speculative Mode Trading: 30-Minute Prices
for Deutsche mark

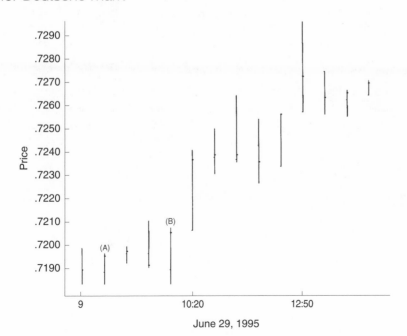

June 29, 1995

T A B L E   4.DM.S30

Trade Results: Mountain/Valley Day Trade Method*
Deutsche Mark: Speculative Mode, 30-Minute Data

Date	Position	Time In	Price In	Time Out	Price Out	$P/L	$Max. Loss	Time	$Max. Gain	Time
6/1/95	Long	952	0.7063	1359	0.7116	662	0	952	662	1136
6/2/95	Short	917	0.7148	1301	0.7089	738	0	917	1025	1200
6/2/95	Long	1301	0.7089	1350	0.711	262	0	1301	262	1350
6/5/95	Long	921	0.7128	1358	0.7122	−75	−75	1358	300	1204
6/6/95	Short	922	0.7089	1056	0.709	−12	−12	1056	138	954
6/6/95	Long	1056	0.709	1206	0.7106	200	0	1056	412	1148
6/7/95	Long	947	0.7142	1115	0.713	−150	−150	1115	0	947
6/7/95	Short	1115	0.713	1359	0.713	0	−75	1145	125	1256
6/8/95	Long	1117	0.71	1359	0.7131	388	0	1117	388	1359
6/9/95	Long	952	0.7168	1359	0.7156	−150	−188	1340	38	1053
6/12/95	Long	1148	0.717	1359	0.7158	−150	−225	1319	0	1148
6/13/95	Short	919	0.7158	1359	0.7131	338	0	919	338	1219
6/14/95	Long	849	0.716	1120	0.7166	75	0	849	300	949
6/14/95	Short	1120	0.7166	1359	0.7164	25	−212	1250	25	1359
6/15/95	Short	1049	0.7108	1149	0.7121	−162	−162	1149	0	1049
6/15/95	Long	1149	0.7121	1359	0.7125	50	−88	1219	50	1359
6/19/95	Short	1119	0.7159	1325	0.717	−138	−138	1325	62	1149
6/19/95	Long	1325	0.717	1359	0.7171	12	0	1325	25	1355
6/20/95	Long	1019	0.722	1359	0.7217	−37	−312	1119	0	1019
6/21/95	Long	949	0.7218	1359	0.7239	262	−138	1119	400	1350
6/22/95	Short	919	0.7237	1359	0.7176	762	−62	949	800	1050
6/23/95	Long	919	0.7202	1245	0.724	475	0	919	625	1149
6/23/95	Short	1245	0.724	1359	0.7241	−12	−25	1319	0	1245
6/26/95	Short	919	0.7208	1149	0.7207	12	0	919	138	949
6/26/95	Long	1149	0.7207	1359	0.7223	200	0	1149	200	1350
6/27/95	Long	949	0.7244	1359	0.7242	−25	−25	1119	138	1319
6/28/95	Short	1019	0.7172	1249	0.7171	12	0	1019	238	1119
6/28/95	Long	1249	0.7171	1359	0.7177	75	0	1249	112	1349
6/29/95	Long	949	0.7209	1359	0.727	762	0	949	850	1249
6/30/95	Long	1225	0.7258	1359	0.7255	−37	−75	1355	12	1255
$Total						4362				
$Ave/Trade						145				

* Settings: Minimum successive high/low closing difference = .0005 dollars
      No. successive high/low closings = 2

T A B L E   4.DM.S60

Trade Results: Mountain/Valley Day Trade Method*
Deutsche Mark: Speculative Mode, 60-Minute Data

Date	Position	Time In	Price In	Time Out	Price Out	$P/L	$Max. Loss	Time	$Max. Gain	Time
6/1/95	Long	1019	0.7063	1359	0.7116	662	0	1019	662	1136
6/2/95	Short	917	0.7148	1333	0.71	600	0	917	938	1215
6/2/95	Long	1333	0.71	1350	0.711	125	0	1333	125	1350
6/5/95	Long	923	0.713	1358	0.7122	−100	−125	1338	162	1122
6/8/95	Long	1238	0.7116	1359	0.7131	188	0	1238	188	1359
6/9/95	Long	1023	0.7166	1359	0.7156	−125	−150	1124	0	1023
6/13/95	Short	920	0.716	1359	0.7131	362	0	920	362	1220
6/14/95	Long	920	0.7183	1120	0.7166	−212	−212	1120	0	920
6/14/95	Short	1120	0.7166	1359	0.7164	25	−100	1318	25	1359
6/20/95	Long	1020	0.7214	1119	0.7195	−238	−238	1119	0	1020
6/20/95	Short	1119	0.7195	1220	0.7218	−288	−288	1220	0	1119
6/20/95	Long	1220	0.7218	1359	0.7217	−12	−50	1320	0	1220
6/22/95	Short	1020	0.719	1359	0.7176	175	0	1020	175	1359
6/23/95	Long	920	0.7207	1359	0.7241	425	0	920	500	1219
6/26/95	Short	920	0.7207	1359	0.7223	−200	−200	1359	25	1118
6/27/95	Long	1320	0.7253	1359	0.7242	−138	−138	1359	0	1320
6/28/95	Short	1020	0.7155	1320	0.7172	−212	−212	1320	0	1020
6/28/95	Long	1320	0.7172	1359	0.7177	62	0	1320	62	1359
6/29/95	Long	1020	0.7238	1359	0.727	400	0	1020	400	1359
6/30/95	Long	1220	0.7263	1359	0.7255	−100	−100	1359	0	1220
$Total						1400				
$Ave/Trade						70				

* Settings: Minimum successive high/low closing difference = .0016 dollars
    No. successive high/low closings = 1

C H A R T   DM–7

Speculative Mode Trading: 60-Minute Prices for Deutsche Mark

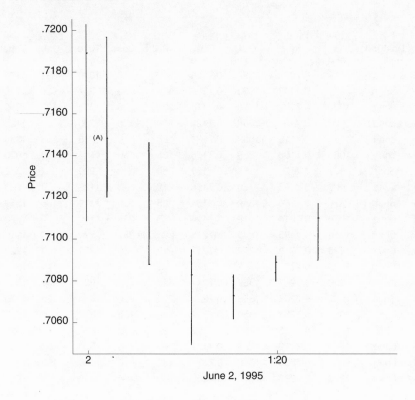

June 2, 1995

SWISS FRANCS

A trender's delight, Swiss francs make big, broad trends over the long term. Because the dollar has been under strong attack the past ten years, prices have traversed broadly between 30 cents to nearly one dollar per franc, giving the trader lots of long-term opportunities. Also, once a trend has started, it takes a long time to reverse. Daily trends in the direction of the trend abound, but also along with a few, but large, reactions to the trend opportunities. Many types of trading interests participate, from speculator to market-making banks, international companies, exporters and importers, and governments. A shopping list of items influences the direction of currency prices in general: international politics, wars, economic cartels, interest rates, local/global investment returns, balance of payments, and inflation.

TYPICAL DAY PRICE MOVEMENTS

Swiss franc prices can swing in both directions in big moves, but with big volatility. Chart SF–1 shows a typical day, May 12, 1995, in which prices did not move terribly much from open to close (.8350 to .8320), but varied 50 points (.0050) several times during the day. If the trader used moving average methods to time trades, he would have experienced several whipsaw nightmarish losses of almost 50 points each.

C H A R T   SF–1

Typical Day Swiss Franc Price Action

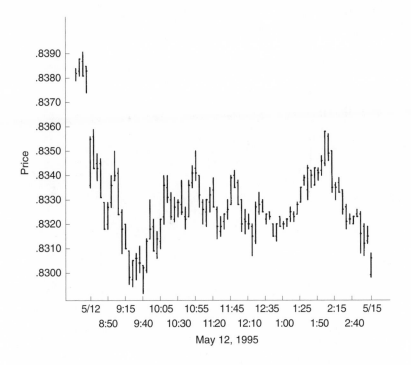

May 12, 1995

Another type of day is presented in Chart SF–2, showing a nicely trended day (80 points from start to finish), one on which trend traders would gladly feast. Unfortunately, these days don't happen that often, and concerted volatility occurs at one point in the day (e.g., 10:40 A.M.), which could whipsaw the trader by reversing a short to a long, resulting in two losses (here).

Finally, a third type of day is prevalent—one where little trend takes place from start to finish, but two or more trends sally back and forth, giving the trader a (rare) opportunity to get into two or more trends, provided his method is nimble enough. In Chart SF–3, prices trend upwards from .8860 to .8910 and then cascade dramatically downwards to .8840 near the end of the trading day.

GREAT SETTINGS FOR SWISS FRANCS

The mountain/valley method was tested on 1-, 5-, 15-, 30-, and 60-minute price data for the month of May 1995. Results for four sets of good results, two speculative and two conservative trading modes, are presented, and accompanying charts are used to explain some examples.

Table 4.SF.C1 is a conservative approach on 1-minute data, using 12 ticks for a significant higher/lower closing difference and requiring five successive closing differences of that magnitude or larger to commence a trade. Eight of 13 trades were successful, for a total profit of $3,200 for the month. The largest loss was $525, far lower than the largest gain of $2,175. Swiss francs surely gave opportunities that month! Chart SF–4 painstakingly follows prices as they bottom on May 18,1995, at around .8200 at 11:10 A.M. or so, methodically make concert-

CHART   SF–2

Typical Day Swiss Franc Price Action

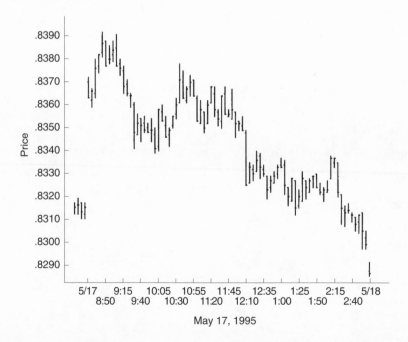

May 17, 1995

CHART   SF–3

Typical Day Swiss Franc Price Action

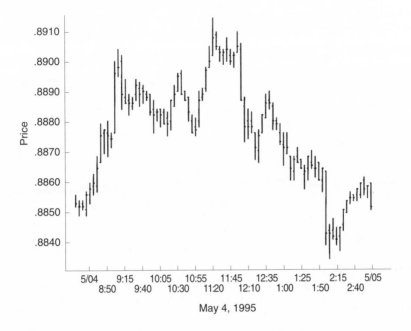

May 4, 1995

TABLE   4.SF.C1

Trade Results: Mountain/Valley Day Trade Method*
Swiss Franc: Conservative Mode, 1-Minute Data

Date	Position	Time In	Price In	Time Out	Price Out	$P/L	$Max. Loss	Time	$Max. Gain	Time
5/5/95	Short	1128	0.8838	1405	0.8848	−125	−212	1133	200	1146
5/9/95	Short	1129	0.8813	1405	0.8798	188	−262	1208	400	1246
5/10/95	Short	1041	0.868	1404	0.8722	−525	−688	1327	62	1044
5/11/95	Short	1050	0.8465	1401	0.8383	1025	−200	1053	1338	1234
5/16/95	Long	1002	0.8346	1405	0.8315	−388	−500	1323	362	1052
5/17/95	Short	1341	0.8307	1404	0.83	88	−62	1348	100	1359
5/18/95	Long	1140	0.8295	1401	0.8334	488	0	1140	812	1258
5/19/95	Short	1328	0.8292	1404	0.83	−100	−125	1338	62	1331
5/22/95	Long	1045	0.8363	1404	0.835	−162	−250	1239	162	1208
5/23/95	Short	1027	0.834	1405	0.8331	112	0	1027	488	1106
5/25/95	Long	734	0.8498	1404	0.8672	2175	−350	741	2250	1353
5/26/95	Long	1128	0.8834	1204	0.885	200	−50	1130	238	1151
5/31/95	Short	745	0.8605	1405	0.8587	225	−188	746	938	835
$Total						3200				
$Ave/Trade						246				

* Settings: Minimum successive high/low closing difference = .0012 dollars
     No. successive high/low closings = 5

C H A R T   SF–4

Conservative Mode Trading: 1-Minute Prices for Swiss Franc

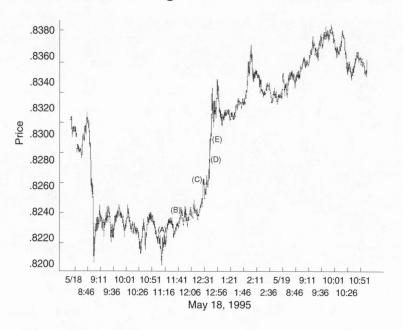

May 18, 1995

T A B L E   4.SF.C5

Trade Results: Mountain/Valley Day Trade Method*
Swiss Franc: Conservative Mode, 5-Minute Data

Date	Position	Time In	Price In	Time Out	Price Out	$P/L	$Max. Loss	Time	$Max. Gain	Time
5/4/95	Short	1259	0.884	1359	0.8855	−188	−225	1349	0	1259
5/5/95	Short	1144	0.8838	1359	0.8848	−125	−200	1311	100	1149
5/9/95	Short	1124	0.8825	1359	0.8796	362	−88	1214	550	1249
5/11/95	Short	1049	0.8477	1359	0.838	1212	0	1049	1488	1234
5/15/95	Long	1344	0.8338	1359	0.8334	−50	−112	1349	0	1344
5/16/95	Long	939	0.832	1319	0.8307	−162	−162	1319	612	1054
5/16/95	Short	1319	0.8307	1359	0.8316	−135	−150	1349	0	1319
5/17/95	Short	1114	0.8332	1359	0.8299	412	−62	1309	412	1359
5/18/95	Long	1139	0.829	1359	0.8329	612	0	1139	988	1259
5/19/95	Short	1305	0.8302	1359	0.8298	50	−62	1310	100	1330
5/22/95	Long	1045	0.8363	1359	0.8354	−112	−225	1240	138	1109
5/23/95	Short	1029	0.8336	1359	0.833	75	0	1029	425	1109
5/25/95	Long	804	0.858	1359	0.8673	1162	−325	824	1162	1359
5/26/95	Long	1139	0.8849	1204	0.885	12	−150	1154	12	1204
$Total						3150				
$Ave/Trade						225				

* Settings: Minimum successive high/low closing difference = .0012 dollars
     No. successive high/low closings = 4

ed steps upwards to establish a long at point (E), and then hold until the close at .8329, resulting in a gain of $612 for the patient, hard working (1-minute price monitoring) trader.

Another conservative mode is available to the trader on a 5-minute basis, so he can breathe a bit between price intervals! This one involves about the same conditions, except it reqires one less successive higher/lower closing to establish a long or short. Slightly different days are traded, giving the trader some thought about diversifying over time frames, etc. Table 4.SF.C5 gives us similar statistics: $3,150 total net profit over 14 trades, 8 of which were successful, with the largest of 6 losses being $188, compared to the largest gain of $1,212. Chart SF–5 shows us how the trader got long. Price (A) starts off more than 12 points higher than the open, then (B) is likewise so much higher than (A), and so on until point (D), when prices closed at .8580 at 8:04 CDT (9:04 EDT) and gave the trader his fourth successively higher closing to go long. The position is held (no reversals occur) until the close for a profit of $1,162.

C H A R T   SF–5

Conservative Mode Trading: 5-Minute Prices for Swiss Franc

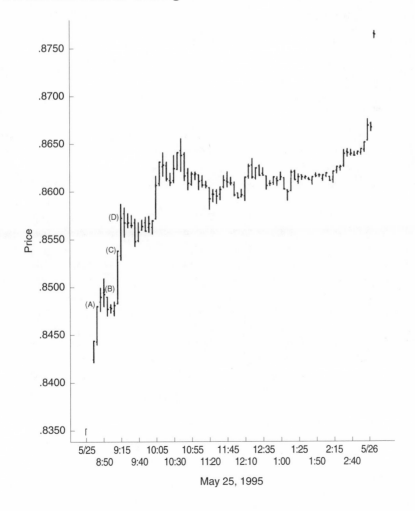

May 25, 1995

The speculative side of this method is portrayed in Table 4.SF.S15 for trading 15-minute prices. There is more activity, because only 5 ticks are needed to define a higher/lower successive closing and four successive ones will trigger the position. The results look good, with $2,837 total net profit, $177 profit per trade, and only 1 loss that shows any sign of being moderately large ($450) but that is made up by the gains being so much larger (e.g., $600, $1,212), and on average. Chart SF–6 shows a steady, strong decline in May 11 Swiss francs beginning around 10:15 EDT and cascading down to point (D), a short signal.

Finally, the lazy man's speculative bonanza—the 60-minute interval trend following. Table 4.SF.S60 requires only two successive higher/lower closings of 12 points or more difference to establish longs and shorts. Again, the table shows more gains than losses, with the gains also averaging more than losses, but the biggest gains are not that big—only $612, $450, and $425. However, the largest loss is only $300, so that is a good trade-off.

Chart SF–7 shows a crystal clear long signal at (B) on May 26, 1995, at 11:20 CDT at .8819, which is held until 12:04 at .8850, resulting in a gain of $388.

TABLE   4.SF.S15

Trade Results: Mountain/Valley Day Trade Method*
Swiss Franc: Speculative Mode, 15-Minute Data

Date	Position	Time In	Price In	Time Out	Price Out	$P/L	$Max. Loss	Time	$Max. Gain	Time
5/3/95	Long	1019	0.8858	1359	0.8854	−50	−175	1204	75	1049
5/4/95	Short	1249	0.8861	1359	0.8855	75	0	1249	262	1304
5/5/95	Short	949	0.8856	1359	0.8848	100	−300	1019	325	1149
5/9/95	Short	1119	0.8844	1359	0.8796	600	0	1119	788	1249
5/11/95	Short	1049	0.8477	1359	0.838	1212	0	1049	1488	1234
5/12/95	Long	1305	0.8359	1359	0.8313	−450	−450	1359	0	1305
5/15/95	Long	1334	0.8308	1359	0.8334	325	0	1334	325	1359
5/16/95	Long	919	0.8307	1319	0.8307	0	−38	934	638	1204
5/16/95	Short	1319	0.8307	1359	0.8316	−116	−150	1349	0	1319
5/17/95	Short	1204	0.8324	1359	0.8299	300	−75	1249	300	1359
5/18/95	Long	1149	0.8325	1359	0.8329	50	162	1204	188	1304
5/19/95	Short	1234	0.8318	1359	0.8298	250	−38	1248	250	1334
5/22/95	Long	1049	0.836	1359	0.8354	−75	−175	1249	175	1134
5/24/95	Long	904	0.8348	1359	0.8339	−112	−112	1134	250	949
5/25/95	Long	1349	0.8647	1359	0.8673	325	0	1349	325	1359
5/26/95	Long	1120	0.8819	1204	0.885	388	0	1120	388	1150
$Total						2837				
$Ave/Trade						177				

* Settings: Minimum successive high/low closing difference = .0005 dollars
    No. successive high/low closings = 4

C H A R T   SF–6

Speculative Mode Trading: 15-Minute Prices for Swiss Franc

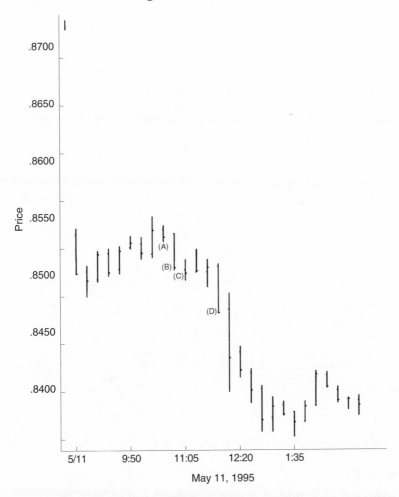

May 11, 1995

T A B L E   4.SF.S60

Trade Results: Mountain/Valley Day Trade Method*
Swiss Franc: Speculative Mode, 60-Minute Data

Date	Position	Time In	Price In	Time Out	Price Out	$P/L	$Max. Loss	Time	$Max. Gain	Time
5/2/95	Long	1020	0.886	1359	0.8838	−275	−400	1220	0	1020
5/4/95	Short	1320	0.8844	1359	0.8855	−138	−138	1359	0	1320
5/5/95	Short	1120	0.8853	1359	0.8848	62	0	1120	188	1220
5/9/95	Short	1120	0.8845	1359	0.8796	612	0	1120	612	1359
5/11/95	Short	1120	0.8414	1359	0.838	425	0	1120	488	1219
5/16/95	Long	1020	0.834	1359	0.8316	−300	−362	1320	100	1120
5/17/95	Short	1120	0.833	1359	0.8299	388	0	1120	388	1359
5/18/95	Long	1320	0.8333	1359	0.8329	−50	−50	1359	0	1320
5/19/95	Short	1219	0.8334	1359	0.8298	450	0	1219	450	1359
5/22/95	Long	1120	0.8368	1359	0.8354	−175	−250	1320	0	1120
5/23/95	Short	1120	0.8315	1359	0.833	−188	−188	1359	0	1120
5/25/95	Long	1320	0.8643	1359	0.8673	375	0	1320	375	1359
5/26/95	Long	1120	0.8819	1204	0.885	388	0	1120	388	1204
$Total						1575				
$Ave/Trade						121				

* Settings: Minimum successive high/low closing difference = .0012 dollars
          No. successive high/low closings = 2

C H A R T   SF—7

Speculative Mode Trading: 60-Minute Prices for Swiss Franc

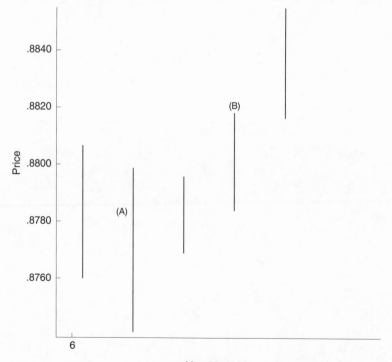

May 26, 1995

JAPANESE YEN

One great currency versus another, the dollar and the yen continually battle and are influenced greatly by their respective government actions to bring about stability and fairness to their common commerce. Long-term big trends are prologue for the continuing dialogue and saga—whether the dollar or yen reigns supreme. All sorts of interests and influences are on both sides (bull and bear) of the market—banks, international companies, exporters and importers, governments, and speculators—all making for big and exciting markets. But buried underneath the big, gargantuan moves are daily moves that reflect the long-term battle. Big moves can and do occur in a day's time, as do meandering, small moves.

TYPICAL DAY MOVES

Good size trends occur within the day, counterpart to long-term overnight moves (e.g., the dollar losing steadily to the yen over a long time). Moves of 100 ticks or more are common, and occasionally a 300 pointer occurs, such as when banks and governments step in to bolster the dollar.

Even with big moves during the day, however, wavelike reactions do take place and can temporarily alter, pause, and even stop a major move. Chart JY–1 displays a yen move from beginning to end of over 200 points on April 10, 1995. Prices did move 60 points by 1:00 P.M. CDT, but significant retreats/advances slowed the trend until massive selling finally came in afterwards. But our mountain/valley method had caught the move far sooner on all time frames (see the four trading results tables, ahead).

C H A R T   JY–1

Typical Daily Japanese Yen Price Action

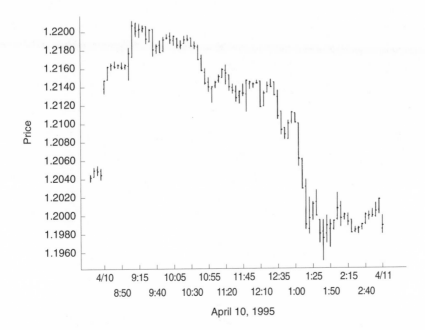

April 10, 1995

On many days there are only moderate to small moves from beginning to end, with lots of turbulence in between. Chart JY–2 perfectly describes this situation. Prices start out around 1.1680, move up rapidly to 1.1700, and then spend almost the entire day vacillating between that price and 1.167, driving the average trader crazy and mauling moving average methods badly (going long, then short, then long, and then short, for many whipsaw losses). This is where a concerted, reliable, strong testing method that looks for significant and continued trend movement does well, rejecting one-time johnnies and spurious little dribbles. (See 9:40 A.M. to 11:20 A.M., and 12:10 P.M. to 2:20 P.M. for trickles that might trigger many an oscillator and moving average to go short.)

GOOD PARAMETER SETTINGS FOR JAPANESE YEN

Japanese yen futures were given a month-long test (April 1995) by the mountain/valley method for 1-, 5-, 15-, 30-, and 60-minute data to see if it generally performed well and to look for better settings.

As with many other commodities, noise and smaller-sized and lesser numbers of big moves kept 1-minute trading from being profitable. (Very few traders would be willing to track yen prices graphically on a 1-minute basis anyway.)

All other databases tests came out well. Two conservative and two speculative modes have been chosen to illustrate profit possibilities and styles of trading and to show the stability and reliability of the method across time frames.

C H A R T   JY–2

Typical Daily Japanese Yen Price Action

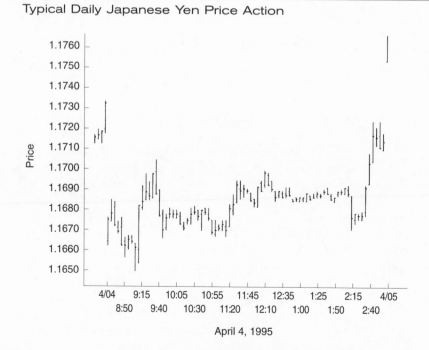

April 4, 1995

Table 4.JY.C5 details and summarizes the trades for the month for a relatively conservative mode which requires a somewhat large difference (8 ticks) between successive higher/lower closings and a relatively stringent number of differences (four) to initiate the trade. Except for two trades in the $500–$600 area, losses remain small and are fewer than gains in number, while gains tend to be larger, and the cumulative total, $4,188, and profit per trade before costs, $161, are good sized. Occasionally there is more than one trade per day: Chart JY–3 depicts

T A B L E   4.JY.C5

Trade Results: Mountain/Valley Day Trade Method*
Japanese Yen: Conservative Mode, 5-Minute Data

Date	Position	Time In	Price In	Time Out	Price Out	$P/L	$Max. Loss	Time	$Max. Gain	Time
4/3/95	Long	829	1.1725	1359	1.1732	88	–475	1029	88	1359
4/5/95	Short	849	1.1733	1109	1.1734	–12	–238	904	825	949
4/5/95	Long	1109	1.1734	1359	1.1745	138	–262	1323	138	1359
4/6/95	Long	924	1.182	1359	1.1828	100	–325	1049	188	1329
4/7/95	Long	1209	1.2018	1359	1.2041	288	–200	1259	400	1349
4/10/95	Short	949	1.2155	1359	1.2011	1800	–60	1014	2188	1234
4/11/95	Long	929	1.2031	1359	1.2071	500	–12	934	550	1344
4/12/95	Long	949	1.2015	1359	1.204	300	–362	1014	375	1244
4/13/95	Short	849	1.2055	1150	1.2096	–512	–512	1150	88	859
4/13/95	Long	1150	1.2096	1200	1.2105	112	0	1150	112	1200
4/14/95	Long	829	1.1725	1359	1.1732	88	–475	1029	88	1359
4/17/95	Long	949	1.2291	1359	1.2288	–37	–212	1044	75	1159
4/18/95	Long	1149	1.2409	1359	1.2491	1025	0	1149	1088	1339
4/19/95	Long	1014	1.2443	1225	1.2441	–50	–200	1044	575	1150
4/19/95	Short	1225	1.2441	1359	1.2408	412	0	1225	950	1325
4/20/95	Long	829	1.2188	1054	1.2134	–675	–675	1054	125	909
4/20/95	Short	1054	1.2134	1359	1.21	425	–238	1104	725	1222
4/21/95	Long	819	1.2122	1359	1.2172	625	–238	934	625	1359
4/24/95	Short	954	1.2092	1359	1.211	–225	–325	1019	150	1004
4/25/95	Long	904	1.2301	1034	1.2278	–288	–288	1034	525	924
4/25/95	Short	1034	1.2278	1059	1.2306	–350	–350	1059	250	1039
4/25/95	Long	1059	1.2306	1359	1.2318	150	–250	1109	362	1334
4/26/95	Short	904	1.2022	1109	1.2011	138	0	904	900	919
4/26/95	Long	1109	1.2011	1359	1.2038	338	–225	1224	612	1304
4/27/95	Short	1015	1.2028	1359	1.204	–150	–275	1230	0	1015
4/28/95	Short	1240	1.1951	1359	1.1957	–75	–125	1305	138	1335
$Total						4188				
$Ave/Trade						161				

* Settings: Minimum successive high/low closing difference = 0.0008 cents
        No. successive high/low closings = 4

C H A R T   JY–3

Conservative Mode Trading: 5-Minute Prices for Japanese Yen

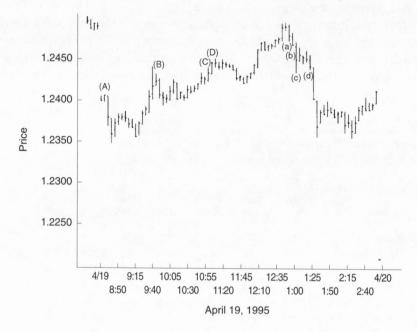

April 19, 1995

a day (April 19, 1995) in which a long is initiated (at 10:14 CDT) at point (D), but is reversed to short at point (d), at 12:25 CDT, for a loss of 2 ticks, but a gain on the short of 33 ticks, for a total day's profit of $362.

A little more speculative stance is taken in Table 4.JY.S15, where the difference size is only 1 tick (anything goes), with the number of differences still at four. The cumulative profits are nearly the same as the previous 5-minute conservative mode and the profit per trade is about the same, but the number of trades and losses are slightly different: the number of losses is less, but the largest loss is a little bigger ($900). One advantage to the trader might be the lesser frequency of graphing (every 15 minutes versus every 5 minutes). Chart JY–4 depicts a typical trade, going long quickly at point (D) around 10:00 A.M. EDT and holding on through lots of volatility until closing at 1.2172 for a 33 point ($412) profit.

Table 4.JY.C15 presents a conservative mode (stiff closing difference and number of successive higher/lower closings requirements), resulting in few trades, but an impressive profit per trade ($219).

Finally, a mode for the long-lunch taking trader: 60-minute price basis speculative trading. Refer to Table 4.JY.S60 for speculative 60-minute results. He needs only two successive higher closings of at least 5 points to initiate a long position. A decent total profit ($2,975) and profit per trade ($157) before costs gives him food for thought.

T A B L E   4.JY.S15

Trade Results: Mountain/Valley Day Trade Method*
Japanese Yen: Speculative Mode, 15-Minute Data

Date	Position	Time In	Price In	Time Out	Price Out	$P/L	$Max. Loss	Time	$Max. Gain	Time
4/3/95	Short	1134	1.1698	1304	1.1709	−138	−138	1304	0	1134
4/3/95	Long	1304	1.1709	1359	1.1732	288	0	1304	288	1359
4/5/95	Short	834	1.1748	1204	1.1738	125	−50	904	1012	949
4/5/95	Long	1204	1.1738	1359	1.1745	84	−288	1319	84	1359
4/6/95	Long	949	1.182	1359	1.1828	100	−325	1049	188	1334
4/7/95	Long	1204	1.2008	1359	1.2041	412	0	1204	525	1349
4/10/95	Short	934	1.2184	1359	1.2011	2162	0	934	2550	1234
4/11/95	Long	934	1.203	1359	1.2071	512	0	934	550	1349
4/12/95	Long	1119	1.2021	1359	1.204	238	−50	1134	262	1334
4/14/95	Short	1134	1.1698	1304	1.1709	−138	−138	1304	0	1134
4/14/95	Long	1304	1.1709	1359	1.1732	288	0	1304	288	1359
4/17/95	Long	934	1.2262	1359	1.2288	325	0	934	412	1249
4/18/95	Short	904	1.2376	1204	1.2448	−900	−900	1204	125	1004
4/18/95	Long	1204	1.2448	1359	1.2491	538	0	1204	538	1359
4/19/95	Long	949	1.2424	1359	1.2408	−200	−612	1304	788	1149
4/20/95	Long	849	1.2177	1119	1.2142	−438	−438	1119	200	904
4/20/95	Short	1119	1.2142	1359	1.21	525	0	1119	825	1220
4/21/95	Long	904	1.2139	1359	1.2172	412	−450	934	412	1359
4/24/95	Short	904	1.2108	1359	1.211	−50	−125	1019	350	1004
4/25/95	Long	904	1.2301	1359	1.2318	212	−288	1034	438	1004
4/26/95	Short	919	1.195	1104	1.2004	−675	−675	1104	0	919
4/26/95	Long	1104	1.2004	1359	1.2038	425	0	1104	700	1304
4/27/95	Short	949	1.2045	1234	1.2048	−36	−36	1234	200	1034
4/27/95	Long	1234	1.2048	1359	1.204	−100	−100	1349	0	1234
4/28/95	Short	1234	1.1959	1359	1.1957	25	−12	1304	200	1334
$Total						4025				
$Ave/Trade						161				

* Settings: Minimum successive high/low closing difference = 0.0001 cents
         No. successive high/low closings = 4

Chart JY–5 details a short taken at 11:20 A.M. CDT on April 20, 1995, and held for almost a $600 profit. (Ignore the first closing, as our chart package counts the opening bell as a closing, not one hour into trading, as it should be). While there are bigger gains (see April 10) and losses than this trade, it is fairly typical of the price movement opportunities we see in the yen.

CHART   JY-4

Speculative Mode Trading: 15-Minute Prices for Japanese Yen

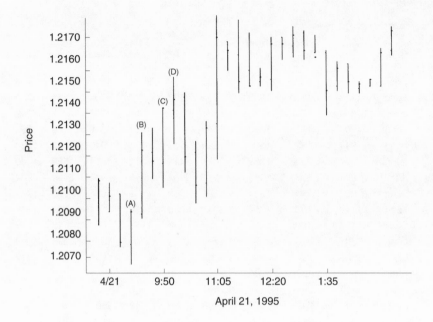

April 21, 1995

TABLE   4JY.C15

Trade Results: Mountain/Valley Day Trade Method*
Japanese Yen: Conservative Mode, 15-Minute Data

Date	Position	Time In	Price In	Time Out	Price Out	$P/L	$Max. Loss	Time	$Max. Gain	Time
4/7/95	Long	1334	1.2035	1359	1.2041	75	0	1334	188	1349
4/10/95	Short	1034	1.2129	1359	1.2011	1475	−225	1104	1862	1234
4/18/95	Long	1249	1.2462	1359	1.2491	362	−62	1304	362	1359
4/19/95	Long	1004	1.244	1359	1.2408	−400	−812	1304	588	1149
4/25/95	Long	949	1.2334	1359	1.2318	−200	−700	1034	25	1004
4/26/95	Long	1149	1.2038	1359	1.2038	0	−350	1234	275	1304
$Total						1312				
$Ave/Trade						219				

* Settings: Minimum successive high/low closing difference = 0.0008 cents
          No. successive high/low closings = 5

C H A R T   JY–5

Speculative Mode Trading: 60-Minute Prices for Japanese Yen

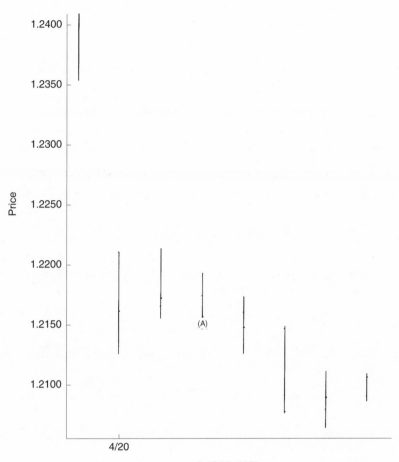

April 20, 1995

T A B L E   4.JY.S60

Trade Results: Mountain/Valley Day Trade Method*
Japanese Yen: Speculative Mode, 60-Minute Data

Date	Position	Time In	Price In	Time Out	Price Out	$P/L	$Max. Loss	Time	$Max. Gain	Time
4/3/95	Long	1120	1.1715	1359	1.1732	212	−162	1221	212	1350
4/4/95	Long	1119	1.1691	1359	1.1715	300	−150	1320	300	1359
4/5/95	Short	1020	1.1687	1220	1.1736	−612	−612	1220	0	1020
4/5/95	Long	1220	1.1736	1359	1.1745	112	−288	1320	112	1359
4/6/95	Long	1220	1.1817	1359	1.1828	138	0	1220	138	1350
4/7/95	Long	1220	1.201	1359	1.2041	388	0	1220	388	1359
4/10/95	Short	1020	1.2157	1359	1.2011	1825	0	1020	2200	1320
4/11/95	Long	1020	1.2048	1359	1.2071	288	−62	1220	288	1359
4/12/95	Long	1120	1.2022	1359	1.204	225	0	1120	225	1359
4/14/95	Long	1120	1.1715	1359	1.1732	212	−162	1221	212	1359
4/18/95	Long	1220	1.2453	1359	1.2491	475	0	1220	475	1359
4/19/95	Long	1020	1.2445	1320	1.2375	−875	−875	1320	200	1120
4/19/95	Short	1320	1.2375	1359	1.2408	−412	−412	1359	0	1320
4/20/95	Short	1120	1.2147	1359	1.21	588	0	1120	888	1220
4/24/95	Short	1120	1.2092	1321	1.2105	−162	−162	1321	0	1120
4/24/95	Long	1321	1.2105	1359	1.211	62	0	1321	62	1359
4/26/95	Long	1120	1.202	1359	1.2038	225	−100	1220	225	1359
4/27/95	Long	1320	1.2046	1359	1.204	−72	−72	1359	0	1320
4/28/95	Short	1220	1.1962	1359	1.1957	60	0	1220	188	1320
$Total						2975				
$Ave/Trade						157				

* Settings: Minimum successive high/low closing difference = 0.0005 cents
        No. successive high/low closings = 2

The Energies

CRUDE OIL

Everyone remembers the Gulf War. When oil products soared in August 1990, oil companies made millions as crude went from under $20 to over $40 per barrel. Just as quickly, and quicker ($10 drop on the following January 15 alone), prices plummeted as allied forces bombarded Iraq and brought the war to a quick conclusion. Prices have stabilized since, ranging just under $20 again, with moderate trends occurring. Many are awaiting another Middle East explosion.

TYPICAL DAY PRICE MOVES

Crude rarely makes gargantuan trends during the day. More commonly, trends will go 20–30 points, but rarely more. To the good fortune of traders, however, price volatility is low. Three typical price movements are shown in Charts CL–1 through CL–3.

A moderate trend is displayed in Chart CL–1, where prices start off in the low 17.50s and progress steadily upwards to close the day in the 17.70s, a net move of 20 points. Price volatility is relatively moderate also, mostly in the 5–8

C H A R T   CL–1

Typical Day Crude Oil Price Action

January 5, 1995

C H A R T   CL–2

Typical Day Crude Oil Price Action

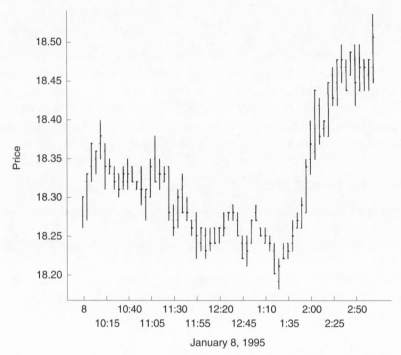

January 8, 1995

range, with the worst reaction to the trend being 10 points. Even though the trader would like more profit potential than 20–30 points, this is really typical of crude, and he has to settle for this potential. That means making sure his costs (commissions and slippage) are good.

Another trend type is displayed in Chart CL–2, where it is possible to capture part of two trends. Prices start off and rise to the 18.35 area and then tumble to 18.20, a 15 point trend, then rise for the rest of the day for a 30 point trend, to 18.50. The trader must be nimble to catch some of each, lest he get whipsawed on one or two trades if he is even a little late in each trend.

The third situation is very prevalent: a sideways, volatile price movement that can be treacherous, especially to traditional trend methods such as moving averages. Chart CL–3 shows us a thrashing picture, as prices oscillate between just above 17.40 to just under 17.30, a range of 20 points. This range is elusive and impossible to capture, however, as prices quickly move towards and away from the range extremes.

GOOD PARAMETER SETTINGS FOR CRUDE OIL

The mountain/valley method was tested on January 1995 price data for 1-, 5-, 15-, 30-, and 60-minute intervals.

C H A R T   CL—3

Typical Day Crude Oil Price Action

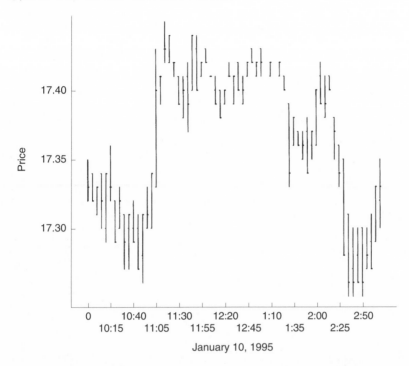

January 10, 1995

As mentioned in the previous section, there were few big profit opportunities in the month (I feel this may be typical), but the method made the most of them. Again, the caution: be sure costs are low, as profits did not rise on average above $50, or five ticks.

Table 4.CL.C15 details a conservative philosophy applied to 15-minute intervals requiring at least three successive higher closes of at least 4 ticks to initiate a long position. The net result is 14 trades, 9 of them winners, and small losses (the worst is $140), with a total of $650 profit and $46 per trade profit. If profit opportunities had been great, this mode probably would have done very well. A typical trade for this mode is shown in Chart CL—4. Prices steadily move lower from the open, and at point (A) through (C) register successive falls of three ticks or more until (C), where a short is taken at 17.75 at 2:04 P.M. EDT and is held until the close at 17.62, for a 13 point, or $130, profit.

A speculative version of the method for the same time interval, 15 minutes, is presented in Table 4.CL.S15. Ironically, to get fairly good results we have to greatly increase the size of successive differences (to 16 ticks) to be able to use less numbers of successive higher/lower closings (here only one required). The results are similar, with profit totals of $520, an average profit per trade of $47, and only three losses in 11 trades. This trading mode looks for large, significant breakouts, as opposed to steady, smaller and more cumulative trades with the conservative version

TABLE   4.CL.C15

Trade Results: Mountain/Valley Day Trade Method*
Crude Oil: Conservative Mode, 15-Minute Data

Date	Position	Time In	Price In	Time Out	Price Out	$P/L	$Max. Loss	Time	$Max. Gain	Time
1/3/95	Short	1503	17.43	1509	17.4	30	0	1503	30	1509
1/4/95	Long	1101	17.61	1509	17.47	−140	−140	1509	0	1101
1/6/95	Short	1404	17.75	1505	17.62	130	0	1404	130	1505
1/9/95	Short	1418	17.41	1509	17.35	60	0	1418	60	1509
1/11/95	Long	1346	17.59	1509	17.63	40	−10	1401	40	1509
1/16/95	Long	1149	17.62	1509	17.76	140	0	1149	160	1503
1/17/95	Long	1248	18.03	1509	18.2	170	−20	1403	170	1509
1/18/95	Long	1432	18.46	1509	18.49	30	0	1432	30	1509
1/20/95	Long	1100	18.45	1509	18.42	−30	−70	1200	30	1317
1/23/95	Short	1159	18.29	1508	18.09	200	−10	1215	200	1508
1/24/95	Long	1201	18.43	1502	18.38	−50	−50	1246	90	1417
1/24/95	Short	1502	18.38	1507	18.38	0	0	1502	0	1502
1/25/95	Short	1045	18.46	1507	18.39	70	0	1045	300	1415
1/27/95	Short	1201	17.92	1509	17.92	0	−100	1504	60	1419
$Total						650				
$Ave/Trade						46				

* Settings: Minimum successive high/low closing difference = .04 dollars
        No. successive high/low closings = 3

CHART   CL−4

Conservative Mode Trading: 15-Minute Prices for Crude Oil

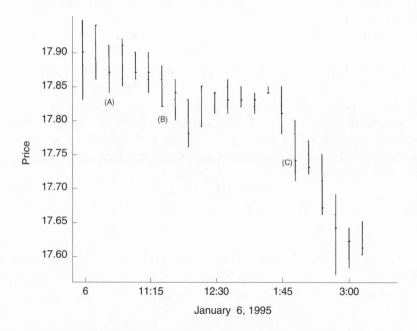

January 6, 1995

T A B L E   4.CL.S15

Trade Results: Mountain/Valley Day Trade Method*
Crude Oil: Speculative Mode, 15-Minute Data

Date	Position	Time In	Price In	Time Out	Price Out	$P/L	$Max. Loss	Time	$Max. Gain	Time
1/3/95	Short	1457	17.46	1509	17.4	60	0	1457	60	1509
1/4/95	Long	1101	17.61	1509	17.47	−140	−140	1509	0	1101
1/6/95	Short	1419	17.73	1505	17.62	110	0	1419	110	1505
1/11/95	Long	1346	17.59	1509	17.63	40	−10	1401	40	1509
1/16/95	Long	1133	17.58	1509	17.76	180	0	1133	200	1503
1/17/95	Long	1233	18.02	1509	18.2	180	−10	1403	180	1509
1/20/95	Long	1100	18.45	1509	18.42	−30	−70	1200	30	1317
1/23/95	Short	1345	18.14	1508	18.09	50	−10	1401	50	1508
1/24/95	Long	1100	18.35	1507	18.38	30	0	1100	170	1417
1/25/95	Short	1045	18.46	1507	18.39	70	0	1045	300	1415
1/27/95	Short	1216	17.89	1509	17.92	−30	−130	1504	30	1419
$Total						520				
$Ave/Trade						47				

* Settings: Minimum successive high/low closing difference = .16 dollars
        No. successive high/low closings = 1

C H A R T   CL–5

Speculative Mode Trading: 15-Minute Prices for Crude Oil

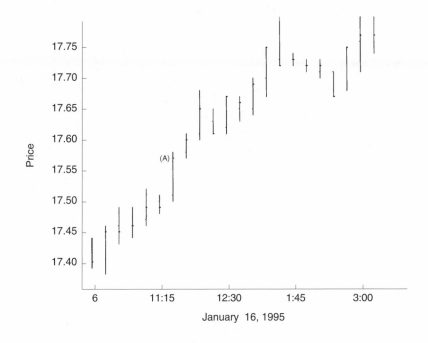

January 16, 1995

T A B L E   4.CL.S30

Trade Results: Mountain/Valley Day Trade Method*
Crude Oil: Speculative Mode, 30-Minute Data

Date	Position	Time In	Price In	Time Out	Price Out	$P/L	$Max. Loss	Time	$Max. Gain	Time
1/3/95	Short	1324	17.51	1509	17.4	110	0	1324	110	1509
1/4/95	Long	1245	17.58	1509	17.47	−110	−110	1509	10	1319
1/5/95	Long	1228	17.68	1509	17.69	10	−10	1429	30	1359
1/6/95	Short	1115	17.87	1506	17.61	260	0	1115	260	1506
1/9/95	Short	1218	17.47	1509	17.35	120	−50	1248	1248	120
1/10/95	Short	1417	17.35	1509	17.33	20	0	1417	80	1447
1/11/95	Long	1215	17.47	1509	17.63	160	0	1215	160	1509
1/12/95	Short	1147	17.55	1349	17.64	−90	−90	1349	20	1216
1/12/95	Long	1349	17.64	1509	17.64	0	−60	1420	0	1349
1/13/95	Long	1216	17.57	1317	17.45	−120	−120	1317	0	1216
1/13/95	Short	1317	17.45	1509	17.44	10	0	1317	50	1450
1/16/95	Long	1149	17.62	1509	17.76	140	0	1149	140	1509
1/17/95	Long	1248	18.03	1509	18.2	170	0	1248	170	1509
1/18/95	Short	1147	18.27	1417	18.41	−140	−140	1417	50	1509
1/19/95	Long	1216	18.44	1347	18.41	−30	−30	1347	30	1246
1/19/95	Short	1347	18.41	1509	18.34	70	0	1347	70	1509
1/20/95	Long	1115	18.4	1509	18.42	20	−10	1145	80	1317
1/23/95	Short	1215	18.3	1508	18.09	210	0	1215	210	1508
1/24/95	Long	1115	18.37	1507	18.38	10	−10	1144	150	1417
1/25/95	Short	1144	18.43	1507	18.39	40	0	1144	270	1415
1/26/95	Short	1214	18.26	1509	18.24	20	−50	1315	20	1509
1/27/95	Short	1115	18.04	1509	17.92	120	0	1115	180	1419
1/30/95	Long	1145	18.1	1509	18.08	−20	−80	1212	0	1145
1/31/95	Short	1145	18.15	1446	18.18	−30	−40	1243	40	1346
1/31/95	Long	1446	18.18	1509	18.37	190	0	1446	190	1509
$Total						1220				
$Ave/Trade						47				

* Settings: Minimum successive high/low closing difference = .02 dollars
     No. successive high/low closings = 2

for 15 minutes. Chart CL–5 shows prices moving steadily upwards, but they don't register that large net increase (from the start) of 16 points until 11:33 A.M. at 17.58. A long position is signaled at (A) and is held until the closing, for a profit of 18 points, or $180.

A very aggressive mode is proposed and used on 30-minute data, with requirements to initiate a position of only two successive higher/lower closes of two or more points. Refer to Table 4.CL.S30 for aggressive 30-minute trading results. This mode results in many trades, with a high total profit result of $1,220 and nearly the same profit per trade as before, $47. Losses are kept small (the largest is $140) and few in number (7 out of 25, for a 72 percent success rate). A nice profit is detailed in Chart CL–6. Prices move pretty much successively lower from the high point of 18.43 just after the opening, retreating only once in upticks thereafter, and signaling a short at (B) at 12:15 P.M. at 18.30 which is held until the close at 18.09, for a 21 point, or $210, profit.

Finally, a conservative stance is taken for us coffee drinkers and socializers who wish to follow prices on an hourly basis. The profit results, as expected, are sedate and involve only four trades, all of which are profitable but small in size, reflecting the generally small profit opportunities for the month. Here the trader is buying safety, with three successive higher closes of at least 3 points required to go long. A typical trade is shown in Chart CL–7. Prices just monotonously move lower hour after hour, from point (A) to point (C), where a short position is finally signaled at 17.46 at 2:57 P.M. right near the close. The day's profit is 6 points, or $60, small but reliable.

C H A R T   CL–6

Speculative Mode Trading: 30-Minute Prices for Crude Oil

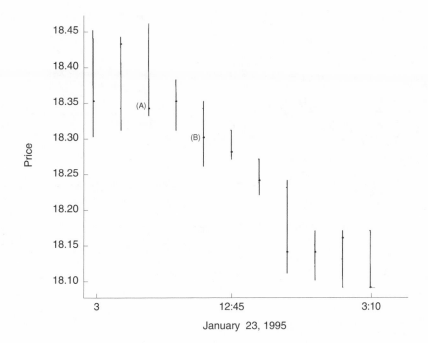

January 23, 1995

C H A R T   CL–7

Conservative Mode Trading: 60-Minute Prices for Crude Oil

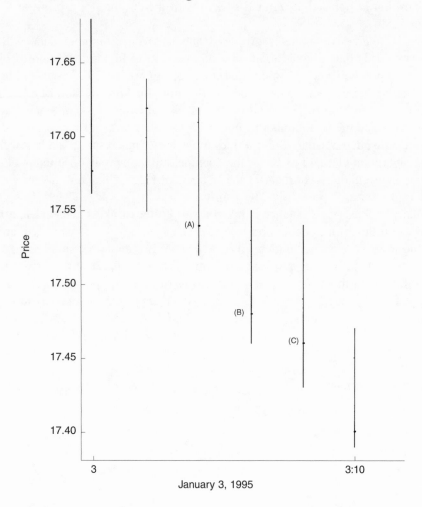

January 3, 1995

T A B L E   4.CL.C60

Trade Results: Mountain/Valley Day Trade Method*
Crude Oil: Conservative Mode, 60-Minute Data

Date	Position	Time In	Price In	Time Out	Price Out	$P/L	$Max. Loss	Time	$Max. Gain	Time
1/3/95	Short	1457	17.46	1509	17.4	60	0	1457	60	1509
1/6/95	Short	1448	17.64	1506	17.61	30	0	1448	30	1506
1/9/95	Short	1448	17.41	1509	17.35	60	0	1448	60	1509
1/23/95	Short	1345	18.14	1508	18.09	50	0	1345	50	1508
$Total						200				
$Ave/Trade						50				

* Settings: Minimum successive high/low closing difference = .03 dollars
         No. successive high/low closings = 3

UNLEADED GAS

As part of the energy complex, unleaded gas generally follows the trends of the others, but it can diverge and show its own style. Some are looking to the Middle East for conflict or choas, and they are also looking at the gas pump for possible long lines, as all consumers faced both in the 1970s. Unleaded gas has had plenty of trends—from the .20 cent area to over $1.20 per gallon, back and forth from .60 to .80 cents, and also at other levels, though with perhaps less width.

TYPICAL DAY PRICE MOVES

Like crude oil, unleaded gas rarely makes big moves within the day. The typical patterns are volatility-riddled days with no or only slight trends; a nice, moderate trend, often with a "kicker" reaction at the end; or a moderate trend with much volatility.

Chart HU–1 depicts a typical churning market day, June 15, 1995. Prices start off at .6190, rise to the day's ultimate high of .6245 by 10:45 A.M. drop to almost the day's ultimate low of .6180 by 11:10, and spend the rest of the day wandering between these two barriers. A moving average approach might have gone long by 10:45, then short by 11:10, lost on both trades, and then possibly entered into another losing long and short during the remainder of the day.

Another good typical pattern is captured in Chart HU–2, for June 13, 1995. A moderate short trend is made early in the day and ends 70 points down by midday with little price volatility, a boon to the trader, only to give another tickler, a

C H A R T   HU–1

Typical Day Unleaded Gas Price Action

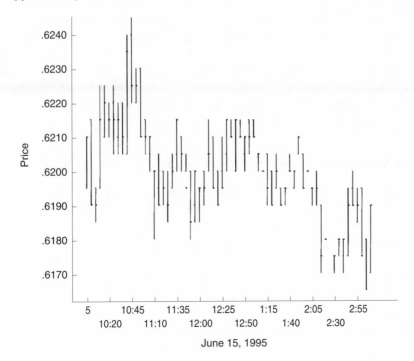

June 15, 1995

C H A R T   HU–2

Typical Day Unleaded Gas Price Action

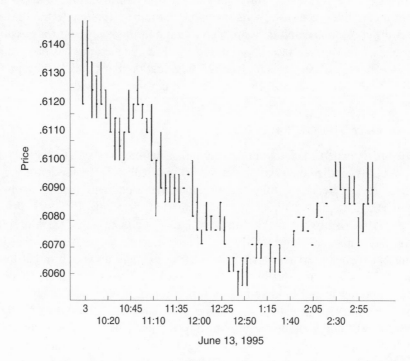

June 13, 1995

possible uptrend and certainly dimunition of the current downtrend, to the trader. This reaction/new trend eventually climbs up 30–40 points, or about half of the original downtrend.

Finally, the other major formation the trader will find in prominence for unleaded gas is the moderate trend with outsized price volatility (as compared to the trend). Chart HU–3 shows another downtrend for unleaded gas on June 8, 1995. It also goes down about 70 points from beginning to end, but has several important reactions/reversals of 30 points and more along the way. This could prove tough for traditional trend followers, who could get whipsawed back and forth on longs and shorts.

GOOD PARAMETER SETTINGS FOR UNLEADED GAS

We tested the mountain/valley method on June 1995 data for price intervals of 1,5, 15, 30, and 60 minutes. Four successful modes of trading, two conservative and two speculative, were found and are presented here. While the trend opportunities were few and small, the method performed decently with good profit per trade numbers.

Table 4.HU.C5 gives results for a 5-minute conservative trading mode. This mode requires eight successive higher closings of at least .10 cents to initiate a long position. The total profit results are modest ($462), while the profit per trade average is $92. But there are no losses (only two breakevens), so this is a very careful strate-

C H A R T   HU–3

Typical Day Unleaded Gas Price Action

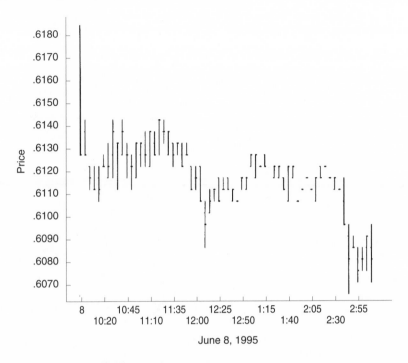

June 8, 1995

T A B L E   4.HU.C5

Trade Results: Mountain/Valley Day Trade Method*
Unleaded Gas: Conservative Mode, 5-Minute Data

Date	Position	Time In	Price In	Time Out	Price Out	$P/L	$Max. Loss	Time	$Max. Gain	Time
6/14/95	Long	1120	0.6165	1511	0.62	147	−210	1211	147	1501
6/21/95	Short	1230	0.59	1510	0.587	126	0	1230	504	1445
6/23/95	Short	1130	0.5705	1457	0.566	189	0	1130	336	1241
6/28/95	Long	1439	0.596	1509	0.596	0	−126	1452	0	1439
6/29/95	Short	1407	0.59	1511	0.59	0	−105	1435	0	1407
$Total						462				
$Ave/Trade						92				

* Settings: Minimum successive high/low closing difference = .10 cents
        No. successive high/low closings = 8

gy. Chart HU–4 details the long trade for June 14, 1995, where prices steadily rise and a long signal is finally triggered at (H), at 11:20 in the morning. Prices dip after that, and there should be concern that it might be a whipsaw, or just plain loss. But prices recover and end up nicely higher, for a 35 point, or $147, profit.

C H A R T   HU–4

Conservative Mode Trading: 5-Minute Prices for Unleaded Gas

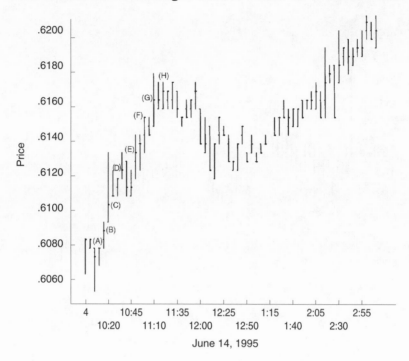

June 14, 1995

T A B L E   4.HU.S5

Trade Results: Mountain/Valley Day Trade Method*
Unleaded Gas: Speculative Mode, 5-Minute Data

Date	Position	Time In	Price In	Time Out	Price Out	$P/L	$Max. Loss	Time	$Max. Gain	Time
6/21/95	Short	1225	0.5915	1510	0.587	189	0	1225	567	1445
6/22/95	Short	1232	0.58	1511	0.583	−126	−252	1441	0	1232
6/23/95	Short	1115	0.5715	1457	0.566	231	−84	1125	378	1241
6/28/95	Long	1159	0.593	1509	0.596	126	−126	1258	126	1439
$Total						420				
$Ave/Trade						105				

* Settings: Minimum successive high/low closing difference = .60 cents
      No. successive high/low closings = 2

A little more audacious is the mode presented in Table 4.HU.S5 for 5-minute data. Here the trader requires only two successive higher closings with differences of .60 cents to get long. The results are about the same as for the conservative version for 5-minute data, with slightly higher profit per trade ($105) and one loss. Chart HU–5 shows a strong downtrend underway early in the day. It is caught early by this mode of trading, at point (B) at 11:15 A.M. at .5715. Some price gyrations intervene shortly thereafter, but prices settle back down again and give the trader a 55 point, or $231, gain at the end.

A conservative stance is taken for 15-minute data in Table 4.HU.C15. Here we need four successive higher closings of at least .20 cents to go long. Not surprisingly, the total profit is still modest at $462 and $77 profit per trade, but the losses are also still very small, the largest being $63. Chart HU-6 shows a short trade for June 21. Prices steadily drop and build up successive lower closings at point (A) through (D), where a short is taken at 12:06 at .5940 and liquidated by the close at .5870, resulting in a profit of 70 points, or $294.

Finally, our old friend the coffee break trader goes for 30-minute price data and uses a speculative entrance requirement of only two successive higher closings of .35 cents or more to go long. Please refer to Table 4.HU.S30 for speculative mode 30-minute trading results. The policy works well—while only five trades are taken, the profit total is a good $777, profit per trade also comes in a good $155, and the only loss is a mere $21. A typical trade is shown in Chart HU–7. Prices move up strongly from the opening, and two successive significant closing differences occur at (A) and (B), where the long is initiated at .5900 at 11:50 A.M., and is held until the close at .5755, a profit of 55 points, or $231.

C H A R T   HU–5

Speculative Mode Trading: 5-Minute Prices for Unleaded Gas

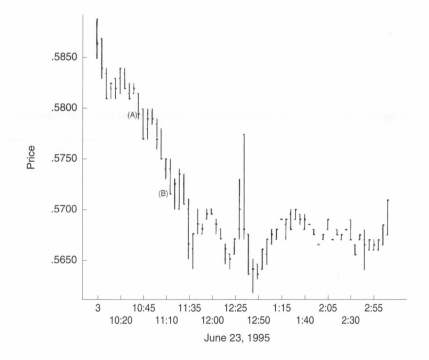

June 23, 1995

T A B L E   4.HU.C15

Trade Results: Mountain/Valley Day Trade Method*
Unleaded Gas: Conservative Mode, 15-Minute Data

Date	Position	Time In	Price In	Time Out	Price Out	$P/L	$Max. Loss	Time	$Max. Gain	Time
6/2/95	Long	1352	0.6085	1511	0.609	21	-42	1407	21	1453
6/14/95	Long	1120	0.6165	1511	0.62	147	-168	1235	147	1511
6/21/95	Short	1206	0.594	1511	0.587	294	0	1206	546	1451
6/22/95	Short	1236	0.5815	1511	0.583	-63	-189	1441	0	1236
6/23/95	Short	1120	0.5725	1511	0.571	63	0	1120	378	1250
6/28/95	Long	1428	0.5955	1510	0.5955	0	-84	1443	0	1428
6/29/95	Short	1407	0.59	1511	0.59	0	-105	1435	0	1407
$Total						462				
$Ave/Trade						77				

* Settings: Minimum successive high/low closing difference = .20 cents
        No. successive high/low closings = 4

C H A R T   HU–6

Conservative Mode Trading: 15-Minute Prices for Unleaded Gas

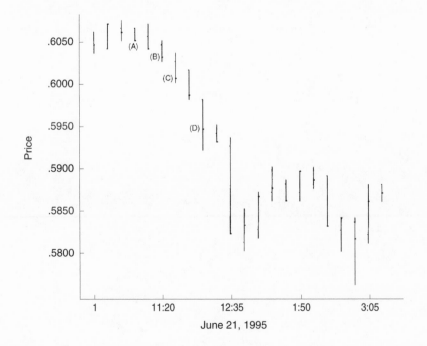

June 21, 1995

C H A R T   HU–7

Speculative Mode Trading: 30-Minute Prices for Unleaded Gas

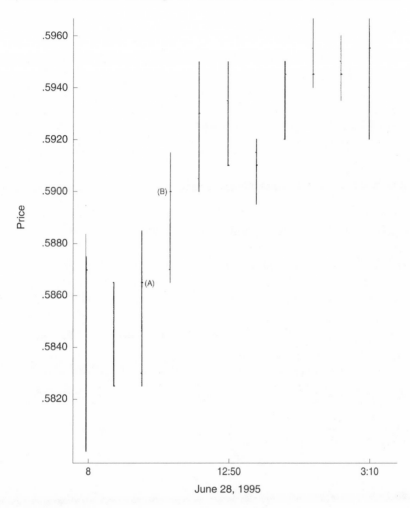

June 28, 1995

T A B L E   4.HU.S30

Trade Results: Mountain/Valley Day Trade Method*
Unleaded Gas: Speculative Mode, 30-Minute Data

Date	Position	Time In	Price In	Time Out	Price Out	$P/L	$Max. Loss	Time	$Max. Gain	Time
6/19/95	Short	1452	0.6025	1511	0.603	−21	−21	1511	0	1452
6/21/95	Short	1151	0.5975	1511	0.587	441	0	1151	693	1451
6/23/95	Short	1120	0.5725	1511	0.571	63	0	1120	378	1250
6/28/95	Long	1150	0.59	1510	0.5955	231	0	1150	231	1510
6/29/95	Short	1427	0.5915	1511	0.59	63	0	1427	63	1511
$Total						777				
$Ave/Trade						155				

* Settings: Minimum successive high/low closing difference = .35 cents
     No. successive high/low closings = 2

Foods & Fiber

COFFEE

Heavily dependent on weather and on some South American government actions, this bean has plenty of action nearly year-round. The freeze weather (from late spring through early fall here in the U.S.) produces great uptrends and hot daily action. Drought can happen quite frequently, however, during the growing season (our winter), since coffee needs lots of moisture.

The day trader will not be disappointed in the profit potential in coffee.

TYPICAL DAY PRICE MOVEMENTS

Coffee price moves can be quite large and numerous during the day: .8 and .10 cent moves (nearly $4,000) are not unheard of. It often seems that half the days have at least one big move sometime within the day.

Chart KC–1 shows a typical big move from the day's opening to the end. Prices gently move downwards one cent in the first three hours, then plummet another six cents in the space of about an hour. The pattern was clear and well-intentioned, but no depth estimator could have called the full extent of the drop. However, when you check the tales of trade results you'll see that the mountain/valley method is up to catching the moves!

However, coffee can also be very volatile and end up nowhere or unchanged by day's end. Chart KC-2 shows coffee starting off at $1.53/lb, falling to below

C H A R T   KC–1

Typical Daily Coffee Price Action

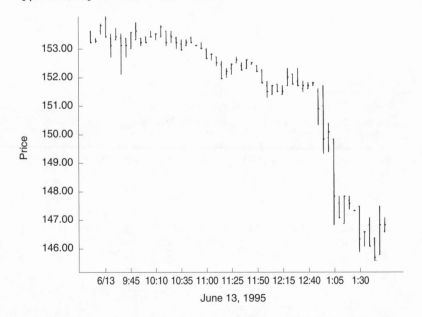

June 13, 1995

CHART   KC–2

Typical Daily Coffee Price Action

June 9, 1995

$1.51, rising again to nearly $1.53, falling yet again to below $1.51, and then finally rising to over $1.53. The trader had to have possessed a strong stomach and fast reflexes for that day. Likewise, his methods must be strong yet flexible, responsive yet patient, for this hot ticket.

GREAT SETTINGS FOR COFFEE

Our method was historically tested on coffee 1-, 5-, 15-, 30-, and 60-minute price data for June 1995.

At all levels the results were not only very good, in some cases they were spectacular. The results are displayed in Tables 4.KC.S1 through S60, a wide panorama of data time frames and combinations of different operating parameters (minimum successive closing differences and numbers of differences required). You will see a wide variety of speculative and conservative modes of trading, all successful in their own rights.

Table 4.KC.S1 starts off the parade with a jump-start. Built for the active, speculative trader, this mode (four succesive higher/lower closings of at least .40 cents) generates approximately 40 trades during the month of June 1995, almost two per day on average (one day, June 23, has four trades), and a total profit before costs of about $6,400 (for only one month!). Gains tend to be larger than losses, and the trade success rate is nearly 50 percent. Occasionally losses get large, but gains can reach nearly $2,000. Though recommended for the speculative trader, this version of the method should be computerized (after all, following the action on 1-minute chart basis could be quite exhausting).

TABLE 4.KC.S1

Trade Results: Mountain/Valley Day Trade Method*
Coffee: Speculative Mode, 1-Minute Data

Date	Position	Time In	Price In	Time Out	Price Out	$P/L	$Max. Loss	Time	$Max. Gain	Time
6/1/95	Long	951	160	1406	161.5	562	−75	952	750	1004
6/2/95	Short	1113	161.7	1300	161.3	150	−300	1203	788	1252
6/2/95	Long	1300	161.3	1407	162.2	338	−488	1336	450	1357
6/6/95	Long	938	159.4	1023	158.25	−431	−431	1023	506	958
6/6/95	Short	1023	158.25	1236	157.95	112	−619	1031	281	1211
6/7/95	Short	1024	157.8	1351	153.35	1669	−19	1043	2494	1330
6/7/95	Long	1351	153.35	1408	153.5	56	−319	1358	244	1353
6/8/95	Short	1035	152.05	1259	153.5	−544	−544	1054	300	1233
6/8/95	Long	1259	153.5	1406	154.5	375	−300	1326	469	1405
6/9/95	Short	955	153.1	1342	154.5	−525	−712	1051	188	1206
6/9/95	Long	1342	154.5	1407	154.05	−169	−188	1404	638	1350
6/12/95	Long	1017	155.9	1407	155.8	−38	−300	1038	225	1227
6/13/95	Short	1158	153.3	1409	148.2	1912	−262	1219	2081	1344
6/14/95	Long	1018	150	1116	149.55	−169	−169	1116	750	1022
6/14/95	Short	1116	149.55	1407	148.75	300	−600	1327	469	1405
6/15/95	Long	1134	151.6	1359	155.5	1462	−131	1139	2400	1344
6/15/95	Short	1359	155.5	1409	154.5	375	−281	1402	375	1409
6/16/95	Short	1043	151.75	1147	152.4	−243	−375	1050	619	1106
6/16/95	Long	1147	152.4	1407	151.5	−338	−806	1302	38	1148
6/19/95	Short	1307	146.75	1406	149	−844	−844	1406	19	1310
6/19/95	Long	1406	149	1407	148.95	−19	−19	1407	0	1406
6/20/95	Long	935	150.35	1224	149.8	−188	−188	953	600	1037
6/20/95	Short	1224	149.8	1406	151.1	−488	−525	1341	75	1227
6/21/95	Long	948	153.7	1041	153.1	−225	−225	1041	544	952
6/21/95	Short	1041	153.1	1400	150.5	975	−319	1114	1350	1347
6/22/95	Short	958	151	1408	149.8	450	−825	1131	450	1408
6/23/95	Short	1044	147.4	1150	144.6	1050	−225	1104	1838	1138
6/23/95	Long	1150	144.6	1318	142.7	−712	−712	1318	56	1153
6/23/95	Short	1318	142.7	1338	144.5	−675	−675	1338	19	1319
6/23/95	Long	1338	144.5	1407	144.1	−150	−188	1405	375	1401
6/26/95	Short	950	143.75	1406	138.3	2044	−56	1029	2438	1330
6/27/95	Long	1027	139.9	1057	138.1	−675	−675	1057	0	1027
6/27/95	Short	1057	138.1	1235	137.35	281	0	1057	1031	1130
6/27/95	Long	1235	137.35	1303	134.8	−956	−956	1303	131	1237
6/27/95	Short	1303	134.8	1321	136.3	−562	−562	1321	188	1305
6/27/95	Long	1321	136.3	1407	138.25	731	−188	1326	938	1406
6/28/95	Long	1002	139.8	1144	138.15	−619	−619	1144	206	1003
6/28/95	Short	1144	138.15	1319	138.95	−300	−300	1319	412	1245
6/28/95	Long	1319	138.95	1356	138.8	−56	−356	1341	112	1331
6/29/95	Short	1106	139.6	1407	136.7	1088	0	1106	1256	1137
6/30/95	Short	1013	133.7	1406	130	1388	−412	1129	1388	1406
$Total						6375				
$Ave/Trade						155				

* Settings: Minimum successive high/low closing difference = 0.40 cents
     No. successive high/low closings = 4

Chart KC–3 details two trades made on June 21, 1995. The first, a long, is kicked off at 9:48 EDT when prices make the fourth successive higher closing at point (D). The long is held until 10:41 when prices had fallen four successive lower closings of at least .40 cents after setting highs around 10:00 A.M. at $1.55 or so. The first trade was a small loss, but it was reversed for a handsome profit on the second trade (a short), as prices plummeted at the close.

A much more sedate trading style is shown in Table 4.KC.C1, the mode of which requires many successive higher/lower closings (12) of a relatively small amount (.15 cents) to establish a long or short position. The stance results in far fewer trades (only 14), larger profit per trade ($378), less total profit ($5,288), and, except for one trade, less and smaller losses (a good batting average of 10/14 gains/total trades).

Another conservative approach is shown in Table 4.KC.C5 for those who would prefer to graph prices (on a 5-minute basis) and make decisions on charts rather than through a computer. The results are quite good: totals of $5,475, a profit per trade of $322, and only six losses out of seventeen trades. A good trade is depicted in Chart KC-4. Prices start off around $1.50, slowly but surely waving upwards until point (G) where the seventh successive higher closing of .05 cents (the minimum tick change allowed) gets the trader long at 1.5160 around 11:30 A.M. and by closing allows the trader a profit of nearly $1,300.

Table 4.KC.C15 shows another conservative trading style for those wanting coffee-break trading intervals (15-minute basis). The profit results are still very good ($5,000) and losses are small, especially compared to gains. The success rate

C H A R T   KC–3

Speculative Mode Trading: 1-Minute Prices for Coffee

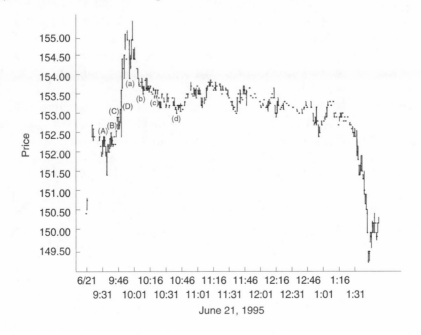

June 21, 1995

TABLE 4.KC.C1

Trade Results: Mountain/Valley Day Trade Method*
Coffee: Conservative Mode, 1-Minute Data

Date	Position	Time In	Price In	Time Out	Price Out	$P/L	$Max. Loss	Time	$Max. Gain	Time
6/7/95	Short	1105	156.25	1408	153.5	1031	−94	1106	1912	1330
6/13/95	Short	1301	151.25	1409	148.2	1144	0	1301	1312	1344
6/14/95	Long	1021	151.75	1407	148.75	−1125	−1294	1405	94	1022
6/15/95	Long	1154	152.6	1409	154.5	712	−131	1159	2025	1344
6/16/95	Short	1100	150.75	1407	151.5	−281	−656	1148	244	1106
6/20/95	Long	1036	151.75	1406	151.1	−243	−806	1227	75	1037
6/21/95	Short	1343	151.1	1400	150.5	225	0	1343	600	1347
6/22/95	Short	1405	150.05	1408	149.8	94	−19	1407	94	1408
6/23/95	Short	1112	146.75	1407	144.1	975	−150	1117	1575	1138
6/26/95	Short	1155	142.15	1406	138.3	1444	0	1155	1838	1330
6/27/95	Short	1124	135.65	1354	137.1	−544	−769	1237	506	1305
6/27/95	Long	1354	137.1	1407	138.25	431	0	1354	638	1406
6/29/95	Short	1109	138	1407	136.7	488	−469	1112	656	1137
6/30/95	Short	1331	132.5	1406	130	938	0	1331	938	1406
$Total						5288				
$Ave/Trade						378				

* Settings: Minimum successive high/low closing difference = 0.15 cents
    No. successive high/low closings = 12

is still high (about 50 percent), with about one trade occurring per day. A nice (short) trade is shown in Chart KC–5. Prices top out early in the day and by point (C) make three successively lower closings of .25 cents or more by about 11:00 A.M. From there, it is all downhill until the closing at 153, when the trader takes in nearly a $1,600 profit.

Two speculative modes at long intervals wrap up the coverage of coffee. Table 4.KC.S30 shows a strong profit total for an active trading stance in which only two successively lower closings of .30 cents or more are required to go short.

Ironically, the most speculative stance, at a really long time interval, 60 minutes, and the equivalent of a single breakout system, can produce very good results which resemble conservative results: total profits of $4,100 before costs, profit per trade of over $300, and only four losses out of thirteen trades. Table 4.KC.S60 shows us results of 60-minute trading in a speculative mode. The simple action of one trade is depicted in Chart KC–6. Right after the initial hour, prices drop by a significant amount, enough at 11:19 A.M. to trigger a short and show substantial profit (almost $2,000) by the close.

T A B L E   4.KC.C5

Trade Results: Mountain/Valley Day Trade Method*
Coffee: Conservative Mode, 5-Minute Data

Date	Position	Time In	Price In	Time Out	Price Out	$P/L	$Max. Loss	Time	$Max. Gain	Time
6/2/95	Short	1254	160.4	1404	162.25	−694	−788	1400	75	1338
6/6/95	Short	1207	158.1	1236	157.95	56	−75	1217	131	1212
6/7/95	Short	1107	156.4	1404	153.25	1181	0	1107	1838	1332
6/8/95	Short	1230	151.4	1404	153.4	−750	−975	1350	0	1230
6/13/95	Short	1159	153.25	1404	148.5	1781	−131	1229	2062	1344
6/14/95	Long	1019	150.5	1403	148.8	−638	−656	1353	188	1023
6/15/95	Long	1134	151.6	1404	155	1275	−131	1139	2400	1344
6/16/95	Short	1059	151.1	1404	151.1	0	−525	1148	319	1104
6/20/95	Long	1104	151.7	1226	149.75	−731	−731	1226	0	1104
6/20/95	Short	1226	149.75	1404	150.6	−319	−543	1341	0	1226
6/21/95	Short	1256	152.85	1400	150.5	881	−169	1311	1069	1346
6/23/95	Short	1114	147	1404	144.5	938	0	1114	1631	1320
6/26/95	Short	1219	140.3	1404	138.45	694	−188	1254	694	1404
6/27/95	Short	1129	135.5	1239	137.25	−644	−644	1239	0	1129
6/27/95	Long	1239	137.25	1404	138	281	−956	1304	281	1404
6/29/95	Short	1059	140.3	1404	137.25	1144	0	1059	1500	1339
6/30/95	Short	1320	133.1	1404	130.35	1031	0	1320	1031	1404
$Total						5475				
$Ave/Trade						322				

* Settings: Minimum successive high/low closing difference = 0.05 cents
      No. successive high/low closings = 7

C H A R T   KC–4

Conservative Mode Trading: 5-Minute Prices for Coffee

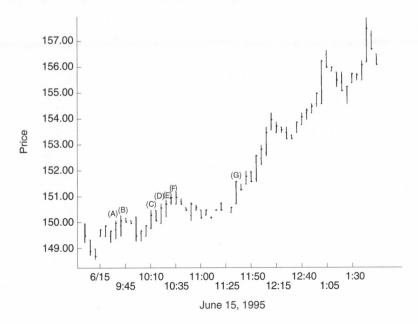

June 15, 1995

TABLE   4.KC.C15

Trade Results: Mountain/Valley Day Trade Method*
Coffee: Conservative Mode, 15-Minute Data

Date	Position	Time In	Price In	Time Out	Price Out	$P/L	$Max. Loss	Time	$Max. Gain	Time
6/1/95	Long	1015	160.9	1403	161.5	225	−281	1143	225	1301
6/2/95	Short	1119	161.5	1404	162.25	−281	−338	1204	712	1252
6/6/95	Short	1232	158	1236	157.95	19	0	1232	19	1236
6/7/95	Short	1102	157.25	1403	153	1594	0	1102	2156	1332
6/8/95	Short	1114	152.4	1317	154	−600	−600	1317	375	1230
6/8/95	Long	1317	154	1404	153.4	−225	−412	1328	0	1317
6/9/95	Long	1348	155.2	1403	154.25	−356	−356	1403	0	1348
6/12/95	Long	1114	155.8	1404	155.8	0	−150	1347	150	1144
6/13/95	Short	1118	153.8	1403	149.1	1762	−188	1133	2175	1333
6/14/95	Long	1029	150.6	1401	148.8	−675	−675	1401	150	1244
6/14/95	Short	1401	148.8	1403	148.8	0	0	1401	0	1401
6/15/95	Long	1146	151.9	1404	155	1162	0	1146	2006	1346
6/16/95	Short	1044	151.9	1404	151.1	300	−38	1146	525	1314
6/19/95	Long	1129	148.9	1404	148.5	−150	−525	1255	0	1129
6/20/95	Long	1059	151.5	1231	150	−562	−562	1231	0	1059
6/20/95	Short	1231	150	1404	150.6	−225	−262	1246	0	1231
6/21/95	Short	1243	153.1	1359	150.7	900	0	1243	900	1359
6/23/95	Short	1044	147.4	1404	144.5	1088	−75	1059	1612	1259
6/26/95	Short	1214	140.4	1404	138.45	731	−131	1229	900	1329
6/27/95	Short	1114	137	1359	137.5	−188	−188	1359	750	1259
6/27/95	Long	1359	137.5	1404	138	188	0	1359	188	1404
6/28/95	Short	1244	137.2	1356	138.8	−600	−600	1356	0	1244
6/29/95	Short	1114	139	1404	137.25	656	0	1114	844	1244
6/30/95	Short	1347	131	1404	130.35	244	0	1347	281	1402
$Total						5006				
$Ave/Trade						208				

* Settings: Minimum successive high/low closing difference = 0.25 cents
       No. successive high/low closings = 3

C H A R T   KC–5

Conservative Mode Trading: 15-Minute Prices for Coffee

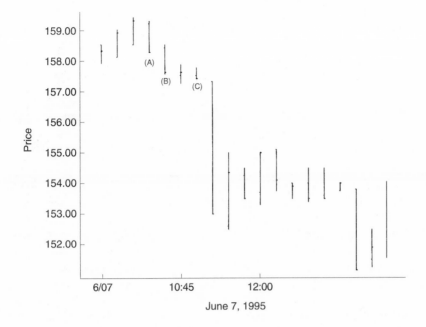

June 7, 1995

T a b l e   4.KC.S30

Trade Results: Mountain/Valley Day Trade Method*
Coffee: Speculative Mode, 30-Minute Data

Date	Position	Time In	Price In	Time Out	Price Out	$P/L	$Max. Loss	Time	$Max. Gain	Time
6/1/95	Long	1217	161.3	1403	161.5	112	−262	1246	112	1403
6/2/95	Short	1119	161.5	1352	162	−188	−262	1148	712	1252
6/2/95	Long	1352	162	1404	162.25	94	0	1352	94	1404
6/6/95	Long	1039	159.5	1217	158.3	−450	−450	1217	0	1039
6/6/95	Short	1217	158.3	1236	157.95	131	0	1217	131	1236
6/7/95	Short	1044	157.6	1216	154	1350	0	1044	1725	1117
6/7/95	Long	1216	154	1404	153.25	−281	−788	1344	0	1216
6/8/95	Short	1114	152.4	1404	153.4	−375	−600	1317	150	1242
6/9/95	Long	1139	154.3	1404	154	−112	−450	1216	338	1348
6/12/95	Long	1114	155.8	1404	155.8	0	−150	1347	150	1144
6/13/95	Short	1213	153.4	1404	148.5	1838	0	1213	1838	1404
6/14/95	Long	1043	150.7	1403	148.8	−712	−712	1403	112	1244
6/15/95	Long	1116	150.8	1404	155	1575	0	1116	2419	1346
6/16/95	Short	1044	151.9	1404	151.1	300	−38	1146	525	1314
6/19/95	Long	1143	148.7	1404	148.5	−75	−450	1314	0	1143
6/21/95	Short	1314	153	1400	150.5	938	0	1314	938	1400
6/22/95	Short	1244	152	1404	150.25	661	0	1244	661	1404
6/23/95	Short	1114	147	1404	144.5	938	0	1114	1462	1314
6/26/95	Short	1214	140.4	1404	138.45	731	−38	1309	731	1404
6/27/95	Long	1043	139.25	1144	136.3	−1106	−1106	1144	0	1043
6/27/95	Short	1144	136.3	1404	138	−638	−638	1404	300	1314
6/28/95	Short	1144	138.15	1356	138.8	−244	−244	1214	356	1244
6/29/95	Short	1114	139	1404	137.25	656	0	1114	844	1244
6/30/95	Long	1116	134.5	1317	133.4	−412	−412	1317	0	1116
6/30/95	Short	1317	133.4	1404	130.35	1144	0	1317	1144	1404
$Total						5869				
$Ave/Trade						235				

* Settings: Minimum successive high/low closing difference = 0.30 cents
          No. successive high/low closings = 2

C H A R T   KC–6

Speculative Mode Trading: 60-Minute Prices for Coffee

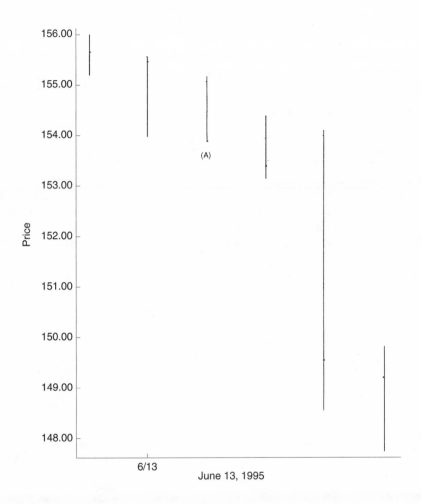

June 13, 1995

T A B L E   4.KC.S60

Trade Results: Mountain/Valley Day Trade Method*
Coffee: Speculative Mode, 60-Minute Data

Date	Position	Time In	Price In	Time Out	Price Out	$P/L	$Max. Loss	Time	$Max. Gain	Time
6/1/95	Short	1122	160.75	1403	161.5	−281	−281	1403	0	1122
6/2/95	Short	1126	162	1404	162.25	−94	−94	1404	525	1323
6/7/95	Short	1119	153.9	1404	153.25	244	0	1119	244	1404
6/13/95	Short	1118	153.8	1404	148.5	1988	−75	1219	1988	1404
6/14/95	Short	1120	149.4	1219	150.5	−412	−412	1219	0	1120
6/14/95	Long	1219	150.5	1403	148.8	−638	−638	1403	150	1320
6/15/95	Long	1225	153.25	1404	155	656	0	1225	806	1326
6/16/95	Short	1122	151.75	1404	151.1	225	0	1122	262	1322
6/23/95	Short	1120	145	1404	144.5	188	0	1120	881	1320
6/26/95	Short	1218	140.4	1404	138.45	731	0	1218	731	1404
6/27/95	Short	1118	137.25	1404	138	−281	−281	1404	619	1318
6/29/95	Short	1117	139.25	1404	137.25	750	0	1117	750	1404
6/30/95	Short	1320	133.1	1404	130.25	1031	0	1320	1031	1404
$Total						4106				
$Ave/Trade						316				

* Settings: Minimum successive high/low closing difference = 0.80 cents
          No. successive high/low closings = 1

COTTON

Like soybeans, cotton is very sensitive to growing conditions. Drought or excessive rain can spur sharp price rises, and perfect weather can kill prices. Recently cotton went through a huge price rise due to drought (hitting a new price record, too). Ironically, cotton is substituted as a crop for soybeans when economics favor the trade-off, and vice versa. Also like soybeans, cotton has been at one time the king of speculation—early in the century and before—when the total dollar value of its trading equaled that of all shares on the stock exchanges combined!

Except for the recent price burst, however, trends have consisted of .10 and .20 cent moves generally, not very big for overnight trend following.

TYPICAL DAY PRICE MOVEMENTS

Cotton prices can range 100 or more points per day, sometimes even 300, but trending that much from beginning to end is another question.

Chart CT–1 exemplifies this well. On April 21, prices start at 107.00, cascade down to below 104.00 by 11:40, sharply rebound to 106.00, and then trade between that and 105.00 the rest of the day. Traditional trend methods would have gone short around 105.00 or lower and then gone back long around 106.00, resulting in a loss of 100 points in a day where prices ranged 300 points and more but ended up only 100 points below where the day began (each point = .01).

C H A R T   CT–1

Typical Daily Cotton Price Action

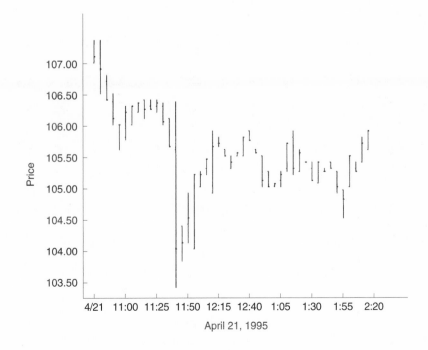

April 21, 1995

Chart CT–2 is a little more encouraging for the trend follower. There actually is a drift, or trend, that, if jumped on, can make profits for the trader. But there is also much price volatility, so the method must be reliable in filtering out meaningful (the upmove) from meaningless (small down reactions) moves. Prices start out around 100.400 (disregard the first interval or bar—its bad data) and "wave" their way up to 101.40, good enough for 50 or 60 points if the trader can jump aboard reasonably and with surety.

GOOD SPECULATIVE AND CONSERVATIVE TRADING STRATEGIES

The mountain/valley method was tested on April 1995 price interval data of 1, 5, 15, 30, and 60 minutes to find good speculative and conservative trading modes and to ensure reliability (not just one fluky or lucky set of parameter values).

The results were good across all bases, and three speculative and three conservative sets were chosen.

Table 4.CT.C1 details 21 trades, over a trade a day on average, taken for a conservative stance on 1-minute price data (five successive lower closings of at least 15 points are needed for a short position) for cotton in April 1995. About 60 percent were successful, and a good profit total of $2,500 results, on an average $120 per trade, before costs. Losses are kept smaller than gains, with the largest loss of $565 and largest gain of $1,100. Chart CT–3 shows us how the trader entered the short that made him the $1,100. Prices start off around 106.00 and

CHART CT–2

Typical Daily Cotton Price Action

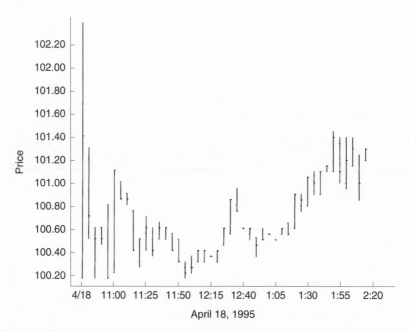

April 18, 1995

T A B L E   4.CT.C1

Trade Results: Mountain/Valley Day Trade Method*
Cotton: Conservative Mode, 1-Minute Data

Date	Position	Time In	Price In	Time Out	Price Out	$P/L	$Max. Loss	Time	$Max. Gain	Time
4/3/95	Short	1140	93	1441	91.15	925	−200	1148	950	1440
4/4/95	Long	1220	90.9	1409	93.1	1100	−200	1253	1100	1409
4/10/95	Short	1222	99	1412	100.15	−565	−1000	1228	0	1222
4/13/95	Short	1107	104.5	1357	104.4	50	−50	1213	600	1335
4/13/95	Long	1357	104.4	1412	104.2	−100	−150	1406	150	1359
4/17/95	Short	1220	102.48	1239	102.15	165	−110	1225	165	1239
4/18/95	Short	1041	100.3	1347	101.25	−475	−475	1347	75	1053
4/18/95	Long	1347	101.25	1411	101.3	25	−175	1409	75	1349
4/19/95	Long	1114	103.05	1254	103.37	160	−75	1141	160	1222
4/21/95	Short	1048	106.1	1155	105.2	450	−150	1117	1150	1141
4/21/95	Long	1155	105.2	1351	104.8	−200	−200	1351	350	1206
4/21/95	Short	1351	104.8	1407	105.7	−450	−450	1407	75	1353
4/21/95	Long	1407	105.7	1411	105.9	100	−50	1409	100	1411
4/24/95	Long	1301	105.75	1409	107.5	875	−75	1304	875	1403
4/25/95	Short	1138	105.8	1410	106.1	−150	−450	1216	1143	1120
4/26/95	Short	1050	104.8	1305	104.05	375	−225	1100	375	1232
4/27/95	Long	1040	104.1	1157	103.8	−150	−500	1101	550	1123
4/27/95	Short	1157	103.8	1336	103.9	−95	−100	1101	550	1123
4/27/95	Long	1336	103.99	1411	105.3	655	−145	1350	755	1410
4/28/95	Short	1123	104.55	1220	105	−225	−225	1220	370	1133
4/28/95	Long	1220	105	1412	105.1	50	−250	1328	200	1403
$Total						2510				
$Ave/Trade						120				

* Settings: Minimum successive high/low closing difference = 0.15 cents
   No. successive high/low closings = 5

tumble in five interval packs, or waves, each time hitting a new low until point (E) at 10:50 A.M., when a short position is signaled. Prices almost recover and give a long signal at around noon, but they don't quite make the last leg (fifth successive high closing of at least 15 points).

Table 4.CT.C5 gives us a conservative trading mode for a higher time frame, 5 minutes. The number of successive higher or lower closings is very stringent and produces only six trades, all but one of which are successful. Chart CT–4 displays the long trade of April 24, when prices bottom around 11:25 A.M. and then start moving successively higher at points (A) through (G), where a long is triggered. The trade was entered at 106.25 at 13:07 and exited at 107.40 on the 5-minute closing at 14:08.

Table 4.CT.S5 takes the opposite stance, a more active role, by requiring only two successive higher closings of 35 points or more to establish a long position. More

CHART CT-3

Conservative Mode Trading: 1-Minute Prices for Cotton

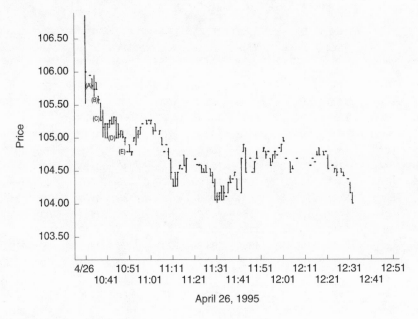

April 26, 1995

TABLE 4.CT.C5

Trade Results: Mountain/Valley Day Trade Method*
Cotton: Conservative Mode, 5-Minute Data

Date	Position	Time In	Price In	Time Out	Price Out	$P/L	$Max. Loss	Time	$Max. Gain	Time
4/3/95	Short	1241	92.85	1357	92.55	150	−225	1320	225	1347
4/4/95	Long	1345	91.75	1409	93.1	675	0	1345	675	1409
4/13/95	Short	1336	103.3	1409	104.2	−450	−550	1401	0	1336
4/17/95	Short	1237	102.3	1239	102.15	75	0	1237	75	1239
4/24/95	Long	1307	106.25	1408	107.4	575	0	1307	625	1403
4/26/95	Short	1134	104.2	1232	104.05	75	−325	1159	75	1232
$Total						1100				
$Ave/Trade						183				

* Settings: Minimum successive high/low closing difference = 0.05 cents
    No. successive high/low closings = 7

trades ensue, but the success rate still stays above 50 percent, and winners generally are larger than losers. The profit total moves up to $1,885, but profit per trade slips down to about $100. Chart CT–5 details a long where the trader got in quickly and captured a large profit ($1,200) by being both nimble (only two successive differences required) and stiff (a high closing difference of 35 points). The two successive higher closing prices occur at (A) and (B), where he goes long until the close.

C H A R T   CT–4

Conservative Mode Trading: 5-Minute Prices for Cotton

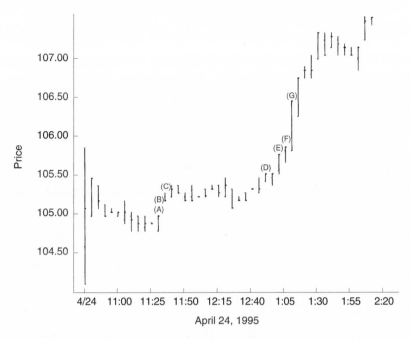

April 24, 1995

Table 4.CT.S15 shows a similar speculative stance for 15-minute intervals, but because the difference requirement is still large, the number of successive closings needed is increased by one, the time frame is bigger, and fewer trades result. The combination produces all winners (three), for a profit total of $1,050.

A similar result occurs when we lessen the difference requirement but increase the number of successive like closings to four: more trades occur, but only one loss, and a good profit total of $1,660 and a hefty profit per trade of $277 result. These results are presented in Table 4.CT.C15

Finally, as shown in Table CT.S30 for 30-minute intervals, a pure speculative mode with a moderate difference requirement and only two successive differences needed to establish a long or short results in a still respectable profit total of $1,350 and average return of $160 per trade.

T A B L E   4.CT.S5

Trade Results: Mountain/Valley Day Trade Method*
Cotton: Speculative Mode, 5-Minute Data

Date	Position	Time In	Price In	Time Out	Price Out	$P/L	$Max. Loss	Time	$Max. Gain	Time
4/3/95	Short	1221	93	1357	92.55	225	−150	1320	300	1347
4/4/95	Long	1219	90.7	1409	93.1	1200	−75	1243	1200	1409
4/10/95	Long	1338	100.3	1409	100.4	50	−125	1354	100	1359
4/13/95	Short	1114	103.9	1401	104.4	−250	−325	1216	300	1336
4/13/95	Long	1401	104.4	1409	104.2	−100	−150	1406	0	1401
4/17/95	Short	1147	102.65	1239	102.15	250	−315	1207	250	1239
4/18/95	Short	1054	100.15	1409	100.9	−375	−575	1402	0	1054
4/19/95	Long	1115	103.15	1254	103.37	110	−125	1232	110	1222
4/21/95	Short	1049	106.15	1204	105.45	350	−100	1109	1075	1139
4/21/95	Long	1204	105.45	1258	105.05	−200	−200	1258	175	1214
4/21/95	Short	1258	105.05	1409	105.6	−275	−275	1409	200	1353
4/24/95	Long	1302	105.7	1408	107.4	850	0	1302	900	1403
4/25/95	Short	1139	106	1409	106	0	−325	1215	75	1144
4/26/95	Short	1109	104.7	1232	104.05	325	−75	1159	325	1232
4/27/95	Long	1119	104.9	1159	103.5	−700	−700	1159	100	1129
4/27/95	Short	1159	103.5	1329	103.7	−100	−225	1207	300	1319
4/27/95	Long	1329	103.7	1409	105.2	750	0	1329	750	1409
4/28/95	Short	1125	104.45	1225	105	−275	−275	1225	200	1130
4/28/95	Long	1225	105	1409	105.1	50	−175	1330	170	1355
$Total						1885				
$Ave/Trade						99				

* Settings: Minimum successive high/low closing difference = 0.35 cents
          No. successive high/low closings = 2

CHART CT–5

Speculative Mode Trading: 5-Minute Prices for Cotton

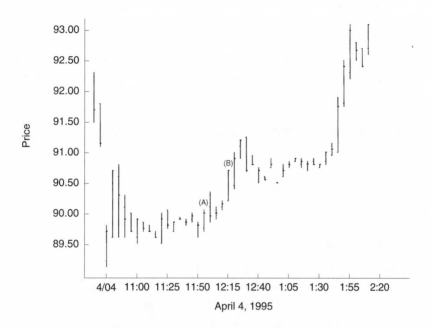

April 4, 1995

TABLE 4.CT.S15

Trade Results: Mountain/Valley Day Trade Method*
Cotton: Speculative Mode, 15-Minute Data

Date	Position	Time In	Price In	Time Out	Price Out	$P/L	$Max. Loss	Time	$Max. Gain	Time
4/3/95	Short	1345	92.75	1408	92.7	25	0	1345	50	1400
4/4/95	Long	1345	91.75	1409	93.1	675	0	1345	675	1409
4/24/95	Long	1316	106.8	1409	107.5	350	0	1316	350	1409
$Total						1050				
$Ave/Trade						350				

* Settings: Minimum successive high/low closing difference = 0.30 cents
        No. successive high/low closings = 3

T A B L E 4.CT.C15

Trade Results: Mountain/Valley Day Trade Method*
Cotton: Conservative Mode, 15-Minute Data

Date	Position	Time In	Price In	Time Out	Price Out	$P/L	$Max. Loss	Time	$Max. Gain	Time
4/3/95	Short	1243	92.8	1408	92.7	50	−175	1328	75	1400
4/4/95	Long	1228	90.8	1409	93.1	1150	−125	1243	1150	1409
4/17/95	Short	1226	102.6	1239	102.15	225	0	1226	225	1239
4/18/95	Long	1343	101.15	1409	100.9	−125	−125	1409	25	1400
4/19/95	Long	1245	103.35	1254	103.37	10	0	1245	10	1254
4/24/95	Long	1316	106.8	1409	107.5	350	0	1316	350	1409
$Total						1660				
$Ave/Trade						277				

* Settings: Minimum successive high/low closing difference = 0.10 cents
        No. successive high/low closings = 4

T A B L E 4.CT.S30

Trade Results: Mountain/Valley Day Trade Method*
Cotton: Speculative Mode, 30-Minute Data

Date	Position	Time In	Price In	Time Out	Price Out	$P/L	$Max. Loss	Time	$Max. Gain	Time
4/3/95	Short	1232	93.1	1408	92.7	200	−35	1333	200	1402
4/4/95	Long	1401	92.5	1409	93.1	300	0	1401	300	1409
4/13/95	Short	1330	103.9	1409	104.2	−150	−350	1400	0	1330
4/17/95	Short	1226	102.6	1239	102.15	225	0	1226	225	1239
4/18/95	Long	1331	101.1	1409	100.9	−100	−100	1409	125	1401
4/24/95	Long	1301	105.75	1409	107.5	875	0	1301	875	1409
4/25/95	Short	1159	106.1	1409	106	50	−150	1230	50	1409
4/28/95	Long	1230	105.2	1409	105.1	−50	−275	1330	0	1230
$Total						1350				
$Ave/Trade						169				

* Settings: Minimum successive high/low closing difference = 0.15 cents
        No. successive high/low closings = 2

SUGAR

Despite Castro and his mercurial influence on sugar production, the sweet can be just that to long-term trend followers who have patience and prescience. Twice, once in 1974–75 and again in 1980–81, sugar has skyrocketed from low prices to many multiples of the beginning price. A $1,000 bet on the long side in 1974 would have returned over $50,000 at its peak, and a similar number would have resulted during the 1980-81 surge. Mostly, trends of 5–10 cents, or $5–10,000 roughly, of profit opportunity predominate. Within these trends, and even in dull times, day trading possibilities do occur.

TYPICAL DAY MOVEMENTS

Most often day moves range from just a few points to over 20 from the beginning to the end of the day. Less often, tight ranges predominate, and occasionally a 30–50 net point move on the day will occur.

Chart SB–1 depicts a typical trading day for sugar. Prices start out around 14.34 cent per pound, bounce between 14.24 and 14.35, and close at 14.25 or so. The net move is minus 7 points, not enough to take a position and make any profits, yet the turbulence is large enough to trigger unsuccessful positions, both long and short. This is truly a tough situation with which to contend.

But sometimes the move from the start to finish, the trend for the day, can slope a little more and give a little opportunity for small to moderate profits—2, 4, or slightly more points—to the careful trader. Chart SB–2 shows a start around

C H A R T   SB–1

Typical Daily Sugar Price Action

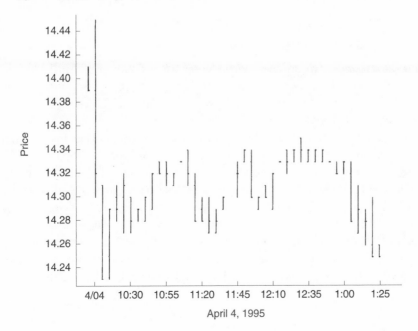

April 4, 1995

CHART SB-2

Typical Daily Sugar Price Action

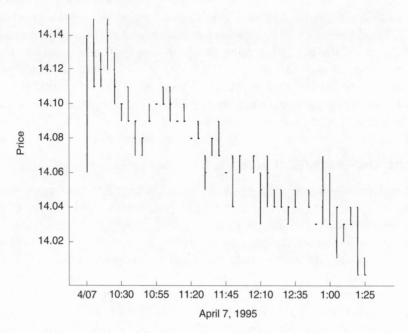

April 7, 1995

14.14 and a finish at 14.00, which may be enough for that elusive, small profit. The volatility—back and forth price changes—is moderate, too.

Finally, Chart SB–3 gives us (a few times a month) the opportunity we were looking for. Prices steadily move lower all day long, moving about 40 points from beginning to end, without too much accompanying volatility.

GOOD SETTINGS FOR SUGAR

We tested the mountain/valley method on sugar for the month of April 1995, on 1-, 5-, 15-, 30-, and 60-minute price data. The results for better settings for conservative and speculative trading modes are chronicled in Tables 4.SB.C1–S30 and accompanying charts.

Table 4.SB.C1 gives results for a conservative trading style for 1-minute data. Losses are kept small (less than $100) and the profit total is good ($840) for the somewhat lackluster profit opportunities for the month. Also, profit per trade is very nice, at $120. This method requires three successive higher 1-minute closings of at least 7 points. Chart SB–4 details an especially interesting set of trades for April 28, 1995. Three quick closings at the start get the trader short at 10:06 at 12.90 (point (C). This position is held until a second position, a reverse to long, occurs at 13:02 (1:02 EDT) at (c) at 12.98 and is held until the close. Even though the first was a loss after making good headway until about 1 P.M., the second

CHART SB–3

Typical Daily Sugar Price Action

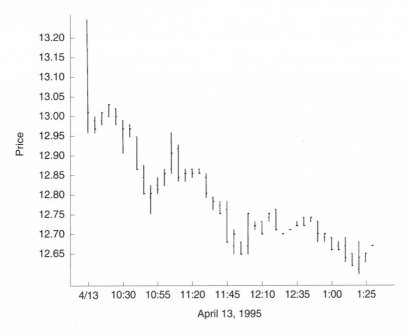

April 13, 1995

TABLE 4.SB.C1

Trade Results: Mountain/Valley Day Trade Method*
Sugar #11: Conservative Mode, 1-Minute Data

Date	Position	Time In	Price In	Time Out	Price Out	$P/L	$Max. Loss	Time	$Max. Gain	Time
4/5/95	Short	1233	14.05	1321	13.9	168	−44	1235	280	1314
4/10/95	Short	1238	13.8	1321	13.71	101	0	1238	134	1250
4/13/95	Short	1133	12.76	1327	12.67	168	−22	1135	168	1316
4/17/95	Short	1156	12.59	1321	12.63	−44	−44	1321	202	1246
4/24/95	Short	1212	12.95	1321	12.93	22	−112	1304	90	1258
4/28/95	Short	1006	12.9	1302	12.98	−90	−146	1025	168	1149
4/28/95	Long	1302	12.98	1319	13.5	582	−33	1304	582	1319
$Total						840				
$Ave/Trade						120				

* Settings: Minimum successive high/low closing difference = .07 cents
    No. successive high/low closings = 3

C H A R T   SB–4

Conservative Mode Trading: 1-Minute Prices for Sugar

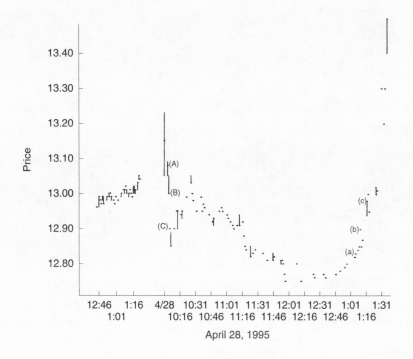

April 28, 1995

makes up for that loss, and then some, as shorts desperately attempt to cover their positions and heavy buying comes in. But be careful: This was the last effective day for trading the May contract, so lots of movement and volatility should be expected (not for the weak at heart!).

Table 4.SB.C5 gives us another viewpoint, trading on a 5-minute basis, a little less harried pace, with no positions signaled on the final day of the month, April 28.

The results are still good, as the trading mode picks up most of the profit potential while experiencing small losses. Net profits total $403 with seven trades, or $58 per trade. A short for this mode is shown taken at point (D) in Chart SB–5 at 12:34 P.M. at 13.85 on April 10, 1995, for an eventual profit of $168 before costs.

A speculative trading approach is depicted in Table 4.SB.S15 for 15-minute prices. As you can see, there is lots of trading (19 trades), most of it successful (10 trades), with profits larger than losses, resulting in a profit total of $1277 and a profit per trade of $67. Two trades are marked on Chart SB–6. The trader quickly gets short at 10:44 at 12.71 at (A), then in late afternoon, at 1:15 P.M. EDT, he reverses the short and goes long at 12.52 at point (a), for a day's total profit of $325. Wouldn't it be nice if all days were like that!

T A B L E   4.SB.C5

Trade Results: Mountain/Valley Day Trade Method*
Sugar #11: Conservative Mode, 5-Minute Data

Date	Position	Time In	Price In	Time Out	Price Out	$P/L	$Max. Loss	Time	$Max. Gain	Time
4/5/95	Short	1224	14.09	1319	13.92	190	0	1224	325	1315
4/10/95	Short	1234	13.85	1319	13.7	168	0	1234	190	1250
4/12/95	Short	1249	13.27	1319	13.3	−33	−33	1319	44	1304
4/13/95	Short	1044	12.84	1319	12.66	202	−100	1104	246	1315
4/17/95	Short	1136	12.64	1319	12.62	22	−11	1151	258	1246
4/24/95	Short	1252	12.95	1319	13	−56	−112	1304	67	1259
4/25/95	Long	1208	12.91	1319	12.83	−90	−134	1247	0	1208
$Total						403				
$Ave/Trade						58				

* Settings: Minimum successive high/low closing difference = .03 cents
        No. successive high/low closings = 4

C H A R T   SB–5

Conservative Mode Trading: 5-Minute Prices for Sugar

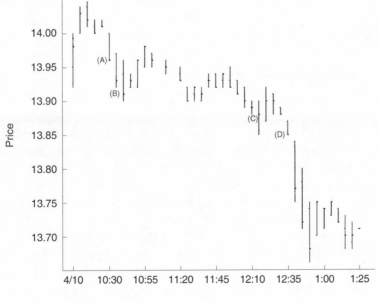

April 10, 1995

T A B L E   4.SB.S15

Trade Results: Mountain/Valley Day Trade Method*
Sugar #11: Speculative Mode, 15-Minute Data

Date	Position	Time In	Price In	Time Out	Price Out	$P/L	$Max. Loss	Time	$Max. Gain	Time
4/3/95	Long	1029	14.42	1312	14.41	−11	−11	1312	55	1115
4/4/95	Long	1211	14.33	1319	14.28	−55	−55	1315	11	1230
4/5/95	Short	1150	14.18	1319	13.92	291	0	1150	291	1250
4/7/95	Short	1242	14.04	1318	14.01	33	0	1242	33	1318
4/10/95	Short	1043	13.93	1319	13.7	258	−33	1100	258	1316
4/12/95	Short	1300	13.24	1319	13.3	−66	−66	1319	0	1300
4/13/95	Short	1044	12.84	1319	12.66	202	−11	1059	235	1314
4/17/95	Short	1044	12.71	1315	12.52	213	−22	1115	336	1245
4/17/95	Long	1315	12.52	1319	12.62	112	0	1315	112	1319
4/18/95	Short	1214	12.63	1312	12.8	−190	−190	1312	0	1214
4/18/95	Long	1312	12.8	1319	12.77	−33	−33	1319	0	1312
4/19/95	Long	1301	12.8	1319	12.82	22	0	1301	33	1316
4/21/95	Long	1156	13.23	1319	13.25	22	−22	1228	22	1319
4/24/95	Short	1214	12.98	1314	12.98	0	−45	1226	100	1259
4/24/95	Long	1314	12.98	1319	13	22	0	1314	22	1319
4/25/95	Long	1059	12.83	1319	12.83	0	−45	1319	0	1300
4/26/95	Short	1300	12.87	1319	12.9	−33	−33	1319	0	1300
4/28/95	Short	1114	12.84	1319	12.95	−121	−121	1304	91	1225
4/28/95	Long	1304	12.95	1319	13.5	616	0	1304	616	1319
$Total						1277				
$Ave/Trade						67				

* Settings: Minimum successive high/low closing difference = .08 cents
        No. successive high/low closings = 1

The final entry is a speculative mode for 30-minute day prices. This requires 16 points difference on only one higher close to initiate a long, and the same for a lower close to go short. Results are detailed in Table 4.SB.S30. The losses get a little bigger (largest is $224), because of the time frame—a lot of time between price readings for something big (and often bad) to happen. The total results and profit per trade are still good, however, coming in at $493 total and $82 per trade. A typical trade is displayed in Chart SB–7. A short is not initiated until 12:31 P.M. at (A) at 14.06. (The price bar before it looks like it might have triggered the sell, but it did not—only a 15 point drop had occurred at that point, and we needed 16 points.) The trade was held until the close at 14.92 for a 14 point profit of $157 before costs.

C H A R T   SB–6

Speculative Mode Trading: 15-Minute Prices for Sugar

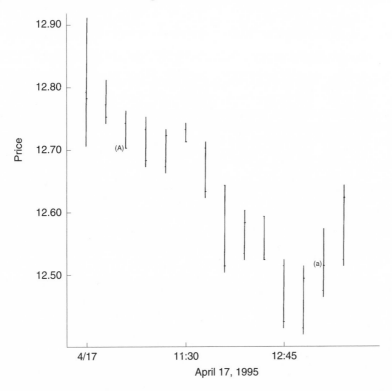

April 17, 1995

T A B L E   4.SB.S30

Trade Results: Mountain/Valley Day Trade Method*
Sugar #11: Speculative Mode, 30-Minute Data

Date	Position	Time In	Price In	Time Out	Price Out	$P/L	$Max. Loss	Time	$Max. Gain	Time
4/5/95	Short	1231	14.06	1319	13.92	157	0	1231	157	1319
4/10/95	Short	1301	13.74	1319	13.7	44	0	1301	44	1319
4/13/95	Short	1159	12.7	1319	12.66	44	−11	1227	44	1258
4/17/95	Short	1201	12.54	1319	12.62	−91	−91	1319	44	1301
4/28/95	Short	1159	12.8	1303	13	−224	−224	1303	44	1225
4/28/95	Long	1303	13	1319	13.5	560	0	1303	560	1319
$Total						493				
$Ave/Trade						82				

* Settings: Minimum successive high/low closing difference = .16 cents
         No. successive high/low closings = 1

C H A R T   SB-7

Speculative Mode Trading: 30-Minute Prices for Sugar

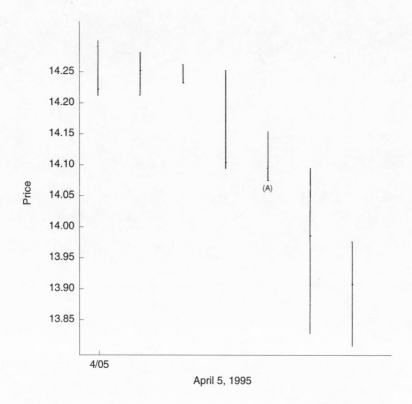

April 5, 1995

The Grains

SOYBEANS

The speculative king of the grains, soybeans have had a history of barn-burning price bursts, both overnight and within the day, for over 30 years. These bursts occur, of course, mostly during the growing season, which occurs from spring to late summer and mostly in the Midwest and South. The fortune of the crop and subsequent pricing depends principally on weather, with drought and other natural catastrophes being the main ingredients for big bull moves, and clear weather with good moisture the determinant for slow, but significant, drops in price.

TYPICAL DAILY MOVEMENTS

Soybean price moves can be large and trended during the day, but the emphasis should be placed on price volatility. Sometimes prices will move .10 and .20 cents, and occasionally more, from start or low point to the close.

However, the pull back and forth can be as large as or even greater than the net move. Chart SY–1 is typical of soybean price moves, starting at one price (610

C H A R T   SY–1

Typical Daily Soybean Price Action

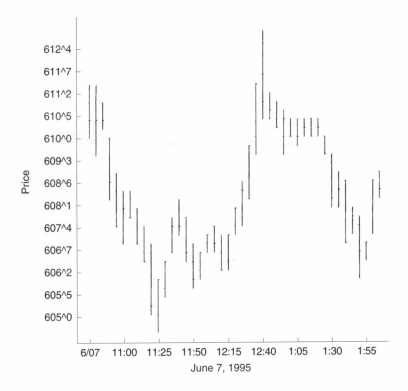

June 7, 1995

area), rising (to 613), falling (to 605), and then ending up not far from the start (at 609). This makes it hard to make money for trend followers and our system.

Chart SY–2 shows another typical soybean profile. Prices on June 15, 1995, start at 604 and end up at 612 for a moderately good trend. In between, however, much volatility predominates. Prices repeatedly vacillate 2 to 3 cents, giving the usual trend-following methods (e.g., moving averages) fits, as these movements force the trader to go long, then short, and then long again, resulting in many whipsaw losses. But our mountain/valley method can avoid many of these whipsaws.

GOOD SETTINGS FOR SOYBEANS

The mountain/valley method was historically tested on soybean 1-, 5-, 15-, 30-, and 60-minute prices for the month of June 1995.

The results for 5-, 15-, and 60-minute price data intervals during the day were good; they are presented in Charts SY–3 through SY–5, and accompanying tables, for two modes of trading, conservative and speculative.

However, profits for 1-minute data intervals were slim to none, using all sorts of closing differences and numbers of successive closings to enter positions. I attribute that to a great deal of noise in the data at that level, with spurious moves

C H A R T   SY–2

Typical Daily Soybean Price Action

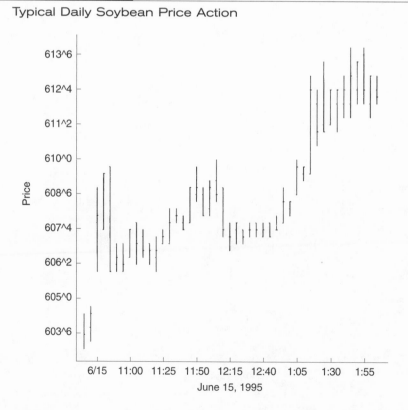

June 15, 1995

occurring as often as good-sized trends. To filter the noisy data, we have to increase the difference size or number of like closing differences required, but that makes us late in entering even good trends, so the total net profit is marginal.

Table 4.SY.C5 shows a moderate/conservative trading stance with 5-minute data intervals. A good success rate results (three out of five, or 60 percent), and losses are small. Gains are moderate in size, reflecting the relatively small day trends made by soybeans during the month of June. Other months, say July, August, and September, could show much bigger individual and total profit sizes due to the critical crop growing period. This is somewhat speculative, because the mode requires only a one cent difference between successive higher and lower closings, although a safety/reliability factor is thrown in by requiring five or more successive closings in one direction to enter a position.

Results for the conservative mode for soybeans 15-minute data are shown in Table 4.SY.C15. Only three trades occur, and a decent profit per trade ($92) results. Again, the totals are small because of the lack of trends, but the risk exposure is very small.

The 60-minute speculative mode strategy displayed in Table 4.SY.S60 gets more out of the profit potential. This strategy gets much of the moderate moves for a per trade average of almost $150, a respectable outcome for the few opportunities presented that month. The total profit is $462, not bad for a slow month, and there is only one loss.

Charts SY–3, SY–4, and SY–5 display price moves and position entries for soybeans using the speculative and conservative modes discussed above.

Chart SY–3 shows a conservative trading stance for soybeans (see Table 4.SY.C5), and shows the details of entering a short position in soybeans on June 12, 1995. The trader needed five successive lower closings of at least 1.0 cents. The first occurred at (A) around 11:25 EDT, with the next occurring right afterwards, another

T A B L E   4.SY.C5

Trade Results: Mountain/Valley Day Trade Method*
Soybeans: Conservative Mode, 5-Minute Data

Date	Position	Time In	Price In	Time Out	Price Out	$P/L	$Max. Loss	Time	$Max. Gain	Time
6/2/95	Short	1206	607.5	1314	603.5	200	−25	1221	225	1311
6/8/95	Short	1114	608.5	1314	609.5	−50	−50	1314	225	1134
6/12/95	Short	1229	596.5	1314	592	225	0	1229	250	1239
6/19/95	Long	1226	630	1314	629	−50	−50	1314	250	1241
6/26/95	Short	1229	601.5	1314	595.5	300	0	1229	325	1259
$Total						625				
$Ave/Trade						125				

* Settings: Minimum successive high/low closing difference = 1.0 cents
           No. successive high/low closings = 5

T A B L E   4.SY.C15

Trade Results: Mountain/Valley Day Trade Method*
Soybeans: Conservative Mode, 15-Minute Data

Date	Position	Time In	Price In	Time Out	Price Out	$P/L	$Max. Loss	Time	$Max. Gain	Time
6/12/95	Short	1244	592.5	1314	592	25	0	1244	25	1314
6/15/95	Long	1244	613	1314	612	−50	−50	1259	0	1244
6/26/95	Short	1229	601.5	1314	595.5	300	0	1229	325	1259
$Total						275				
$Ave/Trade						92				

* Settings: Minimum successive high/low closing difference = 0.5 cents
            No. successive high/low closings = 6

T A B L E   4.SY.S60

Trade Results: Mountain/Valley Day Trade Method*
Soybeans: Speculative Mode, 60-Minute Data

Date	Position	Time In	Price In	Time Out	Price Out	$P/L	$Max. Loss	Time	$Max. Gain	Time
6/2/95	Short	1234	606	1314	603.5	125	0	1234	125	1314
6/9/95	Short	1231	606.75	1314	604	138	0	1231	138	1314
6/12/95	Short	1231	596.25	1314	592	212	0	1231	212	1314
6/20/95	Long	1232	629	1314	626	−150	−150	1314	0	1232
6/23/95	Long	1232	619.5	1314	619.75	12	0	1232	12	1314
6/26/95	Short	1233	598	1314	595.5	125	0	1233	125	1314
$Total						462				
$Ave/Trade						77				

* Settings: Minimum successive high/low closing difference = 0.5 cents
            No. successive high/low closings = 2

around noontime, and then the fifth and short trigger appearing at almost 1:30 P.M. EDT at (E). A profit of 4 1/2 cents, or $225, resulted by the closing.

Chart SY–4 depicts a conservative trading mode on 15-minute data on June 26, 1995, requiring six successive lower closings of 1/2 cent. The first (A) occurs at around 11:15 EDT after reaching a top around 609 just after 11:00 A.M. A cascade of successive lower closes occur right afterwards at (B) and continue until price (F), at which point the trader goes short at 1:29 A.M. EDT (12:29 CDT) at 601.5 and holds to the close at 595.5 for a six cent ($300) profit.

Finally, Chart SY–5 shows speculative trading for 60-minute soybean prices on June 9, 1995. Two successive lower closings of at least 1/2 cent are needed to

C H A R T   SY–3

Conservative Mode Trading: 5-Minute Prices for Soybeans

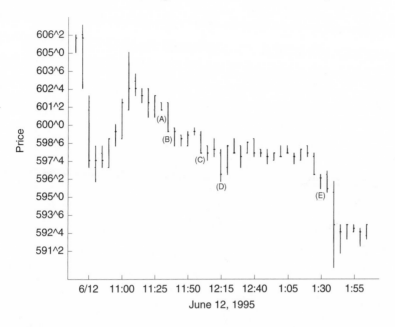

June 12, 1995

C H A R T   SY–4

Conservative Mode Trading: 15-Minute Prices for Soybeans

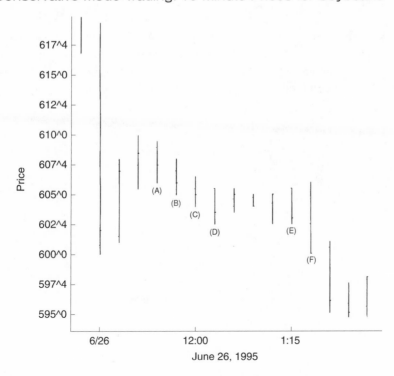

June 26, 1995

C H A R T   SY–5

Conservative Mode Trading: 60-Minute Prices for Soybeans

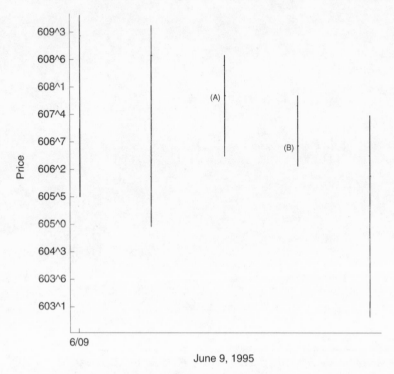

June 9, 1995

trigger a short. The first occurred at (A) around 11:00 A.M. EDT at about 608, and the second occurred at (B) about 12:30 P.M. at about 606.5, at which point the trader went short and then closed out the trade at 604 at almost the close (see closing price caveats at the beginning of the chapter), for a profit of about .3 cents, or $138.

WHEAT

The oldest of the grains, wheat has known boom and bust years—most notably the famous Russian wheat deal years of the mid 1970s, when the Eastern bloc opened up to Western sales and a huge increase in demand occurred. Like soybeans, however, much of the big moves, especially within the day, occur during the growing season, when weather is the main ingredient: Instances of drought or excessive rain send prices skyrocketing or plunging, depending upon long strings of bad weather days.

TYPICAL DAY PRICE MOVEMENTS

Wheat can make bigger moves during the day (see May 12 on Table 4.WN.C30 for an 8 cent profit captured), but it usually makes only moderate moves and shows high volatility. So, the successful trader has to choose his period carefully, get good executions, and have low commission charges.

Chart WN–1 shows a meandering price downtrend from the 363 area to 358 and then a rebound to 360, demonstrating some trend and some volatility (which can take away profits at the end). Another pattern is for real and false moves to be made in both directions, with prices ending up nowhere by day's end. Chart WN–2

C H A R T   WN–1

Typical Daily Wheat Price Action

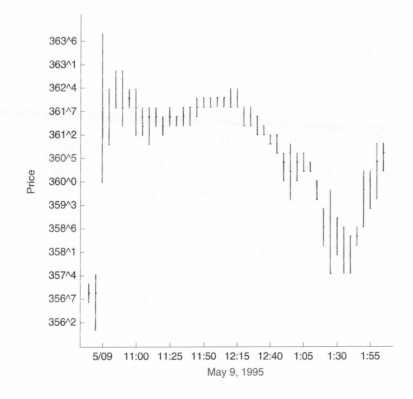

May 9, 1995

C H A R T   WN–2

Typical Daily Wheat Price Action

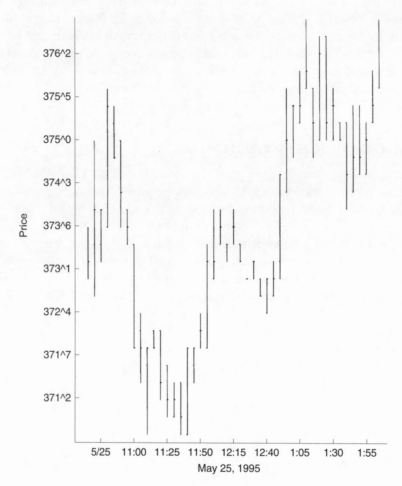

May 25, 1995

tells the sad tale of wheat starting at 373, rising to 375, falling to 371, then rising again to 376 to end the day. Yes, a trader could have made 3 cents, or $150, by being omniscient and simply holding from the opening to the close, but that some trader could have used a sensitive, speculative mountain/valley method on 5-minute prices and accomplished the same thing.

SOME GOOD SETTINGS FOR WHEAT

The method was historically tested on wheat prices for May 1995, on 1-, 5-, 15-, 30- and 60-minute intervals. The results for the 5-minute and 15-minute price data intervals during the day turned out good (although borderline in total profit per trade for those traders not having good execution or low commission costs). Charts WN–3 through WN–5 depict some poignant trades for conservative and speculative modes, and Tables 4.WN.C5, C30,S30, and S60 detail better trade set-

C H A R T   WN–3

Conservative Mode Trading: 30-Minute Prices for Wheat

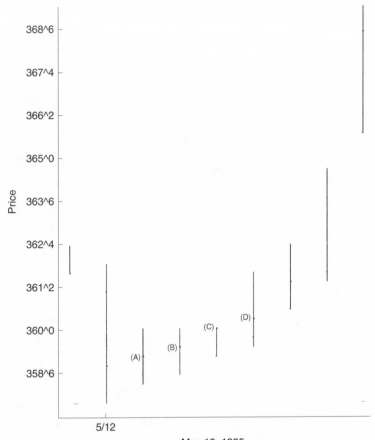

May 12, 1995

T A B L E   4.WN.C5

Trade Results: Mountain/Valley Day Trade Method*
Wheat: Conservative Mode, 5-Minute Data

Date	Position	Time In	Price In	Time Out	Price Out	$P/L	$Max. Loss	Time	$Max. Gain	Time
5/12/95	Long	1256	364.5	1314	368	175	0	1256	175	1311
5/17/95	Short	1254	356.75	1314	356	38	0	1254	38	1314
5/25/95	Long	1209	376.75	1314	376.5	−12	−112	1239	88	1309
$Total						200				
$Ave/Trade						67				

* Settings: Minimum successive high/low closing difference = 0.875 cents
        No. successive high/low closings = 5

T A B L E   4.WN.C30

Trade Results: Mountain/Valley Day Trade Method*
Wheat: Conservative Mode, 30-Minute Data

Date	Position	Time In	Price In	Time Out	Price Out	$P/L	$Max. Loss	Time	$Max. Gain	Time
5/8/95	Short	1231	356.5	1314	356.75	−12	−25	1301	0	1231
5/10/95	Long	1230	359.25	1314	359.25	0	0	1230	12	1300
5/12/95	Long	1200	360.5	1314	368	375	0	1200	375	1314
5/17/95	Short	1304	356.25	1314	356	12	0	1304	12	1314
5/18/95	Long	1301	359.75	1314	359.5	−12	−12	1314	0	1301
5/26/95	Long	1231	384.25	1314	386	88	0	1231	88	1314
5/30/95	Short	1258	377.5	1314	374	175	0	1258	175	1314
$Total						625				
$Ave/Trade						89				

* Settings: Minimum successive high/low closing difference = 0.125 cents
        No. successive high/low closings = 4

tings and total results. Trades for a 1-minute interval did not fare well, with profits per trade not over $30, too small to deal with. It is a situation similar to that of soybeans: There is so much noise around valid trends that stringent filters (large closing difference required or number of differences) make the trader jump aboard the trend too late.

Table 4.WN.C30 shows a very selective, conservative trade stance (four higher differences needed to go long), with only seven trades made (four of them successful), for a moderate total profit. One must be patient for the big moves! The one real successful trade is graphically shown in Chart WN–3. Prices start off waving upwards after 11:00 A.M., and make real, concerted upside moves after 1 P.M. A buy signal occurs at point (D), following four successive higher closings of at least 1/8th cent apart. The trader closes his long at 368, for nearly an 8 cent profit ($400) at the end of the day.

On the other hand, Table 4.WN.S30 goes overboard in the other trading direction—lots of activity. Two trades per day occur, keeping the trader quite busy with approximately thirty trades in May alone. If he can act fast, execute well, and bargain for slim commissions, his trading could be well worth it—to the tune of $1,000 for the month, before costs.

A nice turnaround in a day for this 30-minute speculative trading mode is shown in Chart WN–4. Prices initially start climbing slowly upwards, then turn down after about 11:30 EDT, giving us two significantly lower closings by 12:30, or price (B), and a short position at about 379. Prices continue that way, and the position is closed at 374, for a profit of about 5 cents, or $250.

Finally, a really speculative stance is taken with only one minimal (1/8th cent) difference required to establish a significant successive higher or lower

T A B L E   4.WN.S30

Trade Results: Mountain/Valley Day Trade Method*
Wheat: Speculative Mode, 30-Minute Data

Date	Position	Time In	Price In	Time Out	Price Out	$P/L	$Max. Loss	Time	$Max. Gain	Time
5/1/95	Long	1202	358	1314	358.5	25	0	1202	50	1302
5/2/95	Short	1100	357.25	1200	360	−138	−138	1200	0	1100
5/2/95	Long	1200	360	1314	361	50	−12	1230	50	1314
5/3/95	Short	1101	357.25	1230	358.25	−50	−50	1230	12	1131
5/3/95	Long	1230	358.25	1314	360.25	100	0	1230	100	1314
5/4/95	Long	1054	359	1232	358.5	−25	−25	1232	0	1054
5/4/95	Short	1232	358.5	1314	356.75	88	0	1232	112	1302
5/5/95	Short	1100	351.75	1230	352.25	−25	−25	1230	0	1100
5/5/95	Long	1230	352.25	1314	353	38	0	1230	38	1314
5/8/95	Short	1159	360.5	1314	361	−25	−25	1314	75	1230
5/10/95	Long	1130	358.25	1314	359.25	50	0	1130	62	1300
5/12/95	Long	1100	359.75	1314	368	412	0	1100	412	1314
5/15/95	Long	1130	364.75	1300	361.5	−162	−162	1300	38	1200
5/15/95	Short	1300	361.5	1314	360.75	38	0	1300	38	1314
5/16/95	Short	1059	356.5	1202	358.5	−100	−100	1202	0	1059
5/16/95	Long	1202	358.5	1314	360.75	112	−25	1233	112	1314
5/17/95	Short	1204	360.75	1314	356	238	0	1204	238	1314
5/18/95	Long	1200	358	1314	359.5	75	0	1200	88	1301
5/19/95	Long	1100	362.5	1200	360.25	−112	−112	1200	0	1100
5/19/95	Short	1200	360.25	1314	359.75	25	0	1200	25	1314
5/22/95	Long	1130	366.5	1314	366.25	−12	−12	1314	75	1230
5/23/95	Short	1131	374.25	1314	374	12	−88	1201	12	1314
5/24/95	Long	1132	375.25	1302	373.25	−100	−100	1302	0	1132
5/24/95	Short	1302	373.25	1314	373.75	−25	−25	1314	0	1302
5/25/95	Long	1202	375.75	1314	376.5	38	−38	1232	38	1314
5/26/95	Long	1130	380.75	1314	386	262	0	1130	262	1314
5/30/95	Short	1200	379.25	1314	374	262	0	1200	262	1314
5/31/95	Short	1058	371.5	1314	372.25	−38	−138	1130	0	1058
$Total						1062				
$Ave/Trade						37				

* Settings: Minimum successive high/low closing difference = .125 cents
        No. successive high/low closings = 2

closing and only one succession needed to put on a short or long position. But the trader uses his head—he lengthens the time size to 60 minutes to get more significant movement. The result of the two criteria, extremely sensitive entries on a long interval, produce interesting results, which are detailed in Table 4.WN.S60. A total of 32 trades occur, 19 of which are successful, for a total profit of $1,875. You will note that the losses are very small, never exceeding $100,

C H A R T   WN–4

Speculative Mode Trading: 30-Minute Prices for Wheat

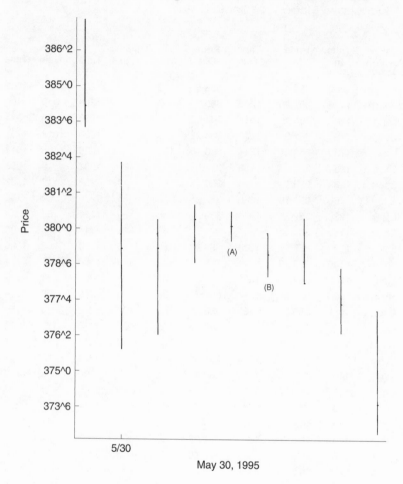

May 30, 1995

while the gains can be larger than $300 and are more numerous—a nice combination. A nice trade is detailed in Chart WN–5, where the trader jumps aboard a short right into the first period possible (11:29) at 362.5 and holds until the close for a 6 cent, or $300, profit.

C H A R T   WN–5

Speculative Mode Trading: 60-Minute Prices for Wheat

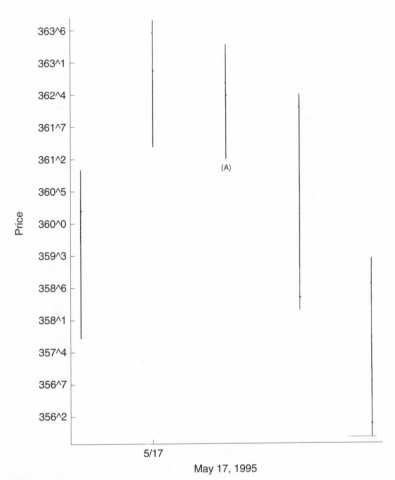

May 17, 1995

T A B L E   4.WN.S60

Trade Results: Mountain/Valley Day Trade Method*
Wheat: Speculative Mode, 60-Minute Data

Date	Position	Time In	Price In	Time Out	Price Out	$P/L	$Max. Loss	Time	$Max. Gain	Time
5/1/95	Long	1132	356.5	1314	358.5	100	0	1132	100	1314
5/2/95	Long	1129	358.75	1314	361	112	0	1129	112	1314
5/3/95	Short	1131	357	1230	358.25	−62	−62	1230	0	1131
5/3/95	Long	1230	358.25	1314	360.25	100	0	1230	100	1314
5/4/95	Long	1132	359	1232	358.5	−25	−25	1232	0	1054
5/4/95	Short	1232	358.5	1314	356.75	88	0	1232	112	1302
5/5/95	Short	1130	352	1230	352.25	−12	−12	1230	0	1130
5/5/95	Long	1230	352.25	1314	353	38	0	1230	38	1314
5/8/95	Short	1130	357.75	1314	356.75	50	0	1130	62	1231
5/9/95	Short	1130	361.25	1314	361	12	0	1130	112	1230
5/10/95	Long	1130	358.25	1314	359.25	50	0	1130	50	1230
5/11/95	Long	1129	362.25	1229	362	−12	−12	1229	0	1129
5/11/95	Short	1229	362	1314	362.25	−12	−12	1314	0	1229
5/12/95	Long	1130	360.25	1314	368	388	0	1130	388	1314
5/15/95	Long	1130	364.75	1230	363.75	−50	−50	1230	0	1130
5/15/95	Short	1230	363.75	1314	360.75	150	0	1230	150	1314
5/16/95	Long	1129	358	1314	360.75	138	0	1129	138	1314
5/17/95	Short	1129	362.5	1314	356	325	0	1129	325	1314
5/18/95	Long	1129	355.75	1314	359.5	188	0	1129	188	1314
5/19/95	Long	1130	362	1230	360	−100	−100	1230	0	1130
5/19/95	Short	1230	360	1314	359.75	12	0	1230	12	1314
5/22/95	Long	1130	366.5	1314	366.25	−12	−12	1314	75	1230
5/23/95	Short	1131	374.25	1231	376	−88	−88	1231	0	1131
5/23/95	Long	1231	376	1314	374	−100	−100	1314	0	1231
5/24/95	Long	1132	375.25	1232	374.25	−50	−50	1232	0	1132
5/24/95	Short	1232	374.25	1314	373.75	25	0	1232	25	1314
5/25/95	Long	1131	373	1314	376.5	175	0	1131	175	1314
5/26/95	Long	1130	380.75	1314	386	262	0	1130	262	1314
5/30/95	Long	1129	380.25	1229	378.25	−100	−100	1229	0	1129
5/30/95	Short	1229	378.25	1314	374	212	0	1229	212	1314
5/31/95	Long	1130	374.25	1229	374	−12	−12	1229	0	1130
5/31/95	Short	1229	374	1314	372.25	88	0	1229	88	1314
$Total						1875				
$Ave/Trade						59				

* Settings: Minimum successive high/low closing difference = .125 cents
    No. successive high/low closings = 1

Interest Rates

T-BONDS

T-bonds, the U.S. government's 30-year security offering, vies with Eurodollars (U.S. dollars on deposit in Europe and reflecting those interest rates) for top position in volume of trading for all commodities. It is that big. Much of commerce and many institutions, governments, and individuals dwell on this instrument as the main ingredient in their portfolios. The T-bond has had some major trend moves in the past 20 years of its existence—most notably the high interest rate period of 1980–81, when rates skyrocketed to nearly 20 percent. There have also been good-sized major moves in the past five years, with moves of 40 full points or more occurring every other year or so. Each point is worth $1,000 on the contract traded. Many moderate and small moves (less than 10 points) have occurred almost regularly, due to bets on Fed Reserve moves, US–Japan government negotiations, unemployment data, PPI, housing starts, GNP, and so on.

TYPICAL DAY PRICE MOVEMENTS

Intraday price moves are a different story. Only very rarely do you get a monster move of 2 full points or more. Most of the time moves occur in the 1/4 to 1/2 point range, though occasional moves of 1 point or more do occur. So the day trader has to make his living going after (and hoping for) a 1/4 point move and content himself with an average of 1/8th or so after losses. Fortunately, the market is big and reliable, so the slippage on trade execution should be very small. I estimate (having been a broker) 1/2 tick each way, or 1 tick (.03125 point) on average, for a mediocre floor trader.

This means a trader could get $80 or so gross profit average and still make about half of that ($40) net after costs. But that is between you and your broker. Good bargaining!

Chart US–1 depicts a very typical day for T-bonds. The day's range is 10–11 points (ticks), with wave-like, reactionary moves from high to low. If the trader is adept, he can make a few points (ticks) profit, maybe 6 points if lucky, and probably, by using a contrary (opposite acting) method—buy a sharp dip, sell a strong rally—make a little profit here and there. But for trend followers, all is grief, for the trader usually gets in longs late, near the top, then sells near the bottom as prices drop hard. Fortunately, the mountain/valley method, though trend following, can avoid and filter out many of the false moves.

Chart US–2, what the trader is really looking for, happens fairly frequently: congestion for a while, then a concerted trend later in the day, affording that 6–8 point profit potential (though we can always hope for the occasional big move).

C H A R T   US–1

Typical Daily T-Bond Price Action

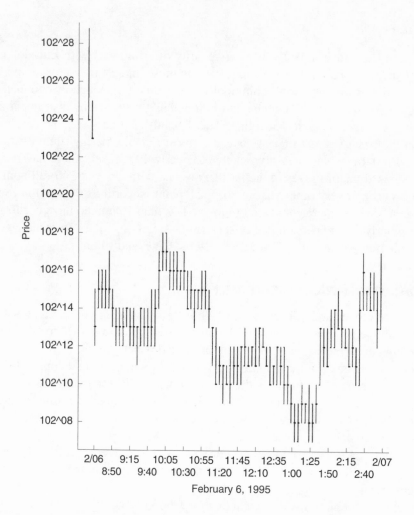

February 6, 1995

A VARIETY OF SETTINGS FOR DIFFERENT TRADING STYLES

Our method was tested on 1-, 5-, 15-, 30-, and 60-minute price data for the month of February 1995. Results were positive for all time frames, with the best option depending upon the style of trading desired.

Table 4.US.C1 takes a conservative stance to trading (six successive higher closings of 1 tick or more needed to trigger a long), yet trades nearly once a day (primarily because of the time frame). Results show that only one trade loses more than $400 and the worst cumulative losing period (days) is $500, yet there are several gains over $400, a cumulative profit total of $1,700, and profit per trade of $82.

Table 4.US.S15, traded on 15-minute price intervals, is for the aggressive trader who is willing to go for the trade with only a slight cautionary reliability

C H A R T   US-2

Typical Daily T-Bond Price Action

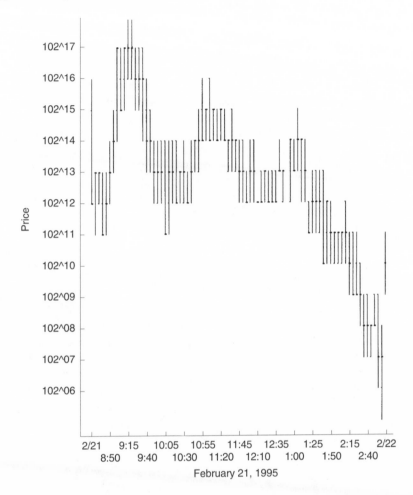

February 21, 1995

(successive number of closing confirmations) built in. Here he wants a moderate size between successive closings (3 ticks), but only two in succession to go long or short. Ironically, the trade totals are very similar to the results for the conservative 1-minute time basis trading program. Results indicate profit totals of $1,800 versus $1,700, an identical average profit per trade of $82, and similar numbers of trades (22 versus 21), but losses are smaller (the largest is $219 versus $469). Oh well, it was intended to be more speculative, and it probably will be in the future, over more time.

Chart US–3 depicts a nice day's labor for our embattled spec trader. Two big price jumps occur right after the bottom at 102-6 made at around 8:00 A.M. CDT, and he takes a long at point (B) on the second large successive higher closing (by 3 ticks or more). However, a top is quickly made just after 11:00 A.M. EDT and two large price drops occur by point (b), at which time he goes short and holds for

T A B L E   4.US.C1

Trade Results: Mountain/Valley Day Trade Method*
T-Bonds: Conservative Mode, 1-Minute Data

Date	Position	Time In	Price In	Time Out	Price Out	$P/L	$Max. Loss	Time	$Max. Gain	Time
2/1/95	Short	1327	101.3125	1410	101.1875	125	−219	1336	156	1400
2/3/95	Long	935	102.343	1410	102.718	375	−218	1006	563	1351
2/6/95	Short	1228	102.218	1409	102.375	−157	−313	1339	0	1228
2/7/95	Short	1315	102.406	1410	102.281	125	−156	1337	125	1409
2/8/95	Short	1235	102.031	1410	102.25	−219	−281	1324	0	1235
2/9/95	Long	1300	102.25	1349	101.968	−282	−282	1349	93	1306
2/9/95	Short	1349	101.968	1410	101.843	125	0	1349	156	1400
2/10/95	Short	743	101.937	1410	101.593	344	−94	801	687	1133
2/14/95	Long	822	102.093	1411	102.3125	219	−281	912	219	1354
2/15/95	Long	824	102.5	1113	102.906	406	0	824	750	1043
2/15/95	Short	1113	102.906	1410	102.687	219	−62	1116	313	1344
2/16/95	Short	829	102.781	1053	102.687	94	−187	901	531	934
2/16/95	Long	1053	102.687	1340	102.593	−94	−187	1128	281	1253
2/16/95	Short	1340	102.593	1409	102.718	−125	−157	1359	0	1340
2/22/95	Short	955	102.343	1101	102.531	−188	−188	1101	218	1007
2/22/95	Long	1101	102.531	1410	103.187	656	−156	1115	687	1359
2/24/95	Short	1213	102.531	1400	103	−469	−469	1400	0	1213
2/24/95	Long	1400	103	1410	103.031	31	0	1400	31	1401
2/27/95	Long	1238	103.593	1409	103.625	32	−250	1325	94	1259
2/28/95	Short	908	103.25	1321	103.375	−125	−125	1321	219	1332
2/28/95	Long	1321	103.375	1410	104	625	−32	1322	625	1359
$Total						1717				
$Ave/Trade						82				

* Settings: Minimum successive high/low closing difference = .03125 points
   No. successive high/low closings = 6

the rest of the day. The total profit equals $93 for the long and $156 for the short.

The conservative version results for 15-minute basis price intervals is displayed in Table 4.US.C15. Because the trader is really stringent in position entrance criteria (4 ticks, or .125 points, for each successive higher/lower closing and five successions to establish a position), few (but good) trades happen. But he is the type who will lie in wait for big opportunities, unconcerned about trading frequency; he can put his money in other (conservative) trades! Chart US–4 details a nice pickup of $344 profit by getting long midway in the day February 3, 1995, at point (E), the fifth successive higher closing of 4 ticks or more.

Finally, Table 4.US.S60 shows the results of a quasi-speculative trading stance for 60-minute basis prices. If the trader requires a big difference between successive higher/lower closings (1/2 full point, or 16 ticks) but only one closing confirmation to trigger a long or short position (the spec part!), he can effectively get stringent

T A B L E   4.US.S15

Trade Results: Mountain/Valley Day Trade Method*
T-Bonds: Speculative Mode, 15-Minute Data

Date	Position	Time In	Price In	Time Out	Price Out	$P/L	$Max. Loss	Time	$Max. Gain	Time
2/1/95	Short	1349	101.3125	1359	101.1875	125	0	1349	125	1359
2/3/95	Long	834	102.03125	1359	102.75	719	0	834	844	1349
2/7/95	Short	1319	102.4375	1359	102.3125	125	−63	1334	125	1359
2/8/95	Long	1049	102.375	1204	102.156	−219	−219	1204	31	1104
2/8/95	Short	1204	102.156	1359	102.25	−94	−94	1304	94	1249
2/9/95	Short	1105	101.906	1250	102.125	−219	−219	1250	31	1205
2/9/95	Long	1250	102.125	1350	101.9375	188	−188	1350	1875	1305
2/9/95	Short	1350	101.9375	1359	101.906	31	0	1350	31	1359
2/10/95	Short	1005	101.5625	1359	101.5625	0	0	1005	281	1135
2/14/95	Long	1336	102.0625	1359	102.3125	250	0	1336	250	1359
2/15/95	Long	834	102.75	1119	102.843	93	−94	849	437	1034
2/15/95	Short	1119	102.843	1359	102.687	156	−125	1219	218	1349
2/16/95	Short	919	102.531	1004	102.562	−31	−31	1004	281	934
2/16/95	Long	1004	102.562	1359	102.75	188	−62	1034	313	1304
2/21/95	Short	1320	102.281	1359	102.218	63	0	1320	63	1359
2/22/95	Long	1050	102.46	1359	103.218	812	0	1050	812	1359
2/24/95	Short	1204	102.593	1349	102.781	−188	−188	1349	31	1219
2/24/95	Long	1349	102.781	1359	102.875	94	0	1349	94	1359
2/27/95	Long	934	103.406	1334	103.406	0	−63	1019	281	1304
2/27/95	Short	1334	103.406	1359	103.531	−125	−125	1359	0	1334
2/28/95	Short	834	103.468	1334	103.625	−157	−157	1334	406	1134
2/28/95	Long	1334	103.625	1359	104	375	−32	1349	375	1359
$Total						1810				
$Ave/Trade						82				

* Settings: Minimum successive high/low closing difference = .09375 points
      No. successive high/low closings = 2

breakout trades at major times of the day. The result is a moderate profit total of $532, with $177 profit per trade. A typical trade for the month is shown in Chart US–5. From the open, then from a lower closing of 102-6 around 11:20 EDT, prices finally go one succession higher by 0.50 points (16 ticks) at 13:20 CDT(14:20 EDT); the trader goes long and collects $406 at the end of the day.

CHART US–3

Speculative Mode Trading: 15-Minute Prices for T-Bonds

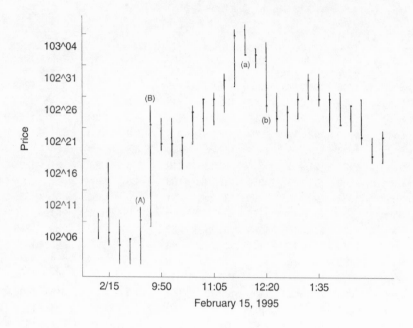

TABLE 4.US.C15

Trade Results: Mountain/Valley Day Trade Method*
T-Bonds: Conservative Mode, 15-Minute Data

Date	Position	Time In	Price In	Time Out	Price Out	$P/L	$Max. Loss	Time	$Max. Gain	Time
2/3/95	Long	1049	102.406	1359	102.75	344	−63	1119	469	1349
2/22/95	Long	1350	103.125	1359	103.218	93	0	1350	93	1359
$Total						437				
$Ave/Trade						218				

* Settings: Minimum successive high/low closing difference = .125 points
   No. successive high/low closings = 5

C H A R T   US–4

Conservative Mode Trading: 15-Minute Prices for T-Bonds

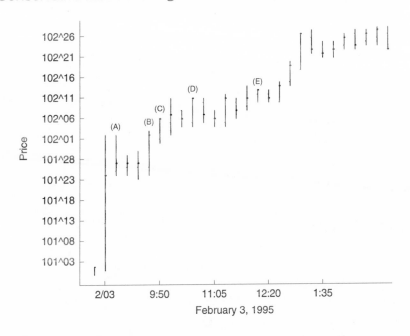

February 3, 1995

T A B L E   4.US.S60

Trade Results: Mountain/Valley Day Trade Method*
T-Bonds: Speculative Mode, 60-Minute Data

Date	Position	Time In	Price In	Time Out	Price Out	$P/L	$Max. Loss	Time	$Max. Gain	Time
2/3/95	Long	1020	102.343	1359	102.75	407	0	1020	407	1320
2/15/95	Long	1020	102.968	1359	102.687	−281	−281	1359	0	1020
2/22/95	Long	1320	102.812	1359	103.218	406	0	1320	406	1359
$Total						532				
$Ave/Trade						177				

* Settings: Minimum successive high/low closing difference = .50 points
      No. successive high/low closings = 1

C H A R T   US-5

Speculative Mode Trading: 60-Minute Prices for T-Bonds

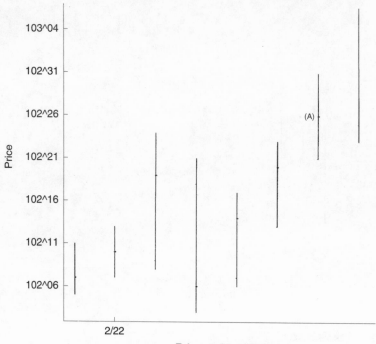

February 22, 1995

T-NOTES

Little is known or observed about this relatively obscure government issue. Because it is a middle rate between short-term T-bills and Eurodollars and long-term 30-year T-bonds, not many think about the midpoint of the yield curve. Most merely acknowledge that it is there, rather than considering it as a leader of the rate curve. The most people think about is the 2/3 rule, which states that if bonds move x amount, notes will move 2/3 of x (roughly).

It is true that the potential for movement of the T-note is constrained by the arithmetic of the older, more influential bond, but it can sometimes deviate enough in a short spell (one day, say) to reflect investor uncertainty about the direction of both long- and short-term rates and provide a trading opportunity.

TYPICAL DAY MOVEMENTS

Like bonds, T-notes can sometimes stage a trend move that is both methodical (building slowly from the beginning to the end of the day) and large in size. Chart TY–1 nicely depicts a typical uptrend for notes. An initial spurt up in the opening 15 minutes moves prices 7 ticks, but this move is followed by a lull period that seems to last an eternity. However, the real substance of the day is revealed when a steady, low volatility drive is made for over three hours to the day's high, nearly 1 full point (32 ticks) from the beginning. Alas, and this is typical, a good chunk of the trend (8 ticks) is given back at the end. The pattern here is a day-long, steady, strong trend (hinted at very early) with small volatility but considerable give-back at the end. This type of day occurs several times a month.

C H A R T   TY–1

Typical Day T-Note Price Action

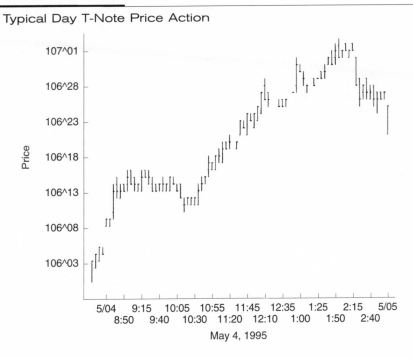

May 4, 1995

Another type of T-note day, however, occurs more frequently.

Chart TY–2 shows a fast-paced T-note moving early in the day of May 24, to the tune of 18 ticks in half an hour. To the disappointment of the excited trader, the price movement completely pancakes after that. This pattern, a sharp initial move followed by nothing, happens often.

BETTER SETTINGS FOR T-NOTES

The mountain/valley method was tested on May 1995 price data for 1-, 5-, 15-, 30-, and 60-minute intervals. Good but somewhat lackluster results resulted from a very tame month. Several profitable settings for conservative and speculative trading modes were found and are presented in Tables 4.TY.C1 through S60, along with charts showing examples of some typical and good trades.

Table 4.TY.S1 takes a speculative stance on 1-minute data by requiring only one successive higher closing (essentially a breakout version) of 1/2 point, or 16 ticks. Surprisingly, there were nine such explosive situations that month, with nearly half being successful, for a net total of $844, or $94 per trade, before costs. The losses, not surprisingly, were small, because of a sedate vehicle (T-notes). Basically, the trader is counting on enough and large enough moves to make the speculative campaign profitable. An especially strong moving T-note for May 5 is shown in Chart TY–3 (look back at Chart TY–1—familiar?), as the long position is quickly picked up at 8:34 EDT (7:34 CDT) at point (A) by the nimble speculator and is held until the close for over a 3/4 point profit, or $781.

C H A R T   TY–2

Typical Day T-Note Price Action

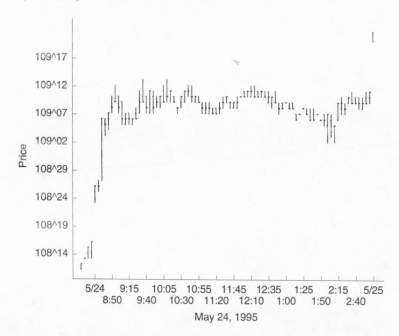

May 24, 1995

TABLE   4.TY.S1

Trade Results: Mountain/Valley Day Trade Method*
Treasury Notes: Speculative Mode, 1-Minute Data

Date	Position	Time In	Price In	Time Out	Price Out	$P/L	$Max. Loss	Time	$Max. Gain	Time
5/3/95	Long	1240	106.156	1400	106.125	−31	−156	1338	0	1240
5/4/95	Long	1045	106.75	1410	106.812	62	−32	1047	312	1251
5/5/95	Long	734	107.187	1409	107.968	781	0	734	813	1324
5/9/95	Long	819	108.468	1409	108.468	0	−218	1329	375	929
5/10/95	Short	1150	108.5	1410	108.093	407	−156	1219	657	1248
5/11/95	Short	943	107.718	1410	107.906	−188	−219	1012	218	1121
5/12/95	Long	1021	107.968	1409	107.875	−93	−218	1047	32	1024
5/17/95	Short	1002	108.593	1409	108.718	−125	−282	1043	0	1002
34843	Long	747	109.312	1411	109.343	31	−219	1257	63	832
$Total						844				
$Ave/Trade						94				

* Settings: Minimum successive high/low closing difference = 0.5 points
          No. successive high/low closings = 1

CHART   TY−3

Speculative Mode Trading: 1-Minute Prices for T-Notes

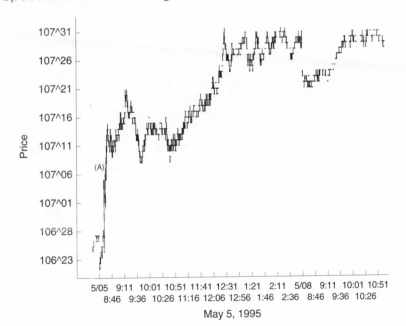

May 5, 1995

T A B L E   4.TY.C1

Trade Results: Mountain/Valley Day Trade Method*
Treasury Notes: Conservative Mode, 1-Minute Data

Date	Position	Time In	Price In	Time Out	Price Out	$P/L	$Max. Loss	Time	$Max. Gain	Time
5/5/95	Long	1127	107.875	1409	107.968	93	−125	1139	125	1324
5/10/95	Short	1233	108.312	1410	108.093	219	156	1238	469	1248
$Total						312				
$Ave/Trade						156				

* Settings: Minimum successive high/low closing difference = 0.03125 points
　　　　No. successive high/low closings = 14

T A B L E   4.TY.C30

Trade Results: Mountain/Valley Day Trade Method*
Treasury Notes: Conservative Mode, 30-Minute Data

Date	Position	Time In	Price In	Time Out	Price Out	$P/L	$Max. Loss	Time	$Max. Gain	Time
5/3/95	Long	1251	106.093	1359	106.125	32	−62	1322	63	1357
5/4/95	Long	1217	106.875	1359	106.843	−32	−63	1350	156	1250
5/10/95	Short	1150	108.5	1359	108.093	407	−125	1220	594	1250
$Total						407				
$Ave/Trade						136				

* Settings: Minimum successive high/low closing difference = 0.03125 points
　　　　No. successive high/low closings = 5

A completely different trading attitude is displayed in Table 4.TY.C1: We'll take sure trades and even give up the big money opportunity, but just don't give us losses! This trader requires 14 (yes, 14) successive higher closings of just one tick to go long, with the expectation of getting higher reliability out of a profitable trade at the expense of more and bigger trades. The results pay off—he trades only twice for a modest total of $312, but there are no losses this time and the average profit is a nice $156.

Table 4.TY.C30 also reflects a conservative stance, but here the trader requires fewer successive higher/lower closings and is checked over 30-minute intervals (between which a lot of good and grief can occur). The result, however, is still good, with again a modest but higher profit total of $407 and profit per trade of $136. The only loss, $32, is small. Chart TY–4 details the first trade, a modest gain. A slow, relentless, steady trickle upwards ticks off five successive

C H A R T   TY-4

Conservative Mode Trading: 30-Minute Prices for T-Notes

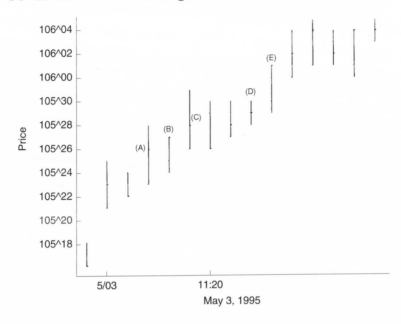

5/03   11:20

May 3, 1995

T A B L E   4.TY.S60

Trade Results: Mountain/Valley Day Trade Method*
Treasury Notes: Speculative Mode, 60-Minute Data

Date	Position	Time In	Price In	Time Out	Price Out	$P/L	$Max. Loss	Time	$Max. Gain	Time
5/10/95	Short	1121	108.656	1359	108.093	563	0	1121	563	1359
$Total						563				
$Ave/Trade						563				

* Settings: Minimum successive high/low closing difference = 0.1875 points
     No. successive high/low closings = 2

higher closings until point (E), whereupon the trader goes long and takes home a modest $31 profit at the close.

Finally, a speculative 60-minute basis strategy is shown in Table 4.TY.S60. The trader needs only two successive lower closings of 6 ticks (.1875 points) or more to signal a short. The only trade, a nice success, occurs on May 10, 1995 (see Chart TY–5). Prices drop steadily and strongly from the start, with the second successive lower closing happening at (B), getting him into a short position and giving him a profit at the close of over 1/2 point, or $563.

C H A R T   TY–5

Speculative Mode Trading: 60-Minute Prices for T-Notes

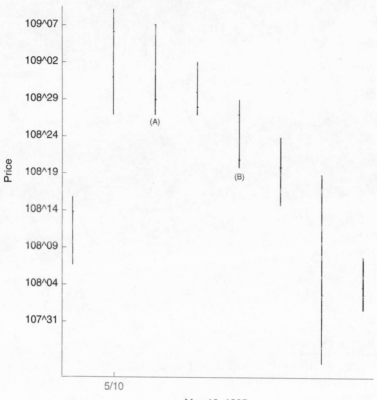

May 10, 1995

The Meats

LIVE CATTLE

Cattle has recently shown an increasing aptitude for enlarging its price moves, to over $1.00 per pound (a new record), and also for incurring big swings on the downside. This could mean ever-widening trends for the future. The old trends might go 10–20 cents, or $4–8,000, moderate in size. Current swings of 20–30 cents and more could propel cattle into serious profit opportunities by trend followers, whether long term or day trading. Because cattlemen depend on grains (corn, soybeans, and wheat primarily) to feed their animals, weather and other long-term influences can not only produce big (up)trends in the grains but in cattle and other livestock as well, so big grain trends can lead to large cattle trends.

TYPICAL DAY PRICE MOVEMENTS

Cattle really moves quite slothfully on most days and is not worth trading from a trend-following standpoint. A 40–60 point range is standard, not enough to get started in a long trend (or, if detected prematurely, it ends quickly and leaves the trader with a loss).

Chart LC–1 well represents the sideways day market for a typical day of May 3, 1995. Prices (5-minute basis) start out at 61.90 or so (sorry for the graph—

C H A R T   LC–1

Typical Day Live Cattle Price Action

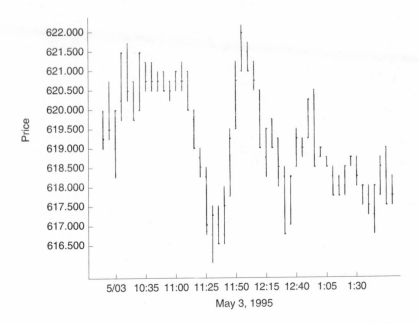

May 3, 1995

prices are off by a decimal place due to the software package settings), swing up to near their eventual daily high of 62.20, then swing down viciously to the day's low of 61.60. All of this takes place in the first hour or so. Not done yet, prices rebound just as quickly to the highs, then oscillate the rest of the day between the two extremes. Trend traders would have gotten short, then long, then short, probably losing on every trade.

What we really want are days like that shown in Chart LC–2. A pronounced downward swing in prices occurs almost immediately, when prices start falling from 62.40. Low volatility accompanies the trend—prices recover only about .40 cents maximum, so that whipsaw trends against the current one do not occur, allowing a trend follower to hold until the end of the day for a good chunk of the 1.00 cent profit potential.

But only a few days a month are like that, unless we are in a very pronounced long-term trend, when daily prices widen and move in a more exaggerated fashion.

Chart LC–3 represents another pattern that increasingly occurs and, for the nimble, quick trader, can mean two trend opportunities. Prices start off the day making a good trend in one direction (here, a downtrend from 62.30 to 61.10), then reverse fairly sharply and recover/make the opposite trend (to 62.00).

GOOD CATTLE SETTINGS

The moutain/valley trend method was tested on live cattle prices for May 1995 on 1-, 5-, 15-, 30-, and 60-minute bases to see what profit opportunities could be

C H A R T   LC–2

Typical Day Live Cattle Price Action

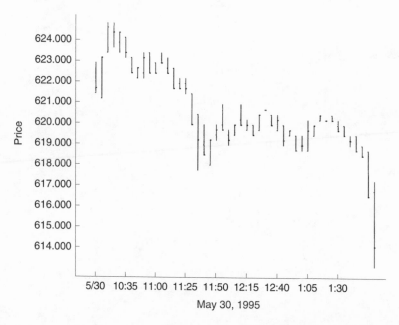

May 30, 1995

CHART LC–3

Typical Day Live Cattle Price Action

May 23, 1995

found. Four good settings, two for speculative modes and two for conservative modes to trading, were found and are presented in Tables 4.LC.C1–S60 and accompanying chart examples.

A conservative mode is shown in Table 4.LC.C1 for 1-minute basis price intervals. This requires six successive higher closings of at least .15 cents (6 minimal trading ticks) before a long position can be taken. Because of this selectivity and few trend opportunities in the month, only four trades occur, but they are all winners, resulting in total profits before costs of $580, with per trade profit of $145. Chart LC–4 depicts a short trade for May 5, 1995. Prices start off at the 62.20 area and saunter their way down the rest of the day. Drops of 0.15 cents, the minimum we stipulated, successively occur at points (A), (B), etc., until point (F), at 12:16 CDT (1:16 EDT on the chart), where a short is entered at 61.17. This position is held until the close, for a 0.375 point, or $150, profit. (Note: part of May 8 is shown, which can be misleading. Prices for May 5 do end at 60.80, upon careful inspection.)

Table 4.LC.S1 illustrates the speculative mode of trading for the 1-minute time frame. This version requires only two successive lower closings of 0.40 cents each to initiate a short position. The results are quite good, except for one loss of $350. The total profit still adds up to $550, or $79 per trade, with only two losers out of seven trades. This mode is ideal for situations where prices move very quickly and strongly, and quick decisions are required. Chart LC–5 shows us a sharply dropping cattle price picture for May 8, 1995. Before the trader has hardly had his coffee and danish, prices have dropped 1.00 cents in a matter of minutes. Two big drops of 0.40 cents or more occurred, and at price point (B), 59.80

T A B L E   4.LC.C1

Trade Results: Mountain/Valley Day Trade Method*
Live Cattle: Conservative Mode, 1-Minute Data

Date	Position	Time In	Price In	Time Out	Price Out	$P/L	$Max. Loss	Time	$Max. Gain	Time
5/2/95	Short	1113	62.125	1307	61.925	80	−80	1126	130	1231
5/5/95	Short	1216	61.175	1310	60.8	150	0	1216	250	1243
5/8/95	Short	1006	59.425	1301	59.25	70	−150	1056	70	1214
5/10/95	Short	1043	59.85	1309	59.15	280	−60	1045	440	1238
$Total						580				
$Ave/Trade						145				

* Settings: Minimum successive high/low closing difference = .15 cents
        No. successive high/low closings = 6

C H A R T   LC–4

Conservative Mode Trading: 1-Minute Prices for Live Cattle

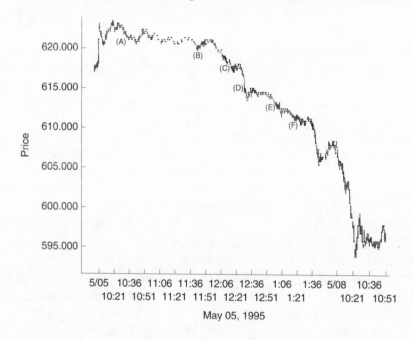

May 05, 1995

at 9:22 CDT (10:22 EDT), he takes his short and holds through a lot of sideways price movement until prices drop to their ultimate low of 59.25 on the close. He pockets $220 profit for the trade.

Moving up the scale timewise, a conservative trading mode for 5-minute time intervals is presented in Table 4.LC.C5. Trading requires nine successive lower closings of a minimal trading tick (.025 cents) to initiate a short. Because of the paucity of trade opportunities and the stringency of our trading requirements,

T A B L E   4.LC.S1

Trade Results: Mountain/Valley Day Trade Method*
Live Cattle: Speculative Mode, 1-Minute Data

Date	Position	Time In	Price In	Time Out	Price Out	$P/L	$Max. Loss	Time	$Max. Gain	Time
5/2/95	Short	1113	62.125	1307	61.925	80	80	1126	130	1231
5/5/95	Short	1131	61.375	1310	60.8	230	−50	1135	330	1243
5/8/95	Short	922	59.8	1301	59.25	220	−30	928	220	1214
5/10/95	Short	1032	60.1	1309	59.15	380	−30	1033	540	1238
5/23/95	Short	1047	61.1	1229	61.975	−350	−350	1229	0	1047
5/23/95	Long	1229	61.975	1308	61.9	−30	−60	1236	10	1252
5/30/95	Short	1300	61.4	1310	61.35	20	0	1300	30	1309
$Total						550				
$Ave/Trade						79				

* Settings: Minimum successive high/low closing difference = .40 cents
      No. successive high/low closings = 2

C H A R T   LC–5

Speculative Mode Trading: 1-Minute Prices for Live Cattle

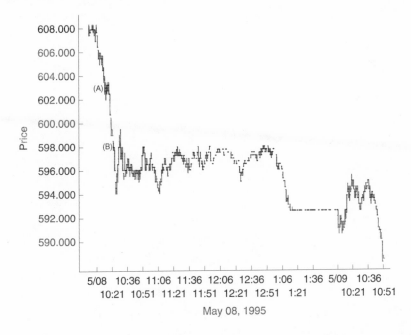

May 08, 1995

only five trades are taken in the month of May. However, all but one are winners, and the loser is small ($100), for a total profit of $690 before costs, or $138 per trade. A typical trade is shown in Chart LC–6, for May 2, 1995. Prices smoothly cascade downwards and make new low points at (1) through (9), where at 10:49

TABLE 4.LC.C5

Trade Results: Mountain/Valley Day Trade Method*
Live Cattle: Conservative Mode, 5-Minute Data

Date	Position	Time In	Price In	Time Out	Price Out	$P/L	$Max. Loss	Time	$Max. Gain	Time
5/2/95	Short	1049	62.35	1259	62.05	120	−20	1054	200	1234
5/5/95	Short	1124	61.75	1259	60.8	380	0	1124	460	1244
5/10/95	Short	1054	59.7	1259	59.15	220	−110	1104	320	1239
5/19/95	Long	1229	61.1	1259	60.85	−100	−120	1244	20	1254
5/30/95	Short	1254	61.75	1259	61.575	70	0	1254	70	1259
$Total						690				
$Ave/Trade						138				

* Settings: Minimum successive high/low closing difference = .025 cents
        No. successive high/low closings = 9

CHART LC–6

Conservative Mode Trading: 5-Minute Prices for Live Cattle

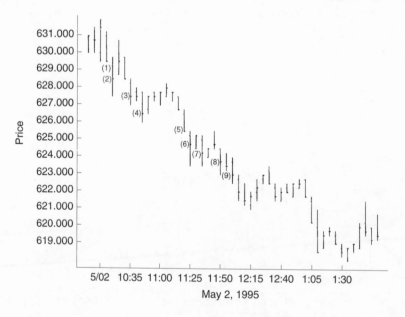

May 2, 1995

CDT (11:49 EDT on our graph), our trader takes a short at 62.35 and holds until the close at 62.05, for a 0.30 cent, or $120, profit.

Finally, a speculative stance on 15-minute intervals is taken, the results of which are shown in Table 4.LC.S15. Only two successive higher closings of at least 0.40 cents are needed to establish long positions. Because of the stringent

T A B L E   4.LC.S15

Trade Results: Mountain/Valley Day Trade Method*
Live Cattle: Speculative Mode, 15-Minute Data

Date	Position	Time In	Price In	Time Out	Price Out	$P/L	$Max. Loss	Time	$Max. Gain	Time
5/2/95	Short	1219	61.95	1259	62.05	−40	−40	1259	40	1234
5/5/95	Short	1204	61.25	1259	60.8	220	0	1204	240	1247
5/10/95	Short	1034	60.125	1259	59.15	390	0	1034	460	1249
$Total						530				
$Ave/Trade						177				

* Settings: Minimum successive high/low closing difference = .40 cents
　　　No. successive high/low closings = 2

size (0.40 cents) requirements and lack of day trend opportunities in May, only three trades result. One is a small loss, but the trader realizes good gains in the other two, for a total of $530 for the month and a healthy per trade profit average of $177.

PORK BELLIES

Pork bellies used to be the premier speculation from the mid 1960s until the early 1980s, but they have fallen on low volume times since then. Prices have moved from the 20 cent area to over one dollar in big, long-term trends with great price volatility, often with dramatic limit moves during the day. Lately, moves have quieted down, so the trader has been content to pick up moderate moves with low to moderate volatility. Prices tend to act liveliest in the spring until late fall because of consumption demand and because this is when, due to perishability, storage supplies are at their most sensitive point.

TYPICAL PORK BELLY DAY MOVEMENTS

Pork belly prices are still volatile, even within the day, whether a trend is present or not. Prices could move a net of one cent from start to finish of the day, with gyrations producing a 2-cent range. Or they could have the same range with no net movement on the day.

Chart PB–1 shows one typical day with moderate trend and moderate to large volatility for pork bellies. There is a moderate move from start (37.50) to end (38.10), but with much up and down, rollercoaster activity in between, enough to sorely test the flexibility and discernibility of trend-following methods (a short moving average might get whipped badly, and a long one not get long or would get in very late).

Chart PB–2 presents a similar day (no trend, much volatility), but the trend collapses at the end, resulting in no net trend for the day. But the price volatility and attendant headaches are there for the assiduous trend follower.

C H A R T   PB–1

Typical Day Pork Belly Price Action

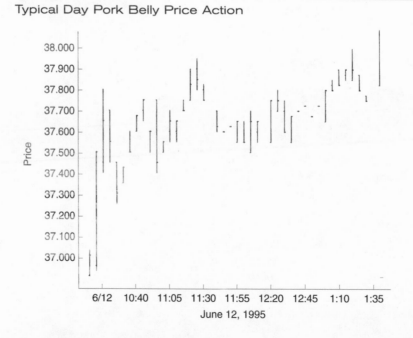

June 12, 1995

C H A R T   PB–2

Typical Day Pork Belly Price Action

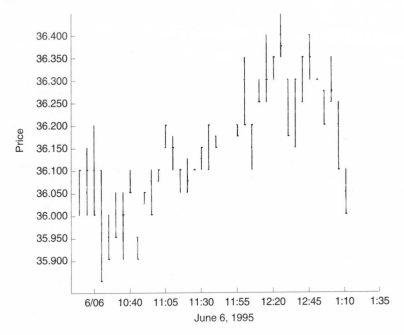

June 6, 1995

Chart PB–3 displays what could be either an opportunity or a nightmare for the trend follower, a day of large range and volatility, with two or more trends to go after.

Prices open around 38.30 on June 13, 1995, move up quickly to almost 39.00, and then plummet to the day's low around 37.60, a move of 140 points. They aren't satisfied with the move, so prices catapult back up to 39.00 by day's end, leaving the trader with either a double dose of trend profits or sharp losses, depending on how quickly and accurately he can react.

GOOD SETTINGS FOR PORK BELLIES

The mountain/valley trend method was tested on historical month of June 1995 price data of 1-, 5-, 15-, 30-, and 60-minute intervals. Because of the paucity of opportunities (basically only June 1 and 19 showed even moderate profit opportunities), few trades were made in any of the mode settings, but four decent returns were shown for two speculative and two conservative modes of trading.

Table 4.PB.C1 displays results for a very conservative mode requiring 16 successive higher closings of a (minimal) change of .05 cents on 1-minute data, or one (effective) tick of trading. Only two trades were recorded, both winners, for a total of $450 profit, or $225 per trade—a good result for patient traders.

Moving up a notch, a similar conservative trading stance is taken in Table 4.PB.C5 for 5-minute data. Here only nine successive higher closings of a minimal 1 tick (.05 cents) are needed to trigger a long position. Chart PB–4 depicts the

C H A R T   PB-3

Typical Day Pork Belly Price Action

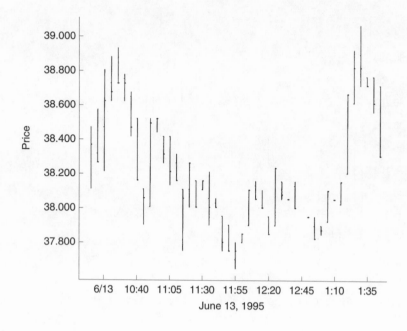

June 13, 1995

T A B L E   4.PB.C1

Trade Results: Mountain/Valley Day Trade Method*
Pork Bellies: Conservative Mode, 1-Minute Data

Date	Position	Time In	Price In	Time Out	Price Out	$P/L	$Max. Loss	Time	$Max. Gain	Time
6/1/95	Short	1046	36.45	1306	35.725	290	−180	1156	340	1242
6/5/95	Long	1021	35.7	1301	36.1	160	−160	1124	170	1232
$Total						450				
$Ave/Trade						225				

* Settings: Minimum successive high/low closing difference = 0.05 cents
No. successive high/low closings = 16

careful, patient trader's count of nine closing upticks from the day's bottom just before 11:00 A.M. EDT, starting at (A) and ending at (I) at 12:15 EDT (11:15 CDT), where he goes long and holds for a profit of .65 cents, or $260.

A more speculative stance is taken in Table 4.PB.S5, where only four higher closings of 3 ticks, or .15 cents, are needed to go long. This stance essentially goes more aggressively for more marginal profit opportunities, letting in a couple of losses (small) and a couple of break-even trades, while picking up more prof-

C H A R T   PB–4

Conservative Mode Trading: 5-Minute Prices for Pork Bellies

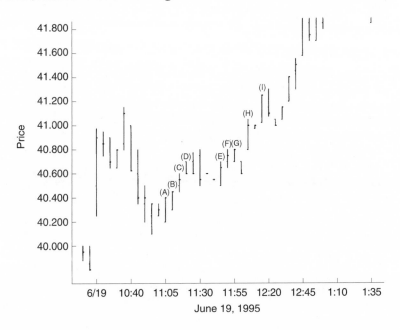

June 19, 1995

T A B L E   4.PB.C5

Trade Results: Mountain/Valley Day Trade Method*
Pork Bellies: Conservative Mode, 5-Minute Data

Date	Position	Time In	Price In	Time Out	Price Out	$P/L	$Max. Loss	Time	$Max. Gain	Time
6/1/95	Short	1054	36.1	1259	35.7	160	−280	1154	160	1259
6/5/95	Long	1226	35.9	1258	36	40	−90	1241	40	1231
6/19/95	Long	1115	41.25	1159	41.9	260	−100	1123	260	1145
$Total						460				
$Ave/Trade						153				

* Settings: Minimum successive high/low closing difference = 0.05 cents
           No. successive high/low closings = 9

its. The total profit is higher ($730), but profit per trade suffers ($91). Still, the result is a low-loss endeavor. Chart PB–5 depicts a long position trade for June 5, 1995. Prices bottom around 10:30 EDT, shoot up twice to points (A) and (B), and then sit a while before making the last two upsurges at (C) and (D), where the trader goes long at 11:08 EDT and holds on until the end of the day for a profit of .70 cents, or $280.

T A B L E   4.PB.S5

Trade Results: Mountain/Valley Day Trade Method*
Pork Bellies: Speculative Mode, 5-Minute Data

Date	Position	Time In	Price In	Time Out	Price Out	$P/L	$Max. Loss	Time	$Max. Gain	Time
6/1/95	Short	1044	36.55	1259	35.7	340	−100	1154	340	1259
6/5/95	Long	1008	35.3	1258	36	280	0	1008	280	1231
6/8/95	Long	1025	37.3	1259	36.95	−140	−160	1255	180	1040
6/9/95	Long	1053	36.8	1259	36.925	50	−80	1106	160	282
6/12/95	Long	1245	38.35	1259	38.35	0	−70	1250	0	1245
6/19/95	Long	1115	41.25	1159	41.9	260	−100	1123	260	1145
6/20/95	Short	1206	41	1258	41.15	−60	−300	1246	40	1211
6/21/95	Long	1243	41.9	1259	41.9	0	0	1243	80	1254
$Total						730				
$Ave/Trade						91				

* Settings: Minimum successive high/low closing difference = 0.15 cents
      No. successive high/low closings = 4

C H A R T   PB–5

Speculative Mode Trading: 5-Minute Prices for Pork Bellies

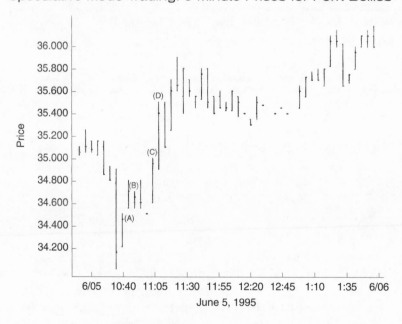

June 5, 1995

T A B L E   4.PB.S30

Trade Results: Mountain/Valley Day Trade Method*
Pork Bellies: Speculative Mode, 30-Minute Data

Date	Position	Time In	Price In	Time Out	Price Out	$P/L	$Max. Loss	Time	$Max. Gain	Time
6/1/95	Short	1107	36.4	1259	35.7	280	−190	1210	280	1259
6/5/95	Long	1033	35.6	1258	36	160	−50	1135	160	1258
6/9/95	Long	1139	36.9	1259	36.925	10	−30	1239	40	1210
6/12/95	Long	1242	38.25	1259	38.35	40	0	1242	40	1259
6/19/95	Long	1140	41.5	1159	41.9	160	0	1140	160	1159
6/21/95	Long	1242	41.85	1259	41.9	20	0	1242	20	1259
$Total						670				
$Ave/Trade						112				

* Settings: Minimum successive high/low closing difference = 0.30 cents
          No. successive high/low closings = 2

Finally, a speculative trading stance is taken on 30-minute data in Table 4.PB.S30. Ironically, the results are steady profits with no losses! The total profit is a respectable $670, and profit per trade comes in at $112. Apparently the interval size smooths out random price fluctuations enough to enable a small trend indication (a breakout) to count for capturing good profit moves.

Metals

COPPER

Copper is often tied in with silver, since they are both byproducts of the same mining process. Their price relationship is often inverse: in times of rising demand and use for silver, production of both is greater, thus causing copper prices to suffer if demand has not increased. Prices for copper keep pace with industrial production and general country wide economic health: if they are up, copper prices will also be up. Prices have vacillated considerably over the past 30 years, alternatively doubling to the 150 cents per pound area in times of tight supply or strong industrial demand and cascading down to the 50 cents area and below in times of general economic malaise.

TYPICAL DAY PRICE MOVEMENTS

Copper prices are volatile, whether in the day or over a long term. Traditional trend-following methods will do poorly, because even in good trended days the price volatility will kick the trader out of perfectly good positions and force him to reverse to even worse ones. The three prevalent types are: (1) well trended but heavy with volatility; (2) trended one way at first, then the other way, definitely bringing in possibilities for whipsaw trades; and (3) whipsaw prices with no trend made from start to finish.

Chart HG–1 depicts a nice trend from start to finish, as prices increase from 131.80 to 133.40 cents/lb. on February 2, 1995—an almost 2.00 point trend! But volatility accompanies every movement, and here price drops of almost 1.00 occur on three occasions—at 10:40 A.M., 12:40 P.M., and 1:10 P.M.—all of which are large enough to trip the average trend-following method and have the trader go short.

Chart HG–2 presents both an opportunity and a trap when prices plunge on February 3 to the 131.00 area from 133.00 and higher, only to bottom and build up to nearly 133.00 again. The results are either great two-trend trading possibilities or whipsaws galore.

The third chart, HG–3, portrays a trend follower's nightmare: no trend from start (130.60) to finish (130.40), but with plenty of worry and gnashing of teeth in between. Possibly four trades, all losers, would have been signaled by a slow moving-average approach.

GOOD SETTINGS FOR COPPER

The mountain/valley method was tested on February 1995 price data of 1-, 5-, 15-, 30-, and 60-minute intervals. Results for four particularly useful strategies for speculative and conservative accounts are detailed in Tables 4.HG.C1 through S60.

Table 4.HG.C1 has a moderate amount of trading for 1-minute prices, requiring 10 successive higher closes of 10 cents or larger to signal longs. The results

C H A R T   HG–1

Typical Daily Copper Price Action

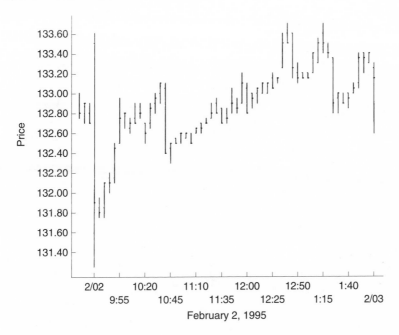

February 2, 1995

C H A R T   HG–2

Typical Daily Copper Price Action

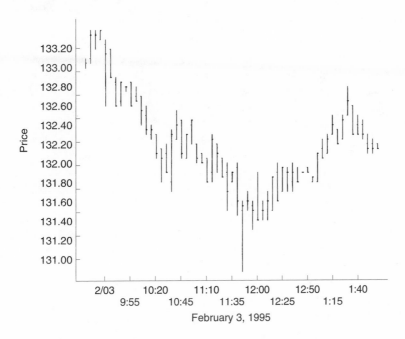

February 3, 1995

C H A R T HG–3

Typical Daily Copper Price Action

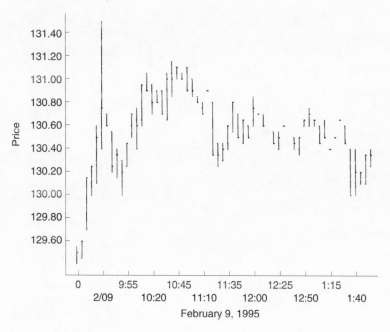

February 9, 1995

T A B L E 4.HG.C1

Trade Results: Mountain/Valley Day Trade Method*
Copper: Conservative Mode, 1-Minute Data

Date	Position	Time In	Price In	Time Out	Price Out	$P/L	$Max. Loss	Time	$Max. Gain	Time
2/1/95	Short	1113	133.75	1445	132.2	388	−88	1248	412	1434
2/2/95	Long	1233	133.5	1443	133.7	50	−175	1324	100	1436
2/3/95	Short	1128	131.5	1437	131.25	62	−325	1329	138	1141
2/6/95	Long	1302	130	1448	131.8	450	−100	1324	550	1437
2/7/95	Short	1222	129.75	1445	129.45	75	−138	1243	412	1312
2/8/95	Long	1304	129.75	1442	130.1	88	−100	1325	188	1400
2/10/95	Long	1334	134.75	1443	134.4	−88	−112	1437	112	1345
2/14/95	Short	1433	134.2	1437	134.4	−50	−75	1434	0	1433
2/17/95	Short	1430	133.15	1437	133.3	−38	−62	1434	12	1432
2/22/95	Short	1409	131.7	1457	131.45	62	−75	1416	125	1429
2/23/95	Long	1435	132.3	1444	132.35	12	0	1435	25	1436
2/27/95	Short	1358	132.9	1414	132.7	50	−25	1401	75	1406
2/28/95	Short	1230	130.6	1419	130.1	125	−150	1249	125	1402
$Total						1188				
$Ave/Trade						91				

* Settings: Minimum successive high/low closing difference = .10 cents
     No. successive high/low closings = 10

are quite good, with only three (small) losses, the largest only $88, out of 13 trades, and a net total of $1,188 before costs.

Another conservative mode is taken in Table 4.HG.C15, where four successive higher closings of at least .20 cents are needed to trigger a long. The results are a bit more risky, since the trader is following prices on a 15-minute basis, and he requires fewer successive closings than with the 1-minute closing conservative mode. Chart HG–4 details one such successful trade for February 6, 1995. The first successive higher closing takes place at (A) at 10:40 A.M. after bottoming out at 1.2875 at 10:25, and then progresses on through (D) at 1.3000 at 13:11 P.M., for a long and eventual profit of $375.

A speculative mode is used in Table 4.HG.S15, with very positive results. For the 15-minute intervals traded during February, a requirement of three successive higher closings of at least .30 cents for a long position produces $1212 total profit, a per trade profit of $121, and only two losses out of 10 trades. Chart HG–5 details one such long trade for February 8, 1995. After bottoming before noon at around 1.2800, prices smartly move up and become significantly, and successively higher at (A) through (C), where a long is signaled. The position is held until the close for a 2.00 cent profit.

Finally, speculative trading is shown in Table 4.HG.S60 for 60-minute intervals. Only one loss (small, at $50) is recorded in nine trades! The total profit is good at $1,575 and per trade profit stands at $175. Only one difference of .60 cents or more is needed to signal a long or short trade. One typical trade is shown in Chart HG–6 for February 28, 1995. Prices drop sharply after the second hour of trading and signal a short at point (A) at 1.3080. This position is held until the close for a profit of $175.

T A B L E   4.HG.C15

Trade Results: Mountain/Valley Day Trade Method*
Copper: Conservative Mode, 15-Minute Data

Date	Position	Time In	Price In	Time Out	Price Out	$P/L	$Max. Loss	Time	$Max. Gain	Time
2/1/95	Short	1324	133.3	1434	132.1	300	0	1324	300	1434
2/6/95	Long	1311	130	1434	131.5	375	−100	1326	375	1434
2/7/95	Short	1209	130	1434	129.5	125	−50	1254	362	1339
2/8/95	Long	1258	129.6	1434	130.1	125	−38	1342	200	1358
2/10/95	Long	1339	134.65	1434	134.65	0	0	1339	50	1354
2/17/95	Short	1346	133.5	1434	133.4	25	0	1346	100	1432
2/22/95	Short	1431	131.5	1434	131.6	−25	−25	1434	0	1431
2/27/95	Short	1334	133	1414	132.7	75	−75	1347	75	1414
2/28/95	Short	1403	130.1	1406	130.7	−150	−150	1406	0	1403
$Total						850				
$Ave/Trade						94				

* Settings: Minimum successive high/low closing difference = .20 cents
   No. successive high/low closings = 4

C H A R T   HG–4

Conservative Mode Trading: 15-Minute Prices for Copper

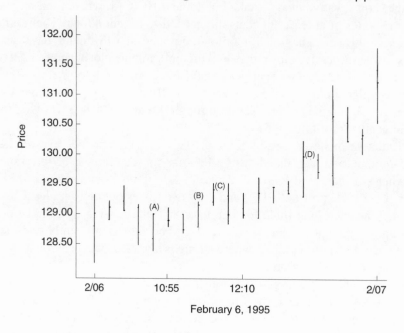

February 6, 1995

T A B L E   4.HG.S15

Trade Results: Mountain/Valley Day Trade Method*
Copper: Speculative Mode, 15-Minute Data

Date	Position	Time In	Price In	Time Out	Price Out	$P/L	$Max. Loss	Time	$Max. Gain	Time
2/1/95	Short	1124	133.65	1434	132.1	388	−62	1154	388	1434
2/2/95	Long	1240	133.5	1434	133.45	−12	−150	1325	0	1240
2/6/95	Long	1341	130.5	1434	131.5	250	−100	1356	250	1434
2/7/95	Short	1209	130	1434	129.5	125	−50	1254	362	1339
2/8/95	Long	1242	129.3	1434	130.1	200	0	1242	275	1358
2/10/95	Long	1339	134.65	1434	134.65	0	0	1339	50	1354
2/17/95	Short	1346	133.5	1434	133.4	25	0	1346	100	1432
2/22/95	Short	1417	131.95	1434	131.6	88	0	1417	112	1431
2/27/95	Short	1334	133	1414	132.7	75	−75	1347	75	1414
2/28/95	Short	1218	131	1406	130.7	75	−50	1330	225	1403
$Total						1212				
$Ave/Trade						121				

* Settings: Minimum successive high/low closing difference = .30 cents
        No. successive high/low closings = 3

C H A R T   HG–5

Speculative Mode Trading: 15-Minute Prices for Copper

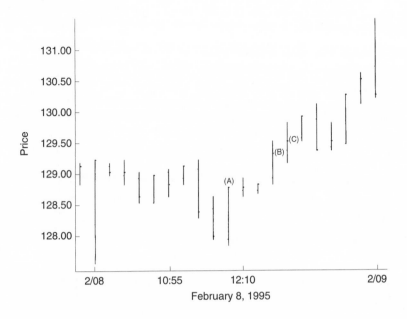

February 8, 1995

T A B L E   4.HG.S60

Trade Results: Mountain/Valley Day Trade Method*
Copper: Speculative Mode, 60-Minute Data

Date	Position	Time In	Price In	Time Out	Price Out	$P/L	$Max. Loss	Time	$Max. Gain	Time
2/1/95	Short	1125	133.7	1434	132.1	400	0	1125	400	1434
2/6/95	Long	1226	129.45	1434	131.5	512	0	1226	512	1434
2/7/95	Short	1227	129.7	1434	129.5	50	0	1227	175	1327
2/8/95	Long	1325	129.35	1434	130.1	188	0	1325	262	1425
2/10/95	Long	1125	134.1	1434	134.65	138	−25	1225	138	1434
2/17/95	Short	1327	133.75	1434	133.4	88	0	1327	138	1429
2/22/95	Short	1430	131.4	1434	131.6	−50	−50	1434	0	1430
2/27/95	Short	1334	133	1414	132.7	75	0	1334	75	1414
2/28/95	Short	1231	130.8	1419	130.1	175	−100	1330	175	1419
$Total						1575				
$Ave/Trade						175				

* Settings: Minimum successive high/low closing difference = .60 cents
         No. successive high/low closings = 1

C H A R T   HG–6

Speculative Mode Trading: 60-Minute Prices for Copper

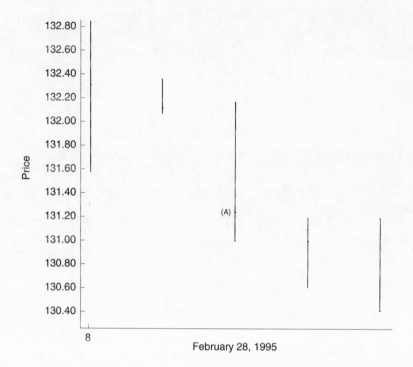

February 28, 1995

GOLD

The yellow metal has long held much of the world in the power of its mystique. Wherever there is choas, war, or natural turbulence, the rich and poor, commerce and government, and the young and old have all fled to the safety of gold. This is especially true in undeveloped and underdeveloped regions of the world and in societies that are not democratic.

Inflation and times of high interest rates, the twin scourges of money retaining its value, have sent gold soaring, as currency effectively became devalued. This happened in 1979–80, when inflation reared its ugly head, as gold skyrocketed to $800 per ounce from less than $100 and ranged wildly in the high interest rate years of 1980–81. Savvy traders know gold leads the way in bad times and can make big trends.

TYPICAL DAY PRICE MOVEMENTS

However, gold has been relatively dormant for more than 10 years, to the great consternation of many a gold bug waiting for the next big move up. But it hasn't come. World political and economic conditions have improved and inflation is very low, so there is no reason for gold to have great overnight swings and trends.

The long-term doldrums have carried over to day price movements. One does not see 15 and 20 dollar moves frequently, if at all. A move of six dollars is a big day. Thus, the trader has to contend with smaller trends during the day, though the volatility and execution slippage are considerably reduced.

Chart GC–1 shows a very typical day of trading, with a small price drift from opening to close of less than 1.0 dollars. Price volatility, however, from local peak to valley is bigger than the day's trend, which gives the trend trader conniptions, particularly moving average methodologists, who would get whipsawed visciously in this type of day.

Almost as bad, and certainly as frustrating, to the trend trader who thinks he has a tiger trend by the tail, Chart GC–2 demonstrates an initially sharply moving uptrend on January 12, from the open to 9:30 A.M. This trend is titillating enough to get the trader long, but it then goes dormant the rest of the day, leaving him with no gain and possibly even a loss.

Once in a while, however, the trader is treated to a moderately profitable trend, as found in Chart GC–3. A steady downbeat gives him ample opportunity to jump aboard the downtrend (refer to the tables to see how the conservative and speculative modes fared). A $2 reaction late in the day tests the resolve and analytics of the trader, but if he holds on he could realize about $200 ($2 per ounce) in profit.

BETTER SETTINGS FOR GOLD

The mountain/valley method was tested on January 1995 data intervals of 1, 5, 15, 30, and 60 minutes. Although most tests showed consistent profits, they were small on average, reflecting the small ranges and trend move opportunities to

C H A R T   GC–1

Typical Day Gold Price Action

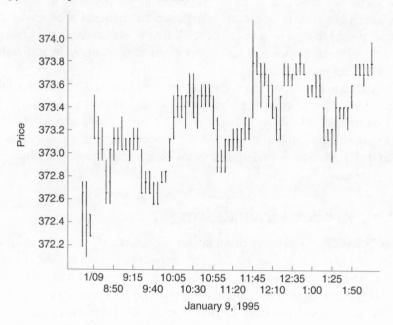

January 9, 1995

C H A R T   GC–2

Typical Day Gold Price Action

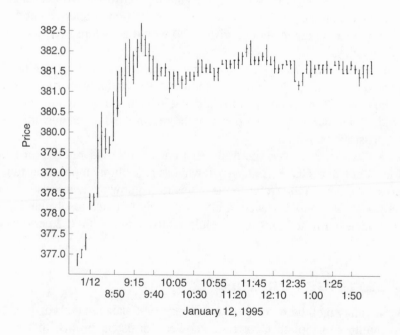

January 12, 1995

C H A R T   GC–3

Typical Day Gold Price Action

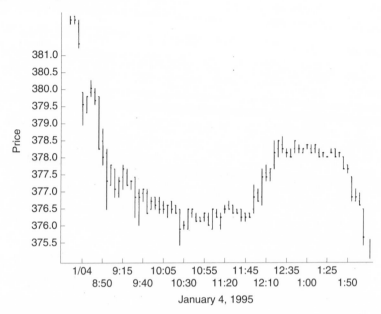

January 4, 1995

which we previously alluded. A fair question has to be the viability of trading with such small trend opportunities. Fortunately, the execution slippage should be small, on the order of 1 tick at most each way, so if the commissions were small, the trader could still make meaningful profits on the speculative and conservative modes presented here.

Table 4.GC.C1 lists the trade on 1-minute data for a conservative mode trading operation (using a requirement of four successive higher closings of at least a half dollar). Losses are very small and only two occur, while profits are much more numerous and larger, giving the trader a total profit of $650 in a lean month and an average profit of $81 per trade.

A more aggressive stance is taken by the trader in Table 4.GC.S5, where only one successive higher closing of at least $1.20 is needed, for 5-minute data. A generous number of trades (15) is generated in searching for quick, powerful trends, and only four losses are recorded. In this mode the trader is ready for the golden 1980 year to return! A total of $980 net profit results, with a per trade profit of $65. Chart GC–4 depicts one successful trade where the trader waited for essentially the first major breakout of $1.2 or more, which happened at (A) at 9:29 A.M., for a short at $384.30 and a profit of $290 by day's end.

Table 4.GC.C5 goes to the other extreme, being very careful about declaring and entering a trend, by requiring seven successive higher closings of the minimally traded tick change of $0.10, for 5-minute data. Again, the losses are few and small (thanks to its conservative analytics), but much of the already small trend is

T A B L E   4.GC.C1

Trade Results: Mountain/Valley Day Trade Method*
Gold(Comex): Conservative Mode, 1-Minute Data

Date	Position	Time In	Price In	Time Out	Price Out	$P/L	$Max. Loss	Time	$Max. Gain	Time
1/4/95	Short	852	377.5	1430	375.3	220	−90	1225	220	1429
1/6/95	Short	1352	374.3	1429	372.2	210	−30	1353	220	1424
1/12/95	Long	856	381	1431	381.4	40	−40	900	150	928
1/17/95	Long	931	380.2	1433	380.6	40	−60	933	120	951
1/19/95	Long	1159	383.7	1431	383.6	−10	−50	1236	40	1226
1/23/95	Short	945	383.3	1434	381.4	190	−10	1227	330	1350
1/27/95	Short	1123	378	1427	377.6	40	−50	1136	370	1357
1/27/95	Long	1427	377.6	1433	376.8	−80	−110	1430	0	1427
$Total						650				
$Ave/Trade						81				

* Settings: Minimum successive high/low closing difference = 0.5 dollars
        No. successive high/low closings = 4

T A B L E   4.GC.S5

Trade Results: Mountain/Valley Day Trade Method*
Gold(Comex): Speculative Mode, 5-Minute Data

Date	Position	Time In	Price In	Time Out	Price Out	$P/L	$Max. Loss	Time	$Max. Gain	Time
1/3/95	Short	1034	381.4	1429	380.8	60	−40	1155	60	1429
1/4/95	Short	854	377.5	1209	377.6	−10	−10	859	140	1024
1/4/95	Long	1209	377.6	1411	375.6	−200	−200	1411	70	1258
1/4/95	Short	1411	375.6	1429	375.3	30	−20	1416	30	1429
1/6/95	Short	1351	375.2	1426	372.3	290	0	1351	290	1411
1/12/95	Long	834	379.5	1429	381.5	200	0	834	300	929
1/17/95	Long	919	379.6	1429	380.6	100	−10	924	130	954
1/18/95	Short	1004	383.3	1429	382.9	40	−40	1158	50	1344
1/19/95	Short	923	382.1	1147	383.5	−140	−140	1147	10	1013
1/19/95	Long	1147	383.5	1428	383.7	20	−30	1150	50	1227
1/20/95	Long	1004	384.8	1429	385.4	60	−90	1119	60	1429
1/23/95	Short	929	384.3	1428	381.4	290	−10	933	420	1359
1/27/95	Short	949	378.5	1418	376.4	210	−70	1044	340	1353
1/27/95	Long	1418	376.4	1428	377.3	90	0	1418	90	1428
1/31/95	Short	939	375.2	1205	375.8	−60	−60	1157	70	949
$Total						980				
$Ave/Trade						65				

* Settings: Minimum successive high/low closing difference = 1.2 dollars
        No. successive high/low closings = 1

CHART   GC–4

Speculative Mode Trading: 5-Minute Prices for Gold

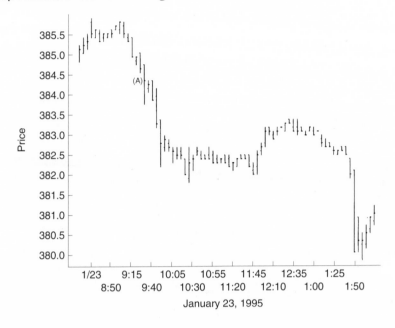

January 23, 1995

TABLE   4.GC.C5

Trade Results: Mountain/Valley Day Trade Method*
Gold(Comex): Conservative Mode, 5-Minute Data

Date	Position	Time In	Price In	Time Out	Price Out	$P/L	$Max. Loss	Time	$Max. Gain	Time
1/3/95	Short	1024	381.8	1429	380.8	100	0	1024	100	1429
1/4/95	Short	1024	376.1	1429	375.3	80	−220	1258	80	1429
1/5/95	Long	1311	376.6	1429	376.7	10	−40	1331	10	1400
1/6/95	Short	1341	375.4	1426	372.3	310	0	1341	310	1411
1/9/95	Long	1144	374	1429	373	0	−90	1315	0	1144
1/12/95	Long	924	382	1429	381.5	−50	−100	1004	50	929
1/17/95	Long	938	380	1429	380.6	60	0	938	90	954
1/19/95	Short	1013	382	1127	383.2	−120	−120	1127	10	1013
1/19/95	Long	1127	383.2	1428	383.7	50	−30	1137	80	1227
1/20/95	Long	1224	384.9	1429	385.4	50	−50	1254	50	1429
1/23/95	Short	944	383.8	1428	381.4	240	0	944	370	1359
1/27/95	Short	1218	377.8	1428	377.3	50	0	1218	270	1353
1/30/95	Long	1056	377.5	1429	376.4	−110	−140	1142	0	1056
$Total						670				
$Ave/Trade						52				

* Settings: Minimum successive high/low closing difference = 0.1 dollars
    No. successive high/low closings = 7

C H A R T   GC–5

Conservative Mode Trading: 5-Minute Prices for Gold

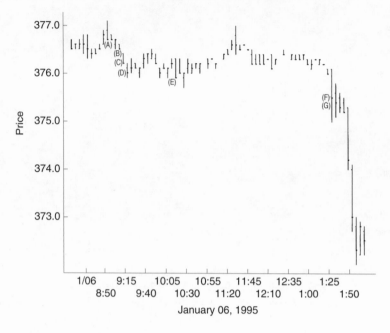

January 06, 1995

T A B L E   4.GC.S30

Trade Results: Mountain/Valley Day Trade Method*
Gold(Comex): Speculative Mode, 30-Minute Data

Date	Position	Time In	Price In	Time Out	Price Out	$P/L	$Max. Loss	Time	$Max. Gain	Time
1/3/95	Short	1048	381.4	1429	380.8	60	−30	1149	60	1429
1/4/95	Short	949	376.9	1429	375.3	160	−130	1219	160	1429
1/6/95	Short	1402	372.7	1429	372.2	50	0	1402	50	1429
1/12/95	Long	919	381.8	1429	381.5	−30	−60	1019	0	919
1/17/95	Long	949	380.4	1429	380.6	20	−40	1049	40	1019
1/20/95	Long	1422	385.5	1429	385.4	−10	−10	1429	0	1422
1/23/95	Short	949	382.5	1428	381.4	110	−70	1219	140	1349
1/27/95	Short	950	378.6	1429	377.3	130	−30	1050	310	1352
$Total						490				
$Ave/Trade						61				

* Settings: Minimum successive high/low closing difference = 1.6 dollars
    No. successive high/low closings = 1

eaten up, so the profit per trade is small. He also hopes for big moves to return! A nice trade is shown in Chart GC–5. Prices pretty much go nowhere during the day, but then they sneakily make five new low closings until a critical point around 1:30 P.M., when big-time selling comes in and prices cave in. The final two suc-

CHART   GC–6

Speculative Mode Trading: 30-Minute Prices for Gold

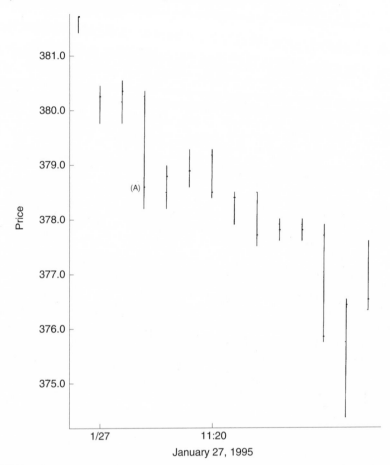

January 27, 1995

cessive lower closings are made at (F) and (G), at which point the short is taken at 13:41 P.M. at 375.4 and held for a $310 profit.

Finally, Table 4.GC.S30 gives us a taste of speculative trading (one successive higher closing of $1.60 or more to trigger a long position) on a 30-minute price basis. The trader is quick to go for any trend-smelling move, but he needs a stiff move to justify the risk. The results are still quite good, with about $500 total profits, $61 average profit per trade, and small and few losses. Chart GC–6 shows a short taken on January 27 right off the opening gong, at 9:50 A.M. at (A), and then held until the close for a $130 profit.

SILVER

Wouldn't it be nice to have silver active and spewing huge price moves the way it did in 1979–80, the time of big bull and bear markets, when prices rode from $5 to over $50 per ounce and then plummeted back down to where they started? Unfortunately, silver has stayed near the bottom ever since that time. Once in a while, prices perk up, as rumors of major strife or choas of some sort make the rounds. But even then, prices move in a relatively tight range, from $5 to $6 or so. Trend methods used on daily-basis prices more often than not get the trader whipsawed with overbought and oversold situations. It seems that only contrary (oppositely directed) methods could do well in this environment.

There are enough moves within the day, however, that trend-following methods can make money.

TYPICAL SILVER DAY PRICE MOVEMENTS

There are occasionally big moves—moves of 15 cents or more—within the day (see results for April 18,19, and 26 in the tables to follow), but the days that predominate are the relatively tight range ones (6–8 cents, typically). Chart SV–1 shows a typical tight range day. Prices actually vacillate quite wildly on the opening two bars (5-minute intervals), making more than the rest of the day's range (I suspect there are errors in the high and low price recordings shown). Prices in the main part of the day effectively range from 538–545, with no sharp trends. The usual trend methods, such as breakouts or moving averages, could quickly get

C H A R T   SV–1

Typical Daily Silver Price Action

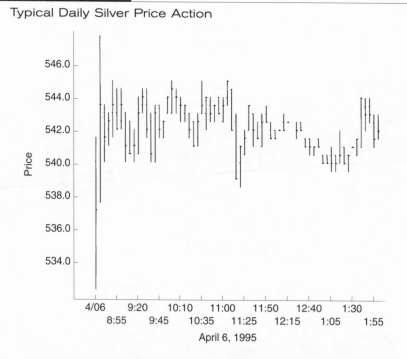

April 6, 1995

whipsawed, going long on very small, temporary price bulges and short on sudden, small drops that come back quickly (see around 11:25 A.M. on the chart).

But there is also a "meat and potatoes" price pattern that occurs fairly frequently, with prices moving in one direction generally for the day and adding up to 12 cents or more, an example of which is shown in Chart SV–2. Prices start off around 572, then start undulating downwards in 4–6 cent movements, followed by price reactions upwards of one-half the down move, or more. By midday prices have settled in a 4 cent trading range, until the final (and strongest) selling wave brings prices to 556 or so. The pattern is: drop 10 cents, go sideways for a good portion of the day, then drop another 10 cents, for a net of 14–16 cents, after upwards retracements, for the day. The trader would aim to make 6–8 cents on this typical day. Most of the strategies that are described below were able to capitalize on these opportunities.

GOOD SETTINGS FOR SILVER

The mountain/valley trend method was tested on historical data for April 1995 on 1-, 5-, 15-, 30-, and 60-minute intervals. All showed varying degrees of real profitability for different trading styles.

Table 4.SV.C1 chronicles the positions taken for a more conservative trader on 1-minute price data. The minimum successive higher /lower closing difference was only 1 tick (0.5 cents) in silver, but 11 successively higher closing were needed to go long. Despite this stringent requirement, 17 trades, almost 1 per day, were

C H A R T   SV–2

Typical Daily Silver Price Action

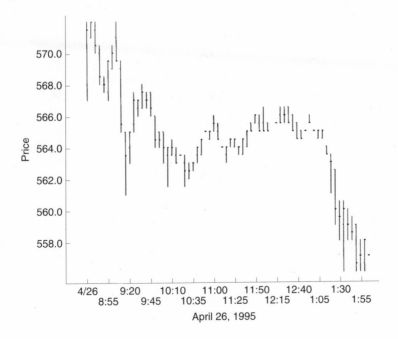

April 26, 1995

T A B L E   4.SV.C1

Trade Results: Mountain/Valley Day Trade Method*
Silver(Comex): Conservative Mode, 1-Minute Data

Date	Position	Time In	Price In	Time Out	Price Out	$P/L	$Max. Loss	Time	$Max. Gain	Time
4/4/95	Long	1140	531	1356	530	−50	−250	1333	25	1141
4/5/95	Long	1250	536.5	1356	540.5	200	0	1250	200	1344
4/7/95	Long	1301	544.5	1357	539	−275	−275	1354	75	1305
4/10/95	Short	1104	523	1359	525.5	−125	−125	1353	100	1112
4/11/95	Long	942	533.5	1356	534.5	50	−150	1004	250	1203
4/13/95	Long	1354	536	1356	538	100	0	1354	125	1355
4/17/95	Long	1307	565	1356	572.5	375	0	1307	550	1350
4/18/95	Long	1232	571	1402	586.5	775	−50	1244	850	1355
4/19/95	Short	1352	587.5	1403	579.5	400	−25	1353	475	1356
4/20/95	Long	917	578	1124	580	100	−150	921	450	1041
4/20/95	Short	1124	580	1357	569	550	0	1124	575	1353
4/21/95	Long	929	572	1400	568	−200	−325	1106	100	1212
4/24/95	Short	927	569	1359	566.5	125	−225	956	225	1352
4/25/95	Long	1116	572	1355	571.5	−25	−100	1316	125	1120
4/26/95	Short	911	564.5	1404	557	375	−150	935	400	1347
4/27/95	Long	1339	569	1357	572	150	−25	1340	200	1347
4/28/95	Short	1355	570	1356	575	−250	−250	1356	0	1355
$Total						2275				
$Ave/Trade						134				

* Settings: Minimum successive high/low closing difference = 0.5 cents
No. successive high/low closings = 11

kicked off. The worst loss was $275, and many gains were considerably larger. This combination led to a profit total of $2,275, before costs, and an average profit per trade of $134, acceptable results if execution costs (slippage) are kept low. A good success rate of nearly 65 percent (11 successful trades out of 17 total trades) occurred.

The action for April 20 is shown in Chart SV–3. A long is entered at 9:17 A.M. after eleven successive higher closings on a 1-minute basis occurs at point 11, at $5.80 per ounce. Prices continue to undulate upwards until reaching a high at 587 or so, whereupon prices steadily drop and reliably start a downtrend. We pick up the short signal at point 11 on the downtrend, at $5.80 at 11:24 A.M. The trader takes in a profit of 2 cents and 11 cents on the long and short positions, respectively.

Table 4.SV.S5 details a speculative mode of trading silver on a 5-minute basis. Only two successive higher closings of at least 4 cents are needed to trigger a long position. The results are also quite favorable, with ten trades and $1,075 in profit to show for it. The success rate is also good, coming in at 60 percent (6 for 10), and losses are small, at $200 or less. Chart SV–4 shows a long being taken near the close at

C H A R T   SV–3

Conservative Mode Trading: 1-Minute Prices for Silver

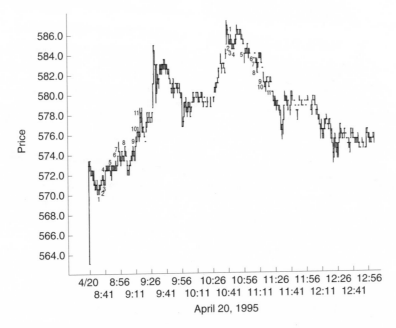

April 20, 1995

Chart SV–3, continued

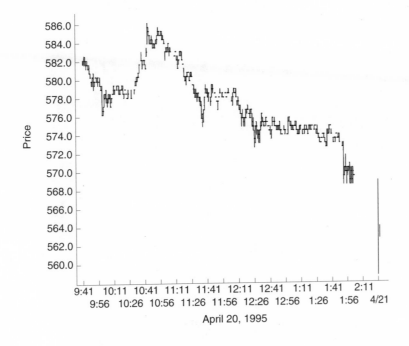

April 20, 1995

T A B L E   4.SV.S5

Trade Results: Mountain/Valley Day Trade Method*
Silver(Comex): Speculative Mode, 5-Minute Data

Date	Position	Time In	Price In	Time Out	Price Out	$P/L	$Max. Loss	Time	$Max. Gain	Time
4/5/95	Long	1309	539.5	1354	540	25	−100	1314	50	1344
4/11/95	Long	1129	537	1354	533.5	−175	−225	1319	50	1204
4/17/95	Long	1314	569	1354	573.5	225	0	1314	300	1349
4/18/95	Long	1234	572	1354	585	650	−100	1244	650	1354
4/19/95	Short	1115	588	1354	585	150	−325	1220	150	1354
4/20/95	Long	929	581	1134	577	−200	−200	1134	275	1054
4/20/95	Short	1134	577	1354	569.5	375	−125	1143	375	1349
4/21/95	Long	924	570	1354	569	−50	−175	1102	125	1332
4/25/95	Long	1119	573.5	1354	572	−75	−175	1319	0	1119
4/26/95	Short	914	561	1354	558	150	−300	929	175	1351
$Total						1075				
$Ave/Trade						108				

* Settings: Minimum successive high/low closing difference = 4.0 cents
No. successive high/low closings = 2

C H A R T   SV–4

Speculative Mode Trading: 5-Minute Prices for Silver

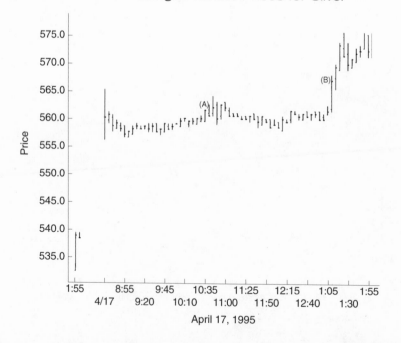

April 17, 1995

569 at point (B), after a second higher closing has occurred (the first at (A) was four cents above the bottom closing for the day around $5.57 at about 9:00 A.M.).

Table 4.SV.C15 shows a conservative strategy for 15-minute price basis trading. The plan requires six successive higher closings of at least 1 cent each to go long. Because it is very stringent, it generates only three trades, all of them winners, that average $183 each. Chart SV–5 shows a short being taken at 12:55 P.M. at point (F) on April 28, 1995, after prices have made a methodical downside drumbeat.

T A B L E   4.SV.C15

Trade Results: Mountain/Valley Day Trade Method*
Silver(Comex): Conservative Mode, 15-Minute Data

Date	Position	Time In	Price In	Time Out	Price Out	$P/L	$Max. Loss	Time	$Max. Gain	Time
4/20/95	Short	1324	573.5	1354	569.5	200	0	1324	200	1354
4/26/95	Short	1341	559	1354	558	50	0	1341	50	1354
4/28/95	Short	1255	577	1354	571	300	−125	1305	300	1354
$Total						550				
$Ave/Trade						183				

* Settings: Minimum successive high/low closing difference = 1.0 cents
No. successive high/low closings = 6

C H A R T   SV–5

Conservative Mode Trading: 15-Minute Prices for Silver

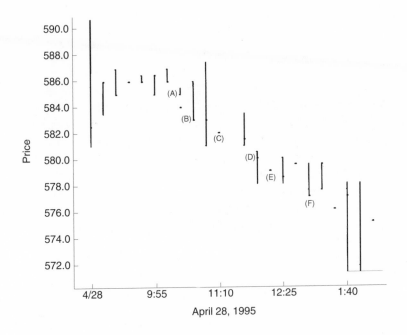

April 28, 1995

T A B L E   4.SV.S30

Trade Results: Mountain/Valley Day Trade Method*
Silver(Comex): Speculative Mode, 30-Minute Data

Date	Position	Time In	Price In	Time Out	Price Out	$P/L	$Max. Loss	Time	$Max. Gain	Time
4/4/95	Short	1024	526.5	1154	530.5	−200	−200	1154	0	1024
4/4/95	Long	1154	530.5	1354	529.5	−50	−100	1324	0	1154
4/5/95	Long	1154	534.5	1354	540	275	−25	1222	275	1354
4/6/95	Short	1256	540.5	1354	541.5	−50	−50	1354	0	1256
4/7/95	Long	1125	542.5	1354	539	−175	−175	1354	25	1300
4/10/95	Short	1059	526	1354	525	50	0	1059	150	1159
4/11/95	Long	1224	534.5	1354	533.5	−50	−100	1323	0	1224
4/13/95	Short	1125	529	1354	536	−350	−350	1354	50	1155
4/17/95	Long	1044	564	1354	573.5	475	−225	1216	475	1347
4/18/95	Long	1224	567.5	1354	585	875	0	1224	875	1354
4/19/95	Short	1123	590.5	1354	585	275	−150	1225	275	1354
4/20/95	Long	954	580.5	1153	578.5	−100	−100	1153	300	1054
4/20/95	Short	1153	578.5	1354	569.5	450	0	1153	450	1354
4/21/95	Long	1347	571.5	1354	569	−125	−125	1354	0	1347
4/24/95	Short	1225	569.5	1354	566	175	0	1225	175	1354
4/25/95	Long	1124	571.5	1354	572	25	−25	1258	50	1330
4/26/95	Short	954	564.5	1354	558	325	−75	1225	325	1354
4/27/95	Long	1012	567	1354	573	300	−200	1220	300	1354
4/28/95	Short	1159	579	1354	571	400	0	1159	400	1354
$Total						2525				
$Ave/Trade						133				

* Settings: Minimum successive high/low closing difference = 1.5 cents
    No. successive high/low closings = 2

Last, but certainly not least, a speculative strategy is undertaken in Table 4.SV.S30, on 30-minute prices. The position requires only two successive lower closings of at least 1 1/2 cent to go short. The total profit, $2,525, is a strong number, as is the $133 average profit per trade. The worst loss is $350, while four gains are larger than that. The success rate is almost 60 percent, and trades occur at the rate of almost one per day. Chart SV–6 details the long trade for April 18, 1995. Prices move sideways and down after the open, then bottom at about 563 just before 11:00 A.M. Two successive significantly higher closings occur at (A) and (B), at which point the trader is long and off to the races. He enters at 567.50 and rides a nice upsurge to 585 at the end of the day, for a profit of $875 before costs.

C H A R T   SV–6

Speculative Mode Trading: 30-Minute Prices for Silver

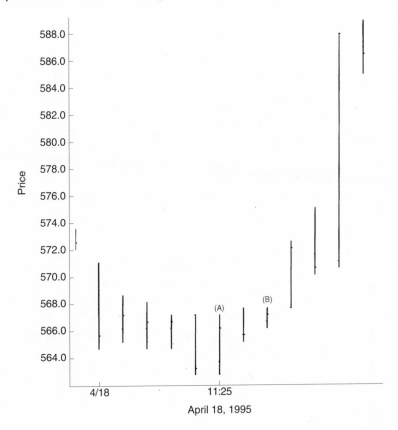

April 18, 1995

Stock Indices

S&P FUTURES

Perhaps the most watched, whether for long-term trend developments or for day-trading opportunities, S&P futures best symbolize the holy grail search for steady, large, predictable profits for commodity traders. Big moves of 100 points or more occur quite frequently, and price volatility gives traders all sorts of different trading mode opportunities. There is no monopoly on S&P price predictability, as neither private nor government economists seem to be able to predict S&P prices with any great degree of certainty, leaving a level playing field for all traders to try their best. Of all futures, S&P is the most watched by day traders, some of whom have concentrated and have only one system and one (this) future in their portfolio.

TYPICAL DAY S&P PRICE MOVEMENTS

Contrary to popular belief, S&P does not make big moves (8–15 full points) regularly (this kind of move once or twice a month is a big deal). Instead, it makes two kinds of moves most frequently: choppy, sideways moves with good-sized price volatility; and moderate moves of 2–4 full points, often with two trends or more.

Chart SP–1 depicts a very typical, choppy market. Prices move very quickly in the first half hour, essentially defining the day's range, 534.50 to 537.50, with

C H A R T   SP–1

Typical Day Price Action for S&P

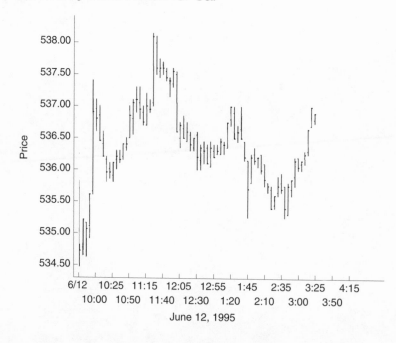

June 12, 1995

most price action occurring between 535.50 and 537.50, a 2-point range. Notice trend-like moves to the day's peak (an uptrend), downward movement to near the bottom (a downtrend), and then a recovery to just above the middle of the day's preponderant activity. A traditional trend method would have been mercilessly whipsawed in this back-and-forth price activity.

Just as common, and giving the trend trader some real profit opportunity, Chart SP–2 shows us again lots of price volatility, but with two distinct trend possibilities. Prices wave downwards from 533.50 to 530, a 3 1/2 point downtrend, then, at mid session, reverse and repeat the same trail, but upwards, for a 3 point uptrend. If the trader can prevent being fooled by the reactions in each trend, he has plenty of opportunity: two trends of 3 points each!

Chart SP–5 presents a bigger, one trend-only situation, the kind most trend followers would prefer. On June 26, 1995, prices move steadily downwards, with only one interruption, or reaction, to the downtrend. However, these opportunities usually only occur a few times a month.

GOOD SETTINGS FOR S&P

The mountain/valley trend method was historically tested on June 1995 price data, on 1-, 5-, 15-, 30-, and 60-minute price intervals. Many parameter combinations were successful, and the two better conservative and two very good speculative modes were chosen and are presented in Tables 4.SP.S1 through S30.

The first one, a speculative mode for 1-minute data, is detailed in Table 4.SP.S1. It requires only two successive higher closes of 80 cents or more to go

C H A R T   SP–2

Typical Day Price Action for S&P

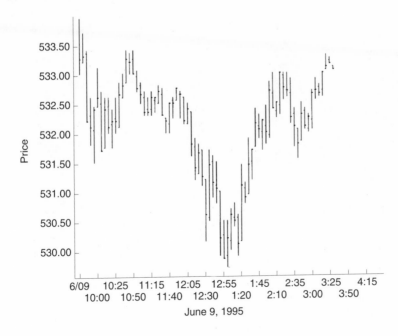

June 9, 1995

T A B L E   4.SP.S1

Trade Results: Mountain/Valley Day Trade Method*
S&P: Speculative Mode, 1-Minute Data

Date	Position	Time In	Price In	Time Out	Price Out	$P/L	$Max. Loss	Time	$Max. Gain	Time
6/1/95	Long	844	539.05	904	537	−1025	−1025	904	325	847
6/1/95	Short	904	537	928	537.4	−200	−200	928	925	909
6/1/95	Long	928	537.4	951	534.9	−1250	−1250	951	150	931
6/1/95	Short	951	534.9	1024	537	−1050	−1050	1024	0	951
6/1/95	Long	1024	537	1356	537.8	400	−650	1049	1450	1347
6/1/95	Short	1356	537.8	1504	538.5	−350	−350	1504	700	1405
6/1/95	Long	1504	538.5	1516	538.4	−50	−175	1512	0	1504
6/2/95	Short	834	534.2	849	536	−900	−900	849	200	840
6/2/95	Long	849	536	942	539.9	1950	−250	859	3150	931
6/2/95	Short	942	539.9	1420	537.4	1250	0	942	2200	1411
6/2/95	Long	1420	537.4	1516	536.5	−450	−475	1428	200	1502
6/5/95	Long	942	539.45	1353	540.9	725	−700	1003	1825	1342
6/5/95	Short	1353	540.9	1515	541.2	−150	−225	1416	625	1356
6/6/95	Long	921	542.2	1056	540.35	−950	−950	1056	50	1000
6/6/95	Short	1056	540.3	1205	541.35	−525	−525	1205	150	1107
6/7/95	Short	1313	537.2	1520	537.85	−325	−400	1437	550	1341
6/8/95	Short	945	536.9	1525	536.2	350	−750	1305	525	1500
6/9/95	Short	931	533	1336	532.3	350	−225	936	1650	1256
6/9/95	Long	1336	532.3	1527	533.05	375	−350	1438	425	1525
6/12/95	Long	952	536	1245	536.1	50	−100	1013	1050	1125
6/12/95	Short	1245	536.1	1523	536.9	−400	−450	1320	375	1441
6/13/95	Long	1112	540.2	1523	540.7	250	−475	1201	650	1335
6/14/95	Long	1159	541.1	1522	540.5	−300	−400	1438	525	1355
6/15/95	Long	901	542.2	1407	541.8	−200	−400	926	1025	1329
6/15/95	Short	1407	541.8	1431	542.2	−200	−200	1431	600	1408
6/15/95	Long	1431	542.2	1516	542.7	250	−225	1441	350	1448
6/16/95	Long	950	544.3	1519	544	−150	−700	1104	225	1357
6/19/95	Long	918	547.35	1523	549.75	1200	−100	931	1450	1442
6/20/95	Short	1259	547.9	1427	549.7	−900	−900	1427	100	1305
6/20/95	Long	1427	549.7	1519	549.2	−250	−350	1444	75	1428
6/22/95	Long	914	552.3	1522	555.35	1525	0	914	1800	1359
6/23/95	Short	1410	553	1515	554.9	−950	−950	1515	250	1413
6/23/95	Long	1515	554.9	1522	555	50	0	1012	75	1516
6/26/95	Short	1012	552.9	1522	548.25	2325	0	1012	2475	1500
6/27/95	Long	904	550.5	1337	549.6	−450	−500	925	600	1007
6/27/95	Short	1337	549.6	1520	547.1	1250	−175	1345	1550	1457
6/28/95	Short	915	545.6	1003	547.5	−950	−950	1003	275	938
6/28/95	Long	1003	547.5	1129	549.3	900	−100	1004	1925	1111
6/28/95	Short	1129	549.3	1432	547.6	850	−175	1329	1750	1425
6/28/95	Long	1432	547.6	1519	549.5	900	0	1432	1100	1502
6/29/95	Short	903	548.5	1244	546.8	850	0	903	1975	1154
6/29/95	Long	1244	546.8	1520	548.4	800	−225	1301	950	1432
6/30/95	Long	1026	550.65	1351	549.2	−725	−725	1351	275	1027
6/30/95	Short	1351	549.2	1518	547.25	975	−300	1417	1200	1449
$Total						4925				
$Ave/Trade						112				

* Settings: Minimum successive high/low closing difference = .80 dollars
              No. successive high/low closings = 2

CHART SP—3

Speculative Mode Trading: 1-Minute Day Prices for S&P

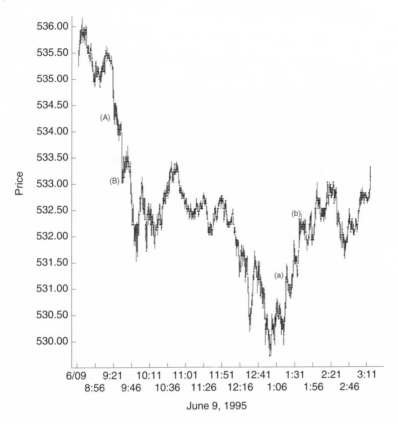

June 9, 1995

long. Hang on to your hats! It traded about 50 times, had nearly a 50 percent success rate, and produced a total profit of just under $5,000, with a $112 per trade profit. It often traded twice a day, and on many occasions traded three or more times a day. On the first day, June 1, 1995, it traded seven times! Chart SP–3 shows 1-minute action for June 9, 1995. Prices started cascading down and fell the required 80 cents by point (A) and then again at (B) at 9:31, to go short at 533. The short is covered at 1:36 at 532.30 at point (b), the second closing from the bottom of 80 cents or more higher, at which point a long is taken and held until the close. Two profits, $350 on the short position and $375 on the long position are accrued by day's end.

Table 4.SP.C1 produces almost the same number of trades and winners, a similar profit total of $5,600, and a similar profit per trade average of $122 before costs. But the attitude is different—it requires many (seven) successive higher closings of at least 15 cents to go long. So, one can trade both ways and still show good results. One part of a day's trading is shown in Chart SP–4, where a long was taken right off the starting gun at 8:50 A.M., at point (7), and was held until going short at the next (7) point at 538.20 at 9:51 A.M. The long closed out for a profit of $950, and the short closed out at 536.50 at the end for a profit of $850—quite a nice day's work!

TABLE   4.SP.C1

Trade Results: Mountain/Valley Day Trade Method*
S&P: Conservative Mode, 1-Minute Data

Date	Position	Time In	Price In	Time Out	Price Out	$P/L	$Max. Loss	Time	$Max. Gain	Time
6/1/95	Long	846	539.55	859	537.5	−1025	−1025	859	75	847
6/1/95	Short	859	537.5	928	537.4	50	−200	902	1175	909
6/1/95	Long	928	537.4	1516	538.4	500	−1250	951	1250	1347
6/2/95	Long	850	536.3	951	538.2	950	−400	859	3000	931
6/2/95	Short	951	538.2	1516	536.5	850	−575	1047	1350	1411
6/5/95	Long	942	539.45	1356	539.65	100	−700	1003	1825	1342
6/5/95	Short	1356	539.65	1515	541.2	−775	−850	1416	0	1356
6/6/95	Long	919	542	1205	541.35	−325	−1000	1107	150	1000
6/7/95	Long	1212	539.9	1233	538.2	−850	−850	1233	0	1212
6/7/95	Short	1233	538.2	1520	537.85	175	−375	1247	1050	1341
6/8/95	Long	1245	538.2	1444	536.3	−950	−950	1444	100	1305
6/8/95	Short	1444	536.3	1525	536.2	50	−175	1504	225	1500
6/9/95	Short	926	534	1328	531.5	1250	−50	929	2150	1256
6/9/95	Long	1328	531.5	1527	533.05	775	−125	1334	875	1525
6/12/95	Long	952	536	1228	536.25	125	−100	1013	1050	1125
6/12/95	Short	1228	536.25	1523	536.9	−325	−375	1320	450	1441
6/13/95	Short	924	537.65	1046	539.2	−775	−775	1046	0	924
6/13/95	Long	1046	539.2	1523	540.7	750	−125	1047	1150	1335
6/14/95	Long	1156	540.6	1522	540.5	−50	−150	1438	525	1355
6/15/95	Long	901	542.2	1407	541.8	−200	−400	926	1025	1329
6/15/95	Short	1407	541.8	1447	542.8	−500	−500	1447	600	1408
6/15/95	Long	1447	542.8	1516	542.7	−50	−500	1502	50	1448
6/16/95	Long	1357	544.75	1519	544	−375	−825	1407	0	1357
6/19/95	Long	851	546.3	1523	549.75	1725	−50	900	1975	1442
6/20/95	Short	1153	548.25	1421	549.3	−525	−525	1421	275	1305
6/20/95	Long	1421	549.3	1519	549.2	−50	−150	1444	275	1428
6/21/95	Short	1013	549	1314	550.3	−650	−650	1314	200	1015
6/21/95	Long	1314	550.3	1426	548.85	−725	−725	1426	0	1314
6/21/95	Short	1426	548.85	1519	549	−75	−300	1435	0	1426
6/22/95	Long	914	552.3	1522	555.35	1525	0	914	1800	1359
6/23/95	Short	1353	553.4	1503	554.45	−525	−525	1503	450	1413
6/23/95	Long	1503	554.45	1522	555	275	−75	1511	300	1516
6/26/95	Short	946	553.15	1338	551.1	1025	−225	952	1950	1238
6/26/95	Long	1338	551.1	1426	549.4	−850	−850	1426	0	1338
6/26/95	Short	1426	549.4	1522	548.25	575	−125	1439	725	1500
6/27/95	Long	902	549.95	1124	550.1	75	−225	925	875	1007
6/27/95	Short	1124	550.1	1520	547.1	1500	−525	1249	1800	1457
6/28/95	Short	909	546	1002	547.25	−625	−625	1002	475	938
6/28/95	Long	1002	547.25	1135	548.8	775	0	1002	2050	1111
6/28/95	Short	1135	548.8	1437	548.15	325	−425	1329	1500	1425
6/28/95	Long	1437	548.15	1519	549.5	675	−100	1444	825	1502
6/29/95	Short	906	547.2	1221	545.9	650	−550	918	1325	1154
6/29/95	Long	1221	545.9	1520	548.4	1250	−325	1225	1400	1432
6/30/95	Short	926	548.8	1000	549.9	−550	−550	1000	100	927
6/30/95	Long	1000	549.9	1400	549	−450	−450	1400	650	1027
6/30/95	Short	1400	549	1518	547.25	875	−400	1417	1100	1449
$Total						5600				
$Ave/Trade						122				

* Settings: Minimum successive high/low closing difference = .15 dollars
    No. successive high/low closings = 7

C H A R T   SP–4

Conservative Mode Trading: 1-Minute Day Prices for S&P

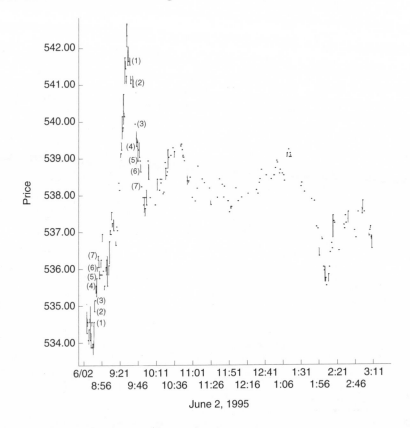

June 2, 1995

Moving up the scale, a conservative trading mode is taken in Table 4.SP.C15, on 15-minute data. This requires five successive higher closings of 15 cents or more to go long. Although this approach doesn't trade that often, it builds up respectable total profits of $2,000 and a $143 per trade profit average. This is a good mode for those who can only follow charts. Chart SP–5 shows a very nice single trade on a good day downtrend. Prices steadily fall at least 15 cents for five lower closings (actually, this time all in a row), beginning at (A) and ending at (E), where a short is signaled at 10:29 A.M. at 552.45 and is held until the close at 548 for a handsome profit of $2,225.

Finally, Table 4.SP.S30 is for those who are more speculative but follow charts only and need some time for coffee and chit-chat. Followed on 30-minute intervals, this mode needs only two successive higher closings of 60 cents or more to go long. The results are still pretty good despite the long price intervals, with a total profit of $3,375, or $130 per trade before costs. Chart SP–6 details a typically successful trade for June 13, 1995. Prices dip at first, move up smartly from the bottom of around 538 early in the morning, rise in an hour and a half to the two higher closings of 60 cents or more, and signal a long at point (B) at 539.70 at 11:00 A.M. The position is held until the close for a profit of $850.

T A B L E   4.SP.C15

Trade Results: Mountain/Valley Day Trade Method*
S&P: Conservative Mode, 15-Minute Data

Date	Position	Time In	Price In	Time Out	Price Out	$P/L	$Max. Loss	Time	$Max. Gain	Time
6/5/95	Long	1305	541.15	1514	540.8	−175	−350	1432	550	1334
6/8/95	Short	1459	536	1514	536.15	−75	−75	1514	0	1459
6/9/95	Short	1214	531.45	1514	532.85	−700	−700	1514	625	1259
6/12/95	Short	1344	535.5	1514	536.4	−450	−450	1514	0	1344
6/13/95	Long	1329	541	1514	541.4	200	−300	1359	200	1514
6/15/95	Long	1229	543.05	1514	542.6	−225	−1050	1414	600	1329
6/19/95	Long	1059	548.6	1514	549.9	650	−150	1114	800	1444
6/22/95	Long	1314	554.7	1514	555.5	400	0	1314	600	1359
6/23/95	Short	1414	552.8	1514	554.6	−800	−800	1514	0	1414
6/26/95	Short	1029	552.45	1504	548	2225	0	1029	2225	1504
6/27/95	Short	1359	549	1514	547.25	875	0	1359	1150	1459
6/29/95	Short	1044	546.2	1414	548.05	−925	−925	1414	525	1144
6/29/95	Long	1414	548.05	1514	548.25	100	−100	1444	100	1514
6/30/95	Short	1359	549.15	1514	547.15	1000	−200	1414	1000	1514
$Total						2000				
$Ave/Trade						143				

* Settings: Minimum successive high/low closing difference = .15 dollars
         No. successive high/low closings = 5

C H A R T   SP–5

Conservative Mode Trading: 15-Minute Day Prices for S&P

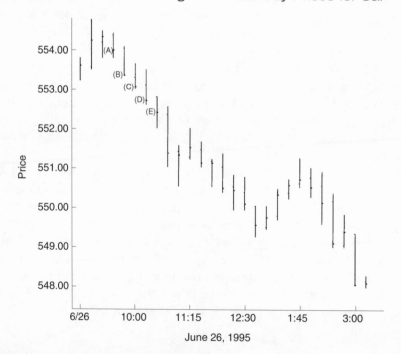

June 26, 1995

T A B L E   4.SP.S30

Trade Results: Mountain/Valley Day Trade Method*
S&P: Speculative Mode, 30-Minute Data

Date	Position	Time In	Price In	Time Out	Price Out	$P/L	$Max. Loss	Time	$Max. Gain	Time
6/1/95	Long	1341	539.1	1513	538.2	−450	−1350	1405	0	1341
6/2/95	Short	1128	537.7	1514	536.8	450	−475	1306	1000	1409
6/5/95	Long	1250	540.6	1514	540.8	100	−200	1450	550	1350
6/6/95	Short	1058	540.3	1205	541.35	−525	−525	1205	0	1058
6/7/95	Short	1316	537.05	1514	537.45	−200	−425	1446	275	1346
6/9/95	Short	1000	532.6	1400	532.7	−50	−50	1400	1200	1300
6/9/95	Long	1400	532.7	1514	532.85	75	−225	1430	75	1514
6/12/95	Long	1130	537.6	1430	535.75	−925	−925	1430	0	1130
6/12/95	Short	1430	535.75	1514	536.4	−325	−325	1514	0	1430
6/13/95	Long	1100	539.7	1514	541.4	850	−150	1200	850	1514
6/14/95	Long	1200	541	1514	540.55	−225	−225	1514	25	1230
6/15/95	Long	1230	542.85	1430	542.05	−400	−400	1430	600	1330
6/15/95	Short	1430	542.05	1514	542.6	−275	−275	1514	0	1430
6/16/95	Long	1400	544.75	1514	543.8	−475	−525	1430	0	1400
6/19/95	Long	1030	547.9	1514	549.9	1000	0	1030	1075	1500
6/20/95	Short	1200	548.25	1514	549.15	−450	−700	1430	150	1300
6/21/95	Short	1030	549.1	1514	549	50	−525	1330	50	1230
6/22/95	Long	1200	554.8	1514	555.5	350	−100	1300	400	1400
6/26/95	Short	1030	552.4	1504	548	2200	0	1030	2225	1500
6/27/95	Short	1401	548.95	1514	547.25	850	0	1401	1125	1501
6/28/95	Long	1030	547.6	1200	548.85	625	0	1030	1800	1100
6/28/95	Short	1200	548.85	1514	549.2	−175	−400	1330	850	1430
6/29/95	Short	1000	547.15	1300	546.4	375	0	1000	1025	1200
6/29/95	Long	1300	546.4	1514	548.25	925	0	1300	1050	1430
6/30/95	Long	1030	550.85	1400	549	−925	−925	1400	75	1100
6/30/95	Short	1400	549	1514	547.15	925	0	1400	925	1514
$Total						3375				
$Ave/Trade						130				

* Settings: Minimum successive high/low closing difference = .60 dollars
     No. successive high/low closings = 2

C H A R T   SP–6

Speculative Mode Trading: 30-Minute Day Prices for S&P

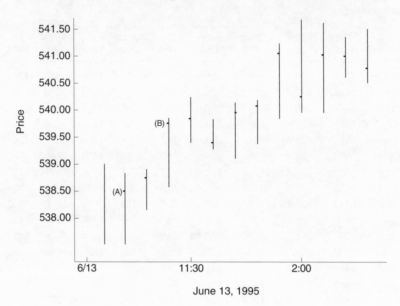

June 13, 1995

CHAPTER 5

Hands-On and Tips

Finally, there are special characteristics and tactics that can improve the performance of day trading. We can take advantage of the short-term nature of day trading (closing out at the end of the day); the nature of the timing method we are using (a trend approach); the miniaturization of price movements; and the symmetry/analog with long-term price patterns (trends) currently in effect.

FILTERING TRADE CANDIDATES

First and foremost to consider is which commodities should be candidates for trading on any given day.

We have a good method for timing trades, but this assumes that there are enough trends around and that they are big enough on average to warrant trading in the first place. Some commodities (like oats, for example) just may not have or may never have big enough moves during the day, especially in relation to the costs involved, or their price changes in the period (even down to 1-minute intervals) may be too large in relation to the average move per day. Oats may move effectively 1/4 cent each time prices change, yet its range may average only 2 1/4 cents per day. The trader will probably get the signal just at the end of the trend (since he probably needs six new highs or lows, for example) and end up with losses every time. He might consider a contrary strategy, but then the average profit before costs would be small with the reaction to the trend, which he was counting on to make those contrary profits, and he would end up just churning trades for commissions.

At the other end of the spectrum would be S&P or coffee, both of which seem to make big moves in relation to costs. It may be unnecessary to filter times for good trading since they have big daily ranges and no apparent cyclicality or long dormant times.

But each commodity is different, and each must go through times of strong trends and dormancy. During strong trend times we can count on big moves with the trend during the day or strong reactions during the day to long-term big trend moves.

There are essentially two types of filters that we can use to thin out those candidates with bigger day move potential. One filter monitors the intraday (day) movement itself to try to find out how far moves are headed, while the other filter ties in day trade move potential to overnight, longer-term trends.

1. *Strong Day Trends*

The first filter looks at day trade trends and asks whether there is regularity or predictability about them. If there is none, then we have to hope that the timing method for trends in the day is not only accurate, but that it also catches big enough trends in each commodity we follow. But we know some commodities always (or nearly so) seem to give mediocre results, so we might have to eliminate some based purely on the fact of lack of long-term profit opportunity. I suspect we could do this anyway (my suspicions are that oats, corn, T-bills, Eurodollars, and several others could easily be eliminated).

The first step is to find an indicator or barometer of what we are trying to detect. We are looking for strong (big) trends during the day, and we would like to trade only during times when such an indicator points to big trends.

One measure of trendedness during the day is the daily price range (low to high price difference), which directly measures at least one big move made during the day (there may be more contained within that range). We know big ranges will give at least one trend opportunity during the day, which is what we want. There may be more than one trend, but my experience with analyzing day movements indicates that there rarely is more than one really big move. More often there are no big moves, just a lot of small and medium-sized ones, which are what we would like to avoid, since our (and any) trend-timing method may not do well in those periods or may, at best, do nothing.

If there is indeed a continuation of trendedness (and our measure of it is range) in store, then one good forecaster of a long-term, steady buildup of day trendedness is a moving average of range. It could tell us that during the period covered we experienced a range of trend opportunities during the day which averaged a certain number. We just have to ascertain what that number is (if it is big enough) to allow our timing method to show good enough trade profits on average. It is also important that the indicator continues to grow or stays at the minimum level in order for us to make good average profits. It will turn out to be a matching or correlating process—we must develop and apply the moving average to ranges and find out what minimal number for it ties in well with those times during which our mountain/valley technique is making money. This should be done separately for each commodity.

In summary, the trader creates a moving average of the daily ranges, trading when the average is at or above a predetermined number (set by examining real or simulated trading results and correlating the average to good results) and not trading when it dips below that number.

The other approach is to trade those commodities showing the *relative* highest moving averages. Basically, the assumption here is that the commodities with highest average will continue to have the highest average and thus the highest current (average of) trend opportunities. The way to put commodities on an equal footing is to divide each commodity average by its basic unit of trading (for example, 1/4 cent for wheat, .05 for cattle, etc.). Then the trader chooses the maximum number of commodities he wants to trade at any one time, say 10, and ranks commodities from highest to lowest based on relative trend size (daily range divided by its basic unit) moving average. The major advantage to this approach is that the trader will get the strongest profit opportunities. The weak point is that if all commodities are in the doldrums he will still be trading a certain number of "dogs" and will possibly get lukewarm results.

   2. *Strong Overnight Trends*

   A second way to obtain better overall day trade results is to take only those trades that agree with the major overnight trend currently in effect. This has the effect of increasing the batting average and boosting up the profit per trade, as trades will tend to occur more in the direction of the trend and be larger in the trend direction, simply because prices are heavily leaning and moving generally in the trend direction. Of course, there could be major corrections to the current trend, offering good counter-trend day trade opportunities.

   Success depends upon how good the longer-term trend method is at picking the major trend. If it is in a strong, prolonged trend mode then everything will be fine. But if the trends are small and don't last long, the major long-term method will get whipsawed with many small- to medium-sized losses. What will happen to day trades is pure conjecture: The trend sizes within the day will probably average smaller, but it is not clear if the mountain/valley method batting average will change upwards or downwards or stay the same. The day trading method will tend to go for trends *counter* to the newly developing overnight direction since the long-term trend method is lagging behind current events. But the new overnight direction may not last long either, so the day trade may be in the right direction (for the wrong reasons).

LATE-IN-THE-DAY TRADING

We should look at the trading day as a miniature of a long time period, like a year. Like trading an option, the value of the option/day trade is zero at the end of the period. It is not good to enter a trade late in the life of the instrument, for there is then little profit opportunity left (although with some options a great deal of price movement, against the instrument, occurs very late in its life). Very little of the trend's move (if you've caught a big one) usually occurs at the very end of the day. Most movement occurs earlier, at inception, midway through the day, or steadily throughout the day.

   Another consideration is the cost of trading. Even if the trader could be assured of getting at least some profit when entering late in the day, he must contend with the definitely smaller average profit and weigh it against the cost of trading (slippage and commissions).

   What constitutes late in the day may be different for each commodity (see Chapter 4 for some commodities with early and late-in-the-day considerations and best operating times). Silver can still make fast, large moves late in the day, whereas T-bonds and Swiss francs have long, steady moves throughout the day, so very little extra profit is left late in the day.

Specific late-in-the-day times vary with each commodity (again, see Chapter 4), but generally a trade will not show significant extra profit in the last hour of trading, so a new trade should not be initiated in that time frame.

ONE TRADE PER DAY

Again, if we look at a trading day as a miniature version of a much larger time frame, say a year, we quickly realize that the safest and most profitable (highest success rate and largest profit per trade) trading style is to go for one big trend.

There simply is not much time for many trends to develop during the day, nor is there much reason for major reversals of direction to occur, as it almost always takes some time and traders' energies for one big trend to start up in the day. Traders do not change their major stances on trend direction that often, so if one trend (side of trading) is predominant well into the day, it is hard for a major counter trend to mount up and reverse the current trend. So the vast majority of counter moves to the one major trend turn out to be reactions to that trend, either profit taking or smaller, oppositely directed ones. Also, the time remaining for a second, third, and other trades severely limits the total profit possible for each trade.

NO REENTRY SAME POSITION

If a trade is stopped out, the trader must decide if reentering the same position makes sense. His stop tells him either that the trend has stopped or that he must protect his position against unwanted open loss. Unfortunately, the first one (trend has stopped) is not a truly valid conclusion because only the mountain/valley timing method can tell him that. The second one, a position-loss protection stop, is likewise unwarranted because the trend again has not stopped (merely increased in price variation); however, the goal is understandable: the trader cannot stand any more loss.

While these arguments for stops seem unwarranted because the trend has not officially stopped, we must constantly remember that the reason for day trading was to cut down on trading account losses, whether for single trades or cumulative ones. Because it sometimes takes long for the trend to reverse, current position profits could evaporate and losses mount. For this reason the really conservative trader may wish to institute stops and not allow reentry of the same (direction) position, because he assumes the stop is accurate and very often presages a turn in the trend (but we need the new trend signal to take a new position).

The key here is that a great amount of testing or actual trade history should show a strong correlation between a stop out and no real current trend continuance. If so, he may save some equity loss on average with each stop out. If not, he has prematurely stopped out a perfectly good trend position and will lose additional profits on balance.

I N D E X